Trance-formations

Neuro-Linguistic Programming™
and
the Structure of Hypnosis

by
John Grinder
and
Richard Bandler

edited
by
Connirae Andreas

ISBN: 0-911226-22-2 clothbound $10.00
ISBN: 0-911226-23-0 paperbound $6.50

Cover Artwork by Rene Eisenbart

Library of Congress Cataloging in Publication Data:

Grinder, John.
   Trance-formations.

   1. Hypnotism--Therapeutic use--Problems,
exercises, etc. I. Bandler, Richard. II. Andreas,
Connirae. III. Title.
RC495.G76   615.8'512   81-15342
ISBN 0-911226-22-2   AACR2
ISBN 0-911226-23-0 (pbk.)

3   4   5   6   7   Printing   90   89   88   87   86   85

Contents

Foreword

Hypnosis is a word that usually gets strong responses from people—some positive and some negative. Some people think it's a hoax or only good for making people act like chickens, some people think it will cure everything from dandruff to flat feet, and others think it is so dangerous that it should be left alone completely. Trance experiences have existed in different forms for centuries, usually surrounded by a mystique of something "magical" and unexplainable. What is unique about this book is that it turns the "magic" of hypnosis into specific understandable procedures that can be used not only in doing "hypnosis" but also in everyday communication.

When John Grinder and Richard Bandler do a seminar on hypnosis together, one of them usually says "All communication is hypnosis" and the other says "I disagree, nothing is hypnosis; hypnosis doesn't exist." There is a sense in which they are both right, and both are saying the same thing.

If I tell you about going snorkeling on my recent honeymoon in the Yucatan and describe to you the swift movements of the brightly-colored tropical fish, the rhythmic sound of the gentle waves against the shore, and the feeling of rising and falling with the warm waves as I scan the underwater scenery, hopefully I will alter your state of consciousness so that you can experience some representation of what I experienced. If you become excited about going there yourself, I will have used the same patterns of communication that are used by successful hypnotists . . . and by successful poets, salesmen, parents,

1

politicians, religious leaders, etc. If you think of hypnosis as altering someone's state of consciousness, then any effective communication is hypnosis.

One of the simpler hypnotic patterns is the "negative command." If I say "Don't think of blue," you *have* to think of blue in order to understand my sentence. If a hypnotist says "I don't want you to relax too soon" the listener often finds himself beginning to relax as a way of understanding what those words mean. Beginning with a negation simply takes any pressure to respond off the listener.

The same pattern is often inadvertently used to get *unwanted* responses. The well-meaning parent may say to her child "Don't spill the milk," or "Don't stumble." The well-meaning husband may say "Don't get upset," or "I don't want you to worry about what happens while you are gone." The listener has to represent the unwanted behavior somehow in order to understand what has been said, and this makes the unwanted behavior *more* likely. Unknowingly, he or she in a sense "hypnotizes" the child or spouse into an *unwanted* response.

The same pattern can be used to get more useful responses from people, whether they are in "trance" or not. "Don't be too curious about what you'll learn from reading this book." "I wouldn't tell you to be eager to discover how you'll change comfortably in the coming weeks." Since hypnosis is fundamentally no different than any effective communication, "There is no such thing as hypnosis" as a separate and distinct process.

Most books present hypnosis as something that you sit down and do with yourself or someone else for a discrete period of time, usually to solve problems. Then you get up and do something else. If you still think of hypnosis in that way after you have read this book, you will be depriving yourself of the most important ways you can use these tools—in your living. The communication patterns described in this book are far too useful to leave on a hypnosis chair somewhere. Most of the satisfactions that we all want in life don't take place in a hypnosis chair; they happen with the people we love, the work that we do, and the ways that we play and enjoy life.

You can use the information in this book in many ways, both personally and professionally. One way is to make *remedial* changes by solving problems and removing limitations. This is the way hypnosis is usually used to stop smoking, lose weight, deal with unreasonable fears, and so on.

But you can also use this information in evolutionary ways to develop yourself and continually increase your abilities and choices in life—learning to do *better* what you already do well You can do this in simple ways such as learning to communicate with family and associates more effectively, make love more enjoyably, learn new skills more easily, and so on. You can also learn how to make even more pervasive changes in how you live.

Much of the material in this book is derived from Bandler and Grinder's careful and systematic observation of the work of Milton H. Erickson, M.D. Until his death in 1980, Erickson was wide'v considered to be the world's greatest medical hypnotist. He was widely known for his successful and often "miraculous" work with "impossible" clients, as well as for his extensive writings on hypnosis.

Several years ago I went to visit Milton Erickson at his home in Phoenix. After he described some of his remarkable work with clients, I asked him how he knew to use one approach with one client, when he had used an opposite approach with another client who apparently had the same kind of problem. He responded "You just trust your unconscious mind."

That approach to hypnosis works great if you have Milton Erickson's unconscious mind. But how is it possible to learn to automatically and unconsciously respond as effectively as Milton Erickson did—to have an unconscious mind like Erickson's? Grinder and Bandler's special genius is the ability to observe someone like Erickson and then describe in detail what Erickson does, what cues he responds to, and how it all fits together. This makes it possible for others to learn how to repeat the same procedures and get similar results. After a period of practice, these patterns can become as automatic as knowing which muscles to move in order to reach across a table and pick up a glass.

Erickson wrote the following in the preface to Bandler and Grinder's book *The Patterns of the Hypnotic Techniques of Milton H. Erickson, M.D.:*

> *"Although this book by Richard Bandler and John Grinder, to which I am contributing this Preface, is far from being a complete description of my methodologies, as they so clearly state it is a much better explanation of how I work than I, myself, can give. I know what I do, but to explain how I do it is much too difficult for me."*

In addition to modeling the behavior of "wizards" such as Milton Erickson, Grinder and Bandler have added their own wide array of effective communication skills to the body of knowledge that they teach others. It is unusual to find two people like Bandler and Grinder who are such powerful and effective communicators. It is even more unusual to find two people who are so capable of teaching others to do what they do so exquisitely.

The material presented in this book is detailed and specific and carefully sequenced, beginning with simple concepts and exercises, and proceeding step-by-step to more advanced procedures. This book has been created from verbatim transcripts of 10 different seminars on hypnosis, edited together so that it appears as a single workshop. No distinction is made between when Richard is speaking and when John is speaking, and the names of most participants have been changed.

As you read this book, keep in mind that Bandler and Grinder are usually *doing* what they're talking about. Sometimes they're explicit about this, and sometimes they're not. The astute reader will find much more in the text than is overtly commented upon.

This book has been edited so as to keep redundancy with other NLP books to a minimum. Some material from the original workshops which is already available in other books has been omitted. You will find that the books *Frogs into Princes, Patterns of the Hypnotic Techniques of Milton H. Erickson, M.D., Vol. I,* and *They Lived Happily Ever After* are very useful additions to the information in this book.

If you are reading with an interest in acquiring and developing hypnotic communication skills, you will serve yourself by taking the time to enjoy practicing each small piece that is presented so that you can become systematically effective. If the pieces are too big for you to do comfortably, break them into smaller and more digestible chunks.

If you are reading this book simply for entertainment or out of curiosity—enjoy! Grinder and Bandler's teaching is more interesting and entertaining than most comedians.

Connirae Andreas

I

Introduction

Our topic here is hypnosis. We could immediately launch into an argument about whether there is such a thing, and what it might be if there were. However, since you already paid your money and came here for a seminar in hypnosis, I won't bring up that particular argument.

I hope that in the three days we spend here together, you will come to understand the sense in which that might be a fruitful argument. I hope you will discover that you already know a great deal about hypnosis under other names, or under no name at all. You can discover that certain experiences many of you have had are really excellent examples of altered states of consciousness. In the course of these three days, I will call upon both of each of you to enjoy and learn from what takes place here.

I assume that each of you is here with at least two objectives in mind. One is to discover how hypnotic patterning might be useful and effective for you in whatever area you are in, whether it's psychotherapy, management, education, nursing, sales, or something else. I assume that you want to discover what new choices hypnotic patterning offers that you might add to your present repertoire to become even more effective in doing what you do. In addition, I am sure that many of you are interested in making a number of personal changes as a part of your experience here.

I invite you to participate with both those objectives fully in mind. In dealing with this material, we will be doing demonstrations, we will

5

discuss what is going on, and we will ask you to do exercises under our supervision after we've explained what we would like you to do.

Hypnotic patterning is the same as any skill that can be learned. In order to be learned, it has to be practiced. I assume that most of you here drive automobiles. If you don't drive automobiles, you can find some comparable perceptual-motor skill that you have mastered, whether it's riding a bicycle, roller skating, or playing some athletic sport. If you remember the first occasion on which you attempted to master the complex skill of driving a car, there were many things that you had to keep track of. Your hands were doing several things. At least one of them was on the wheel, presumably, and the other one was working the gear shift, if the car you were learning to drive had one. At the same time you were taxed with the task of being able to pay attention to what your feet were doing. There were three things they might do down there, and some of those things had to happen in coordination. You may remember putting the brake on and failing to put the clutch in at the same time, and the disastrous results of that. You had to pay attention to all of this, in addition to having some consciousness of what was going on outside of the car itself.

As with any complex perceptual-motor skill, what's required is that the task be organized into small pieces or chunks, so that you can practice each small chunk individually until you've mastered it. Once you have succeeded in practicing each chunk to the point that it becomes an automatic, effective, unconscious skill, you are free to attend to new possibilities: other components of the task. You can then practice these new chunks until they also achieve that same status of an unconscious, effective, perceptual-motor pattern that you do not have to give any conscious attention to.

The easiest way to become skilled at hypnosis is to practice small chunks one at a time, in the same way that you learned many tasks such as driving a car. I assume that the ultimate test of your skill in hypnosis is whether you can walk in and begin to interact with someone in such a way as to induce the specific kind of hypnotic outcome that they request—without having to strategize at the conscious level. Three days is not long enough, in my opinion, to achieve the kind of graceful, systematic, unconscious functioning that is required of a really fine hypnotist. However, our task in these three days will be to organize the overall task of hypnosis into chunks, and ask you to practice the various pieces. Our job will be to balance the amount of time we have you practice specific skills with the time we spend making sure we complete a coherent whole that will give you an overall strategy for hypnosis. I trust that you, and particularly your unconscious mind, will continue to practice such skills after this seminar. I also hope that you will continue to add alternative ways of achieving the same outcomes to the repertoire you will be acquiring here.

What we do for a living is an obscure thing called modeling. When we model, we try to build descriptions of how to do something. As modelers we are interested in two things: one is asking really good questions about what needs to be known, and the other is making descriptions of what seems to work. It's something akin to writing a cookbook.

During the next three days, we'd like to teach you a model for doing hypnosis. It is not the truth. It is not an answer. It is not real. If you think you know what's "really" going on and want to argue with me about what's really going on, I'm not going to be able to argue with you because I don't know. There *are* some things that I *do* know about; I understand how hypnosis is done. Why it works, I don't know. I do know that hypnosis works in the same way that you learn and remember and everything else. It works in the same way that you understand language.

Although hypnosis is not different from anything else, in the configuration we're going to teach it to you, it's a very powerful tool. And I would like you to think of it as a tool that accomplishes something specific. It's an amplifier. No matter what you do, whether you're selling cars, doing psychotherapy, or working with juries, you can do it and elicit more intense responses from people. Hypnosis will allow you to do whatever you do and have a greater impact with it. By itself it won't do anything.

I also want to point out that hypnosis is not a panacea. I have been using hypnosis for seven years, and I still sometimes wake up tired in the morning. Since I'm not a person who ordinarily drinks coffee, if I drink a cup of coffee in the morning, my body vibrates. If I fall down, I still get bruised. If I have a toothache and I remove the pain with hypnosis, I still have to go to a dentist to do something about the tooth. I consider these to be limitations not in hypnosis as a tool, but primarily in myself. Right now, hypnosis and communication arts in general are in their infancy as disciplines.

The process of learning to do hypnosis is somewhat unusual,

8

because unlike most things you learn, you already know how to do it. The problem is noticing it. So rather than going through a long and detailed description this morning, I am going to ask you to do something and then afterwards take a look at it.

Exercise 1

I'm going to ask you to get into groups of three people. I want one of you, person A, to think of something that fits the following description: *a situation in which you become deeply involved, with a limited focus of attention.* For some people that's jogging; for others it's reading a book. It might be writing, watching television, going to the movies, driving your car on a long trip—anything which fits that description.

If you're A, I want you to tell the other two in your group, B and C, what the experience is. Give them only the name of the experience: jogging, sailing—just a word. If you give them too much detail, it makes it too easy for them. Just give them a word, sit back and close your eyes, and pretend that you're in hypnosis—it's all pretend anyway. I want the other two people to describe what they believe would *have to* be there in sensory terms if you were having that experience. The magic words are "have to" because if someone is jogging and you say the bright sun is shining down on your body, that doesn't *have to* be there. People can jog at night, or on a cloudy day. However, they do have to have some skin temperature. So you're going to have to be *artfully vague.* I want B and C to take turns saying two sentences or phrases each. One will say "You can feel the temperature of the air on your body, and the place where your foot touches the ground." The other one might say "You notice the beating of your heart. You can feel the temperature of your skin." Those are experiences that have to be there.

I'm not going to give you any more description than that to begin with. I want you each to take a turn, and I want you to observe the person who has his eyes closed, and notice how he responds to what you say. When you are the person sitting there with your eyes closed, I want you to notice which things allow you to get into the experience more, and which things make it more difficult. I'm going to leave it at that and have you use your own experience as a teacher. Let's start. Take about five minutes each.

* * * * *

I didn't want to talk to you too much in the beginning because whenever I begin to teach a hypnosis course it's a little bit difficult for me to keep from demonstrating at large. I asked you to notice what kinds of things seemed to allow you to go back to the state of consciousness that you were in when you actually had the experience you mentioned, and which things seemed to make it harder for you. Which things seemed to jar you, and which seemed to lead you more into being relaxed? Which things seemed to be disjointed, and which allowed you to forget where you were a little bit?

Woman: Anything that had to with my body put me in deeper, and anything that had to do with my mind, like what I thought about it or my reactions to it, took me out a little.

I want to know exactly what the other person actually did. Give me some examples.

Woman: OK. I was playing the piano. When the person said "You can feel the contact of your fingers on the keys," it made me go deeper. If he said something like "You think the music is you," then I came out.

Man: It was easier for me when the tempo of his voice was the same rate as my breathing.

What kinds of things made it harder?

Man: Um, when something he said was incongruous with what I had been thinking. I saw myself in an indoor skating rink, and it threw me when somebody suggested something outdoors.

Yeah, you're in an indoor skating rink and somebody says "You look up and notice how beautiful the sky is."

Woman: My partner said to me "You can hear and feel your breathing." That really jarred me, because I couldn't do them both at the same time. I thought "No, just a minute. I can't do that."

OK, what kind of things made it easier?

Woman: When she just said one thing to do at a time, like "You can hear your breathing."

Man: I was swimming underwater when someone said "You can feel the splash of your hand hitting the water." I thought "No, I'm underwater. I can't."

Woman: We were talking about music, and at some point he said something about being in tune with the world, and it just really took me in deeper.

What made it harder?

Woman: He didn't do anything that made it harder.

OK, he can go home now.

10

Woman: There was one thing. If one person had slowed down the speed of his voice, and then the other one speeded up, that brought me back up.

So one of the people would go (slowly) "and you'll feel . . . very . . . relaxed" and the other one would say (quickly) "and more and more and more relaxed."

Man: I noticed that my partners used nothing but feeling terms. At first that made it very easy, because I was just using one sensory system, but after a while I heard myself saying "I want to see something." I wasn't seeing anything.

So it was really the absence of something. After a while the instructions became what is known as redundant.

Man: One thing really distracted me and pulled me out after I was in the experience: the phrase "as all other experiences fade." When he said that, suddenly—bang!—I was back.

You had to find out what the other experiences were so they could fade. What made it easier?

Man: Sensory things: feeling the guitar, feeling my fingers moving, looking at the music.

Woman: The omission of something very obvious made it more difficult for me. I was painting a picture and my partners never talked about the feel of the brush in my hand.

How did that make it more difficult for you? How did it cross your mind that they weren't talking about it?

Woman: I kept feeling that there's an incompleteness here; I've got to fill it in. They were talking about mixing paint and looking at the view and how beautifully the picture was progressing.

And that's not what you were doing?

Well, I had to get from mixing the paint to having a brush in my hand and painting before I could stand back and look at the picture.

OK. So it wasn't a natural transition for you. It was kind of like "You're standing on the beach, and you feel the warmth of the sun on your body, and you look back at the beach and notice how far you've swum."

Now what I hope you come to understand in the next three days is that many of the answers to questions about what leads somebody into an altered state have just been described. The difficulty that people have going into hypnosis is not a genetic one. It's not that some people just *can't*. In fact, everyone does it all the time. The difficulty is that no one really notices. Hypnosis is a very natural process, and hypnosis is only a word that describes the tools that you use to systematically take someone into an altered state of consciousness. People go into altered states all the time. Perhaps at lunch you can get in an elevator and ride up to the top of this hotel with some people whom you don't know, and watch what happens to them. People don't get into an elevator and act the way they do normally. They kind of go "on hold" and watch the floors go by. In fact, if the door opens before they're ready to get out, very often they'll wake up and start out. How many of you have walked out of an elevator on the wrong floor? There's a universality to that experience. Finding things that are universal in people's experience is the key to both inducing hypnosis and using it for whatever you want to accomplish.

Another important thing is making a natural sequence. If somebody says to you "Well, I was driving down the road, and I was on my way to Texas, and I was looking out the window and seeing the other cars go by, and it was a beautiful sunny day, and I said to myself 'It's raining so hard!'" that last phrase will jar you out of listening. Usually that's the point at which somebody will ask a question or begin to argue or disagree. Natural transitions lead people into an altered state without jarring them.

There are ways to induce an altered state by jarring someone as well. Both ways of using communication can induce altered states. People often use what is called the confusion technique as an induction procedure. When you use the confusion technique, you do *not* build in meaningful transitions. You induce a state of mild confusion in people, and *then* you begin to build natural transitions from that point. We'll get to that later.

If you listen to the kinds of things that jarred people, usually they were things that weren't sensory-based, or things that weren't universal to the experience. If you're playing the piano, you are going to have contact between the keys and your fingers, but you are not necessarily going to feel that "the music is you." For example, if you were playing "Chopsticks" would you feel like a chopstick? It wouldn't necessarily work that way.

Exercise 2

Soon I'm going to ask you to do the same thing again, only this time I want you to restrict yourself to descriptions of what *must be there in sensory experience* and to *be non-specific.* If you say "You can hear the splash of the water" and the person is *under*water, it won't work. But you can say "You can hear the sounds that the water makes" because there will be some sounds.

This time I'd like you to add one other important piece: I'd like you to have a steady voice tempo and use the other person's breathing as the *speed* . . . and *rate* . . . and the *pace* . . . of the *speech* . . . that you *generate*. Matching someone's breathing with anything in your behavior—whether it's your own breathing rate, the tempo of your speech, or anything else—has a very powerful impact. Try it and find out what impact it has. I want you to use the same experience and keep the same groups. Take two minutes apiece and don't talk about it. It should take eight to ten minutes at most for everybody in your group to do it. Notice if it feels different this time.

* * * * *

I'd like to ask you if you noticed any difference in your own experience, even with just that small amount of instruction. Was it different at all for you? Some of you are nodding. Is there anyone here for whom it was not different at all? . . . One person. Even with just that little bit of instruction, that little bit of change, the experience changed for everyone but one person in this room. That difference to me is a profound one, because the instructions I gave you are just a *tiny* bit of what's available.

Hypnosis itself, as far as I'm concerned, is simply using yourself as a biofeedback mechanism. You were doing that when you matched the other person's breathing rate with your voice tempo. Your behavior became an ongoing feedback mechanism for his behavior. Whether you're going to use altered states for inducing personal change, for some medical purpose, for the purpose of relaxing, or as a form of meditation, the things that allow you to be able to respond to another human being by going into an altered state are not genetically predetermined. They're simply the mechanisms of communication.

If I tell you that I want you to think about this (speaking rapidly) "very-slowly-and-carefully," the incongruity between what I say and how I say it gives you two contradictory instructions. But if I tell you I want you to stop . . . and consider . . . very . . . slowly . . . just exactly . . . what the change . . . in your own experience . . . was . . . then . . . the tempo . . . the rate of my speech . . . the movements of my body (he has been swaying to the rhythm of his speech) don't interfere with the words that I'm saying. In fact they *embellish* them and amplify their impact.

I heard somebody here say the word "up" as he lowered his voice. That's an incongruity. Those two things don't match. It's like talking about being really excited in a monotone. Hypnotists do this sometimes. There's an old notion that you're supposed to talk in a monotone when you do hypnosis. It is actually much more effective to sound thrilled if you are taking someone back into a thrilling experience. Being in trance doesn't mean that you have to be dead. A lot of people tell me "Well, I don't think I was in a trance because I could still hear things and feel things." If you can't see things and hear things, that's death; that's a different state. In hypnosis, what you hear and see and feel is actually amplified for the most part.

I believe that people in a state of hypnosis have much *more* control over themselves than they think they do. Hypnosis is not a process of taking control of people. It's a process of giving them control of themselves by providing feedback that they wouldn't ordinarily have.

I know that each of you in here is capable of going into any trance state—even though Science has "proved" that's not true. And given how researchers have proved it, they're right. If you use the same hypnotic induction with a group of people, only some of them will go into a trance. That's the way traditional hypnotists work. However, we're not going to study traditional hypnosis. We're going to study what's called Ericksonian hypnosis, after Milton H. Erickson. Ericksonian hypnosis means developing the skills of a hypnotist so well that you can put someone into a trance in a conversation in which the word hypnosis is never mentioned.

I learned a long time ago that it isn't so much what you say as how you say it. When you try to convince somebody consciously by overpowering him, it elicits from him the response of resisting you. There are some people who don't resist being overpowered, and who go into a trance. However, neither resistance nor cooperation is a demonstration of anything except the ability of people to respond. Everybody who is living can respond. The questions are: how and to what? Your job when you do hypnosis is to *notice what people respond to naturally*.

People come into my office and say "People have tried to hypnotize me for years and it has never worked." They sit down and say "go ahead and try to hypnotize me." And I say "I can't hypnotize you." They say "Well, go ahead and try." I say "I can't do it. There's nothing I can do; if I decided to force you to keep your eyes open, that would make you keep your eyes open. I'll try. Keep your eyes wide open. Stay totally alert. Everything you do will make you stay right here and right now." Then they resist me right into trance. The principle I was using was simply noticing the response of the person in front of me, and providing him with a context that he could respond to appropriately in a way that was natural for him. Most people are not that radically resistant. Every once in a while you find one. If you realize what he's doing and alter your behavior, it can be really easy.

A stage hypnotist usually pulls twenty people up from the audience and gives them a series of commands. Then he throws out all the good hypnotic subjects and keeps the people who are just obedient. To me that's not an indication of skill; that's a statistical approach to doing hypnosis. I want to teach you to see how someone is responding so that you can vary your behavior to provide a context in which he can respond appropriately. If you can do that, anyone can go into an altered state in which you can teach him whatever you want him to learn.

One thing I've noticed is that people are more apt to respond easily when they're in a state that hypnotists call rapport. Rapport seems to be built on matching behaviors. Disagreeing with people won't establish rapport. Talking faster than people can listen won't build rapport. Talking about feelings when people are making visual images won't build rapport. But if you gauge the tempo of your voice to the rate of their breathing, if you blink at the same rate that they blink, if you nod at the same rate that they're nodding, if you rock at the same rate that they're rocking, and if you say things which must in fact be the case, or things that you notice are the case, you will build rapport. If you say "You can be aware of the temperature of your hand, the sounds in the room, the movement of your body as you breathe" your words will match the person's experience, because all of those things are there. We call this kind of matching "pacing."

A universal experience in this country is driving down the freeway and noticing that somebody next to you is driving at the same rate. If you speed up, they speed up with you, and if you slow down, they slow down with you. When you begin to match somebody, you build an unconscious biofeedback loop, and there's a tendency for the other person to do whatever it is that you do, or whatever it is that you talk about. If you gauge the tempo, the rate, and the rhythm of your speech to someone's breathing and then very slowly begin to slow down that rate, their breathing will slow down too. If all of a sudden . . . you pause, so will they. So if you begin by matching someone's behavior, either verbally or nonverbally, it puts you in the position of being able to vary what you do and to have them follow.

The next time you do this exercise, I want you to begin by matching the person's *present* experience. Last time you described what would have to be there in some *previous* experience the person had. This time you'll begin by describing what has to be there in the person's experience *now*. So if I'm doing it with Charlie, I would say something like "And you are listening to the sound of my voice . . . and you can feel the warmth where your left hand is resting on your thigh. . . ."

There's an artistry to choosing these statements. "Until I say this sentence, you will be unaware of the temperature and feeling in your left ear" and suddenly you are aware of that. If I say to Ann "You can be aware of the feeling of warmth where your hand touches your chin" she was probably not aware of that before I made the statement. But when I said it, she could immediately verify that my verbalization was in fact an accurate representation of her experience. I come to gain credibility, and I also begin to amplify things that are true, but were unconscious in her before I mentioned them.

If I continue with kinesthetic statements and then say "And you can be aware of the sound of people shuffling paper in the room" she will again shift consciousness in order to determine whether my verbalization is accurate for her experience. I'm feeding back things that are a part of her experience, but are normally outside of awareness for her. So I'm building rapport, and at the same time I'm already altering her consciousness by that maneuver.

Today we're only going to explore the principles for *inducing* altered states. What you do to *utilize* an altered state after you get it is a separate topic, which we'll get to tomorrow.

For a long time hypnotists have worried about how "deep" you were. They used depth as an indication of what you could and could not do. As far as I can tell, depth is not a meaningful way to think about trance; in some altered states some hypnotic phenomena are possible, while others are not. But hypnotic phenomena *per se* are not that valuable. Being able to have positive or negative hallucinations is not something which is really that valuable in and of itself. Hallucinations can be used as tools to accomplish other ends, but they are not themselves that valuable.

I have discovered that you can even teach people to do hypnotic phenomena—positive hallucinations, negative hallucinations, pain control, and so on—in the waking state. There is somebody in this room right now who can do these things in the waking state. Is there anybody here who can still see an imaginary friend or animal that you had as a child? Anybody? You can raise your hand, we won't arrest you. (Someone raises his hand.) OK, you can hallucinate in the waking state. *That's* a hallucination. I hope you realize that. If you don't, we have a psychiatrist waiting outside with an electric shock treatment machine.

There are many of you who can do negative hallucination; that is, you can look at somebody and not see them. Many of you have looked down at a table to try to find something on it, and you looked all over the place and didn't see it. Yet all that time it was lying right out in the open. That is not different from what people do in deep trances. Children negatively hallucinate their parents speaking to them all the time! How many of you can smell a rose when there isn't one? How many of you can take a deep breath and smell a rose right now? On a hypnotic chart that means you're three quarters of the way into the deepest trance you can be in! This either means that you've never been in the waking state, or that the people who make the charts don't know what they're talking about.

It's not a question of depth; if one of you in here were to experience the conscious state of the person sitting next to you for a moment, it would make LSD look trivial. Trance is only taking your conscious experience and altering it to something else.

In California the legislature is passing a law which says only licensed hypnotists can induce altered states. The ramifications of that particular law are going to be very interesting, because when people make love, they certainly induce altered states in one another. At least I hope making love is not the same as mowing the lawn! I'd like to know how they're going to enforce that law. Everybody's going to have to go out and become a licensed hypnotist so that they can get married.

Now back to your task. In addition to matching people's experience with your statements to get rapport, you need to be able to do something with the rapport you'll have. The key to this is being able to make *transitions.* You need to have a graceful way of guiding someone from his present state into a trance state—going from describing his present state to describing the state you want him to go to. Using transitional words allows you to do this smoothly. Transitional words such as "as" or "when" are words which imply that there is some meaningful relationship between two utterances. "*As* you sit there, it's possible for you to realize that I'm about to tell you something." There's no relationship between your sitting there and realizing something. However, it *sounds* meaningful, and it's the tone of voice and the transition "as" that imply meaning.

Beginning with sensory-based information allows you to make transitions and elicit responses that induce altered states. The sensory base for transitions needs to be something that the person with whom you are working can find. It doesn't need to be something he already has in awareness, but something that he can find. If I sit here and look down at Stan and say "Stan, you can feel the texture of your moustache *and as* you slide your finger, you can notice that you smiled and stopped. You can even feel your elbow with your other hand *and* sense the rise and fall of your own chest *as* you breathe. *And* you may not know it yet, but you're about to become aware of the temperature of your right foot."

Joe: I still don't understand what you mean by the term transition.

If I say to you "You asked a question *while* you were sitting in a chair" I am making a transition. I'm using the word "while" to define that two things are related. "You asked this question *because* you want to know something that's important." Now most things aren't necessarily related, but using the word "because" gives them a relationship. If I say "*As* you sit in that chair you are breathing in and out" it relates those two things by time. They are not necessarily related, but I relate them in time by saying "as."

I'm talking about relating the sentences by using transitional words. If I say to somebody "You're sitting in this chair. You are blinking your eyes. You are waiting," that doesn't have anywhere near the flowing quality of "You are sitting in the chair *and* you are blinking your eyes *and* you are wondering what the point of all of this is." Words like "and," "as," "while," "because," and "when" all build a relationship between parts of a sentence. The particular relationship is one of time. That relationship allows people to move from one idea to another without disjunction. It's the same thing as saying "You're standing on the beach feeling the warmth of the sun on your body, and you look back at the beach as you take another stroke in the water." Even though the ideas aren't related, they *become* more related simply by adding those connecting words. You can take ideas that don't fit together and fit them together by gracefully using those kinds of words. When people listen to language, part of what allows them to flow from one idea to the other are these particular kinds of words. *And* you are here *because* you want to learn to be able to do a certain phenomenon called hypnosis. *And as* you go through the next three days, I'm going to teach you a lot of things that allow it to work easier. Why it works I don't know. But *as* you begin to try some of these things, you will find in your own experience that they have an impact. *Even as* I'm talking to you now, I'm using the same kinds of words *and* that's part of what makes it more meaningful.

Joe: Is the "even as" that you just used, another example of a transition?

Yes.

Joe: OK, then I understand what you're saying. You're saying figure out words that will allow bridging between the different sentences you're making.

Yes. I could say "*As* you sit in that chair, you can feel the warmth of your hand on your arm *and* you can feel the notebook on your legs. *If* you listen, you can even hear your own heart beating *and* you don't really know . . . exactly . . . what you're going to learn in the next three days *but* you can realize that there are a whole lot of new ideas *and* experiences *and* understandings that could be useful."

Now those things don't necessarily connect together logically. The fact that your hand is touching your arm and your notebook is on your leg does not mean that you're going to learn things. However, it sounds meaningful and serves a purpose. The purpose is not one of deception, but one of transition.

A lot of people have the idea that hypnosis is a contest, but to think of hypnosis as a contest is really a waste of time. The question is "How can I structure my communication to make it *easiest* for someone to accomplish what he wants to?" If somebody comes in wanting to go into a trance to make therapeutic changes, or if I'm using hypnosis for some medical purpose, or control of pain, or to remember things, I want it to be as easy as possible for me to accomplish these things. I want the same thing for the people I communicate with. And as I communicate with people, I use words like "as" to connect ideas together so that they don't have to jump from one idea to another.

Man: Are you saying that you try to link up the suggestion with something in the person's immediate concrete experience to make the suggestion more credible?

Absolutely. You *can,* in fact, feel your hand on your leg and you *can* feel your notebook. So I can link something about learning to that. Not only does it become more credible, but it is no longer a jump. I used to think that what made transitional words powerful was only that they made a statement more credible. In addition to that, the fact that people don't have to jump simply makes it much easier for them to actually engage in the process.

When I was working with people doing things like pain control, I used to build upon things that they could verify. "You can feel the pain in your arm, and it hurts you very badly, but you can also feel the beating of your heart, the movement of your toes, and you can feel the sound in your ears as your heart beats. You can feel your glasses on your nose, and it's possible for you to begin to feel that other hand, and that other hand can become very intense in its feelings. You can notice each finger, and in fact, you can take all the feelings in one hand and put them in another."

I used to think that it was the logic of that kind of statement that made it convincing. That so-called logic is part of what makes these statements effective, but more than being logical and convincing, these statements are a set of instructions about what's plausible. That plausibility becomes easier for people to respond to when they stay in a constant, uninterrupted state of consciousness. You see, hypnosis makes it possible for somebody to control his heart rate. But usually when people begin to try to do something like control their heart rate, they start talking to themselves, and then they start thinking about their Aunt Susie, and then they say "I wonder if this will work." Those jumps between ideas represent changes in consciousness—not radical ones but subtle ones.

Building transitions maintains a relationship between statements so that rather than jumping from one state of consciousness to another, you move through them smoothly. And as you move more gracefully from one state of consciousness to another, it's easier to accomplish tasks, especially ones that have to do with your involuntary systems like heart rate and blood pressure. It's not a mechanism of conviction; it's a mechanism that makes it *easier*.

One of my main criteria for the validity of something is not only whether or not it works, but also how *easily* it works. I don't believe therapy should be hard on the client *or* the therapist. When something is hard, it's an indication of what we don't know. Hypnosis should not be difficult or unnatural. It should be the most natural thing in the world. Whenever people have to force themselves and try, that is an indication that the technology you're using is not sophisticated enough. That doesn't make it bad, but it is an indication that there's much more to know. Does that make sense?

Man: I really wasn't following the last sentence.

Thank you. You did that beautifully. What I'm saying doesn't really make sense; however, it works. I elicit a very different response if I stop using phrases like "as" or "when" or "while" and suddenly use a disjunctive sentence like "Does that make sense?" You start to go back through what I said, and it's difficult to make the transition to the last sentence because there wasn't one. Now while I'm describing this to you, if you consider your experience of what's occurring right at the moment that I'm talking to you, you're moving from one idea to the other. The grace with which you're moving from one idea to the other is what we're talking about. And if I want to know if you consciously understand that—which is a different thing than experiencing it or being able to do it—I'm going to have to be able to make a smooth transition to your conscious understanding. As you sit here considering that, does that make more sense to you?

Man: It seems that you're talking about using a number of bridges; for example the thing about making your style like the patient's, or adopting maybe the mannerisms—

No, I didn't say mannerisms. You might want to mirror body posture, but if the person scratches himself, it's not necessary for you to scratch yourself. If you adopt a person's mannerisms overtly, it has a tendency to intrude into consciousness, and the one thing you don't want to do as a hypnotist is to intrude into that person's consciousness. You want to find more subtle mechanisms: for example, breathing at the same rate. That's not something a person is apt to become conscious of. But unconsciously he will be aware of it and he'll respond.

Man: OK. Those things are another way of making a link between the ideas that you're trying to put across. I don't know quite how to articulate what I'm thinking: that somehow you're going to be more persuasive if there's a similarity in various subtle means.

Yes, and I do something else that makes it much easier to be successful as a hypnotist. I don't think of it as persuasion. Many people who do hypnosis and write about it talk about it as "persuasion," being "one-up," being in "meta-position," or being "in control." They sometimes refer to themselves as "operators," which I always thought was an interesting thing for hypnotists to call themselves. People who do that also write about "resistance," because thinking of hypnosis as control and getting resistance go hand in hand. One way of describing what I'm suggesting is that it is more persuasive. The other way of describing it is that it is more *natural.* It's more natural for you to respond to things that fit together than to things that don't.

Try something. Close your eyes for a minute. Most of you here have been standing near a grove of trees at some time in your life. And as you stood there and looked up at those trees, you could see the leaves and the branches, and you could smell the air that surrounded the trees. You could feel the weather, the temperature of the air; you might even begin to hear a breeze, and as you hear that breeze you might notice the branches and the leaves responding with movement. You might turn to your left and see a large rhinocerous charging at you.

If that doesn't disjoint your reality, nothing will. In terms of inducing an altered state, disjointing can have a value and a function. But its function is not one of gently gliding someone somewhere.

Disjointed communication is a very powerful tool in family therapy. People come in and say things like "I wish my wife would just leave me alone" and I say "OK, lock her in a closet."

"Well, that's not what I want."

"OK, what *do* you want?"

"I just want her to stop telling me she wants things."

"Do you want her to write you letters?"

Those are not natural transitions, and they elicit different kinds of responses. They are very useful in the context of family therapy when things have got to go quickly, and you often have to work around the limitations of the conscious mind by battering it back and forth.

You can use the absence of transitions to elicit very, very powerful responses. Here we're talking about smooth inductions into altered states. You can also pump people into altered states very quickly by communicating without transitions that are logical, meaningful, and smooth. We'll get to that later on. That's a more radical method, and I don't want to teach you both at the same time. I want to teach you one and then the other. It's always easier to understand when things are sorted into pieces.

In my teaching I've noticed something I'll mention to you. It's a funny thing about learning and the way people make generalizations. If you tell people "You know, I really think that Kansas City is a nice town" they'll say "What's the matter with Dallas?" This isn't idiosyncratic to psychological and communication arts; it's a very pervasive thing. In my teaching around the country if I tell people "This is something that will work" somehow or other they get the idea that something else *won't* work. And I'm not saying *not* using transitions won't work. I'm saying using transitions is helpful. It amplifies what you're doing and makes it better. The opposite can work just as well, but you have to use it differently.

In the context of hypnosis, you do not go fast by going quickly. You go fast by going slowly. You simply put your subject's conscious mind in abeyance. Or you can describe it as switching what is in consciousness by leading him into an altered state of consciousness. It's not that he loses his conscious mind and he can't see or hear or think; it's that the same paradigm that operates his conscious mind is not at work. It's still there, it hasn't disappeared, but when you shift him to an altered state, you can logically and systematically and rigorously build new learning. The first step is to learn to get a person into an altered state by using gentle transitions.

Man: I've seen the utility of transitions, especially when you're dealing with relatively unrelated concepts. Is it necessary when they're related—say in relaxation, when you're dealing with words like "feelings of tranquility, peaceful, feeling quiet, feeling very good"? Is it necessary to keep tying transitions onto those types of phrases?

Well, "necessary" is a funny word. Necessary always relates to the outcome. It's certainly not necessary; the question is "What is it that you want to accomplish?"

Man: What becomes the measuring device for knowing how often it's most beneficial to use those transitions?

Your eyes. As you begin to do this you're going to notice that people look different in altered states than they do when they're in their normal waking trances; and as you begin to notice that, you begin to notice when you do things which create discontinuity in their experiences. Very good vision is necessary in order to use hypnosis, because most of the time people are not providing you with as much feedback as they would normally. They're not talking much, and they're not behaving as obviously. In one sense this makes it easier, because there's not as much to confuse you, but it also requires that you have more visual acuity. If you don't have that, you'll end up doing what many hypnotists do—relying completely on finger signals to get yes/no answers to your questions. That isn't necessary. It's a good thing to know about in case you're not getting the feedback you want, or to use while you develop your sensitivity. However, if you have good vision, you can get any feedback you want without having to build in a feedback mechanism artificially. People respond externally, in ways that you can see, to what's going on in them internally.

If people have the internal experience of being disjointed when you say "quiet," "relaxed," or "comfortable" because they don't feel that way, you will see nonverbal responses which will indicate that. And if you see those kinds of things, it makes sense to mention them. "Someone says 'Why don't you relax?' and you try to relax, but it's difficult and you can't, and you say to yourself 'If only I could.' I could tell you 'Be comfortable' but it's hard to *be comfortable* deliberately. But it's very easy to think about a raindrop resting on a leaf." Even though those two things aren't related, people will relax a lot more thinking about a raindrop than they will *trying* to relax.

One of the things that impressed me more than anything else about Milton Erickson was that he did not use hypnosis as a direct tool. If he wanted someone to be colorblind, he didn't say "Become colorblind." He'd say "Have you ever read a book? What does it mean to have a book read (red)? It doesn't mean anything at all. Somebody told me one time that there was a 'blue Monday.' I said to myself 'a blue Monday. That doesn't mean a thing. These things go together somehow, but they don't have any meaning.' They don't mean anything to me. They don't *need* to mean anything to you."

The difference between Erickson and the other hypnotists that I've watched and listened to and studied with, is that Erickson didn't have any resistant clients. Either he selected his patients really well, or he did something important that other people weren't doing. Milton watched how people responded, and he gave them what was appropriate for them. Using transitions is one thing that is appropriate with anyone who is a native speaker of English, *because* transitions are part of the basic structure of English; they are part of how our language is built. *And as* you do hypnosis, *if* you use transitions, they will help you.

I saw Milton do an official trance induction once, which was a very rare phenomenon, believe me. Most of the time people went in and started talking to him about intellectual things . . . and suddenly the time had passed. But once he officially induced a trance. He had a person sit down, and he said "*And as* you sit there I want you to stare at a spot on the wall, *and as* you stare at that spot you can realize that you're doing the same thing now that you did when you very first went to school and learned the task of writing numbers and the letters of the alphabet. You're learning . . . learning about something that you really don't know about. *And* even though you haven't realized it, already your breathing has changed (his voice tempo slows down), *and* you're becoming more comfortable *and* more relaxed." Those transitions helped to build continuity. Now what going to school and learning about numbers and letters of the alphabet have to do with becoming more relaxed is tenuous at best.

However, the meaning of *any* communication—not just in hypnosis but in life—is not what you think it means; it's the response it elicits. If you try to compliment somebody and he's insulted, the meaning of your communication is an insult. If you say he's insulted because he didn't understand you, that's a justification for your inability to communicate. The communication itself was still an insult. You can either justify things and explain them, or you can learn from them. My preference is to learn from them. So if I communicate and someone takes it as an insult, next time I change the way I communicate. And if in the future I want to insult that person, I know exactly how to do it!

While transitions are not the whole ball game, they are a useful tool. There's no set formula in hypnosis. The only thing that you can count on is that when you communicate with people, they will respond. If you provide them with enough different communications, you can find what they will respond to appropriately.

What I've told you so far is just the beginning. I also want you to pay attention to your tempo. Tempo is very, very powerful. A rather traditional hypnotist named Ernest Hilgard proved after forty years of research that there's no relationship between a person's ability to alter his state of consciousness and the hypnotist's voice tempo. He has statistical proof of this. But if you pay attention to your own experience as I am talking to you right now and when . . . I change my tempo . . . to another tempo . . . which is distinctly . . . different . . . and slower . . . it has a noticeable impact. As long as it has a noticeable impact, I don't care what "science" says.

Now, I said in the beginning that I'm a modeler. A modeler only builds descriptions. The descriptions are only ways of getting you to pay attention to things. Right now these descriptions are designed to get you to pay attention to your voice tone and tempo. The first hypnotist I ever met was sitting down trying to put someone in a trance when I walked in the room. He was going to teach me how to do hypnosis, and he was talking in an unpleasant high nasal voice saying "I want you to feel very relaxed." Even *I* recognized that I couldn't feel relaxed with a whining person talking to me. But he "knew" that all you needed to do was have one tone of voice, because it says in all the books that you're supposed to use a monotone. He "knew" that it doesn't matter what tone you use, as long as it's the same one.

Now, talking in a monotone is only a way of avoiding being incongruent, as far as I can tell. If you use the same tone of voice all the time then you probably won't be incongruent. If you *are* incongruent, no one will notice it, because there's no variation in your voice. However, the variation in your voice can also be a vehicle that will *add* to what you're doing.

Man: I noticed that when you were giving suggestions, you sometimes used words that imply control; words like "you will feel" or "you are feeling" versus "this is something that may happen." Do you differentiate between when you choose controlling versus non-controlling words?

Yes. The guideline I use is this: I don't want anyone that I do hypnosis with to ever fail at anything. If I'm making a suggestion about something that can be verified easily, I will probably use words such as "could" or "might"—what we call "modal operators of possibility." "Your arm *may* begin to rise. . . ." That way, if what I've asked for doesn't occur, the person won't have "failed." If I'm making a suggestion about something that is completely unverifiable, I'm more likely to use words that imply causation: "This *makes* you sink deeper into trance" or "That *causes* you to become more relaxed." Since the suggestion is unverifiable, he won't be able to conclude that he's failed.

If I've used five or six modal operators of possibility, and the person responds to them all, at that point I'm probably safe switching to words that imply causation. However, if my next suggestion is very critical, I may continue to use modal operators of possibility. The basic guideline is to make sure no one fails at anything.

Many hypnotists push people to the limits of what they can do by giving them what are called susceptibility tests. These hypnotists put their clients in an altered state and attempt to do a series of graded hypnotic tasks, and the clients accomplish some and fail at others. What usually happens is that somehow or other both the hypnotists and the clients get the idea that there are things they can't do.

When I was teaching at the university and was running hypnosis courses in the evening, a lot of people would come to those courses and say "Well, I've been in lots of trances, and I can only go to a certain level." I don't know where this idea about levels came from. Somehow or other the quality of your hypnotic trance is measured in height—self-esteem goes up, but in hypnosis you go down. It takes a really altered state for some people to see a positive hallucination. Other people see positive hallucinations all the time; they call it thinking. It

I'm a hypnotist and I push someone into a position, it sets him up for failure. If I say "You will open your eyes and see a six-foot French poodle" and he opens his eyes and there's no French poodle, he may think he can't have positive hallucinations. If he takes that instruction as a comment about himself rather than about that particular hypnotist, he will probably believe that he can't do it.

Typically, clients will come in and say "Well, gee, I've always wanted to be able to have a positive hallucination, but I can't." *I* know that everybody is capable of it and has probably already done it a number of times. When they tell me they can't, it's an indication that something has *convinced* them that it's outside the range of their capabilities, which will only make it that much harder for me to be able to do it. I have to sneak around their beliefs in order to get them to have that experience. Alteratively, I can simply accept this belief and say "Well, you know, it's a genetic limitation, but it isn't a necessary phenomenon to be able to accomplish things, unless you're a civil engineer."

That's what civil engineers do for a living, you know. They go out and look at valleys that have nothing in them and hallucinate freeways and dams, and then they measure them. They just have to have *certain* hallucinations and not others. Seeing a freeway where there isn't one is "natural," it's called "work." If they see little blue men walking up and down the freeway, *then* they're in trouble.

Since I don't want people to fail and make generalizations which are not true, I proceed very, very slowly in producing verifiable effects like the classic hypnotic phenomena. I haven't known many people who have a great need to have arm levitation or negative hallucinations. Most people have those all the time and don't know it. Those phenomena don't have any value in and of themselves.

What I'm concerned about is that I lead people through experiences that convince them they can get whatever changes they want for themselves. Whether they want to be able to control pain when they go to the dentist, to change their sleeping habits, or to make very pervasive psychological changes, I want to help them get those results, because hypnosis can be a very powerful tool to expedite psychotherapeutic change.

Many people ask "What can you use hypnosis for?" The question is not "*What* can you do with hypnosis specifically?" but "*How* can you use hypnosis to do whatever you want to do?" Hypnosis is not a cure; it's a set of tools. If you have a set of mechanic's wrenches, that doesn't mean you can fix the car. You still have to use the wrenches in a particular way to fix it. This is the most misunderstood aspect of hypnosis; it's treated as a *thing*. Hypnosis is not a thing; it's a set of procedures that can be used to alter someone's state of consciousness. The question about which state of consciousness you use to work with a particular problem is really a different issue. It's an important issue, and it's one we're going to deal with later. But the first thing to learn is how to move somebody quickly and gracefully from one state of consciousness to another.

Exercise 3

I want you to take another ten minutes and do the same exercise that you did before in the same group of three. This time add the refinements that we have been talking about. Some time has passed since I described them, so I want to go back through them in detail. This time, rather than first describing the experience to the person, have him sit back and close his eyes, and begin by describing elements of his present experience. I want you to use three statements that are pacing statements—descriptions of verifiable experience. "You're sitting in a chair. . . . You can feel where your body touches the chair. . . . You can feel how your arms are crossed . . . where your foot touches the floor . . . the temperature of your face . . . the movement of your fingers. . . . You can hear the sounds in the room of other people moving. . . . You can feel the temperature of the air. . . . You can hear the sound of my voice. . . .

All of those statements can be verified. I want you to say three sentences that can be verified, and then I want you to attach something which is *not* readily verifiable. You can attach any statement that is a description of where you want them to go: ". . . and you're becoming more relaxed." ". . . as you continue to get more comfortable." ". . . and you don't know what I'm going to say next." So you make three pacing statements, use a transitional word, and add one statement that leads them in the direction you want them to go. "You are breathing. . . . There are sounds in the room. . . . You can hear people moving . . . *and* you wonder, really wonder, exactly what you're doing." Make the transitions sound as natural as possible. One of you will be the subject, and the other two will take turns saying a set of pacing and leading statements. After each of you has done two sets, I want you to begin to include descriptions of the same experience you used the first two times you did the exercise in your pacing and leading statements. ". . . while you take time and go back and think about when you were jogging." Notice how it's different this time.

Again, it will help if you pace nonverbally: breathe at the same rate as the person you're talking to, or use the tempo of your voice to match his breathing. And it's essential that what you say is congruent with how you say it.

When your subject appears to be into the experience as deeply or deeper than he was before, I want you to start violating these principles, one at a time. Suddenly make your voice tempo totally different. Notice whether or not that has an impact. Then go back to what you were doing before, and then change your tone. Then try not using transitions. "You're sitting there. You're comfortable. You're relaxed. You don't know what's going to happen." Notice what happens when you do that. Try adding things that are not relevant. "You can feel your fingers on the keys . . . and you know that there's a kitchen somewhere in this building." "You can feel your feet against the floor . . . and you feel the enthusiasm and interest of politicians in Washington."

Concentrate first on using all the elements that we have discussed. When you have established a good solid state, vary just one little piece and notice what happens. Then go back to using all the elements and then vary another little piece. Notice what happens to the person's face, to her breathing, to her skin color, to her lower lip size, to the movement of her eyelids. People don't talk much in trance, so you're going to have to get your feedback in other ways. If you check it out afterwards, it will be too late. You have to be able to check it out while it's going on at each moment, and the best tool to do that with is going to be your vision.

Take three or four minutes each to do this. Go ahead.

* * * * *

Did you notice that doing the exercise this way amplified the process even more? What I have been trying to show you this morning by grading these things—by having you just do it, then giving you a little more instruction, and then having you do it again—is that I'd like you to think of hypnosis as a process of *amplification.* If you think of hypnosis as a way of *persuading,* in the end you won't be able to do nearly as much with it. If you think of it as a way of *controlling,* you won't be able to do nearly as much. We picked one situation in a person's experience in which she responded in a particular way, and as you used these particular techniques, you could amplify that response.

Woman: What about getting arm levitation and things like that? Is that amplification?

Hypnotists are very clever in going after responses that they *know are going to happen anyway.* Arm levitation is one of the things many hypnotists go for. And one of the first instructions to lead to arm levitation is "Pay attention to your hand and it will begin to feel lighter." Try taking a really deep breath, and notice what happens to your hands. . . . Your hands have a little light feeling, because when you breathe in and your chest goes up, that pulls your hands up. So if you give your instruction for light hands when the person breathes in, it will be true.

Good hypnotists pick things like that which they know will happen. However, they're not all conscious of how they're doing it. There's an old induction method you see in the movies where the hypnotist swings a watch back and forth. The hypnotist says "The watch is going back and forth slowly, and you're looking at the watch, and you see it as time passes before you. As you watch that watch go back and forth, your eyes are going to begin to grow tired." Of course they're going to grow tired! If you stare at *anything* long enough, your eyes will get tired.

Around the turn of the century people used to do hypnosis by having the subject look up at something. The subject would be sitting down and the hypnotist would stand up in front of her, hold up two fingers, and say "OK, I want you to stare at these two fingers, and as you look at those fingers, I want you to watch them intensely. . . . And as your eyes begin to feel tired, your eyelids are going to grow heavy and you'll *know* that you're beginning to go into a hypnotic trance." If you stare at anything that's above you long enough, your eyes are going to grow tired. "And as your eyes begin to grow tired, you begin to notice changes in the focus of your vision." If you stare at anything long enough, your focus will change. "And your eyelids are going to begin to grow heavy. You're going to feel the need to close them." Of *course* you will. Everyone does all the time. It's called blinking.

If I then tell you "And when your eyes close, they're going to stay shut" the odds are pretty high that they will. I've taken three pieces of verifiable experience, and I've connected them with one which is not verifiable. I've done it with a natural transition and with a flow that matches everything in your experience. I've built a step-by-step process that leads to an outcome. I'm saying "You are having this experience, and that leads to this experience, which leads to this experience" and these three are all verifiable. Your eyes *are* going to grow tired; your eyelids *are* going to want to close; your focus *is* going to change. You don't know consciously that those things are a natural part of experience, but as I describe them, one naturally leads to the next. Then when I add on something which is *not* a natural part of your experience, you are already following step by step, so you just go on to the next one. It's not that you're convinced. You never even thought about whether it was true or false. You're just following along. Using transitions like that allows you to follow along easily.

If you think of hypnosis as if it's a state of controlling someone or persuading someone, the loser is going to be you. You will limit the number of people you will be effective with. You'll also lose in your own personal life, because you're going to start worrying about who's in control of you. My experience is that people are much more respectful of themselves in hypnotic altered states than they are in the waking state. I can give someone a suggestion which is negative and harmful in the waking state, and she will be much more apt to carry it out than if she is in a trance. If you think about the things that people have told you to do which were unpleasant, but which you did anyway, you were probably in the waking state at the time you did them. In trances it's very difficult to get somebody to do something which does not lead toward something meaningful and positive. People seem to be more discerning in altered states. It's a lot easier to trick or take advantage of someone in the waking state than in any other state of consciousness I know of.

I believe that hypnosis is really biofeedback. However, a biofeedback machine does not tell you to slow your pulse down. It only tells you where it is now. You have to aim toward the outcome of your pulse being slower, or your blood pressure being different. The machine only provides the feedback. As a hypnotist you can do both. You can provide people with communications that match what's going on, just like a biofeedback machine. You can then start adding other things step by step that lead them to somewhere else, and they will be able to go along naturally and comfortably. You can create a situation in which all they have to do is *respond*—the one thing people do all the time, and the thing they do best.

It is a lot easier to make personal changes in an altered state than it is in the waking state. The fact that you don't have the choices that you want is a function of the state of consciousness that you're in. Your normal waking state, by definition, is a description of the capabilities and the limitations that you have. If you are in a state in which you are limited, and you try to make changes in those limitations with your normal state of consciousness, it's a "catch-22" situation. Those limitations will constrain the way you try to deal with the limitations, and you're going to have a lot of difficulty. If you go into an altered state, you will not have the same limitaions that you usually do. You will have limitations, but they will be *different* ones. If you go back and forth between altered states, you can change yourself so much that your waking state won't resemble what it was before.

How many of you in here are clinicians? How many of you at some time have changed so much that you never went back to who you were? . . . And how many of you have never done that? . . . I was hoping one of you would raise your hand so I could say "How dare you be a clinician!" An agent of change unable to change—that would be the ultimate hypocrisy. To me, hypnosis is only a way of expediting change. All we're working on here is learning to make natural transitions from one state to another.

Man: I keep wondering how you can tell when someone goes into a trance. You asked us to notice the changes, and I saw some, but how do I know if that means she's going into a trance?

OK. What kinds of changes did you all see when you did the inductions? I asked you to pay attention to what resulted in change. What changes did you notice?

Woman: Her face muscles seemed to relax, and her face got flatter.

That is characteristic. In trance there is a flattening or a flaccidity of the muscles in the face, and there is a symmetry which is uncharacteristic of the waking state. I've found that first there is an intensification of facial asymmetry as the person begins to enter a trance. You know you've got a fairly deep trance when you get symmetry again—a symmetry that is more balanced than the typical symmetry in the waking state. As a person comes back out of a trance, you can determine where they are in the process of coming back to the normal state of consciousness. They go from extreme symmetry in their face through a relatively asymmetrical state to whatever their normal symmetry is. What else did you see?

Man: There were little twitches of the fingers or other parts of the body.

Any unconscious movements—jerky, involuntary kinds of shudder movements—are really good indicators of a developing trance state.

32

Woman: The breathing really changed.

I'm glad you said it that way. People's breathing patterns vary considerably in their normal state, and when they go into an altered state, whatever breathing pattern is characteristic for them will change. If you have a very visually-oriented client who breathes shallowly and high in the chest in a normal state of consciousness, she'll often shift to breathing deeply from lower in her stomach. If you've got a very kinesthetically-oriented person who typically breathes slowly from her stomach, she'll shift to some other breathing pattern. Breathing patterns are linked to sensory modes, and they will change as a person alters consciousness.

Woman: If you see a person who typically has an asymmetrical face, does that mean that there is a lot of polarity, or a lot of difference between his conscious and unconscious?

I wouldn't draw that conclusion. If you see an exaggerated amount of facial asymmetry, you know something unusual is going on. I conclude that there's some imbalance: either chemical, or behavioral, or both. I wouldn't label this a difference between conscious and unconscious.

Man: I noticed that as people went deeper, their hands got warm and flushed.

Especially as you get into the deeper stages of trance, there will be muscle relaxation and an increased flow of blood in the extremities.

Man: What's the relationship between the eyes rolling completely backwards and altered states?

None that I know of. If the eyes roll all the way up in the head, that's a good indicator of a fairly deep trance. However, lots of people go into a profound trance with their eyes open, so it's not necessarily an indication of an altered state.

Man: What does it mean when you get eye movement?

There are two kinds of movement. One is an eyelid flutter, and the other one is seeing the eyeball moving behind the eyelid, but the lid itself is not fluttering. The latter is called "rapid eye movement" and is an indicator of visualization.

OK. There are these general signs of entering trance, and in addition there will be many other changes that you can observe which will be unique to the person you are working with. These changes will simply be indications that the person is shifting states of consciousness. When you ask what a trance state looks like, the question is "which state?" and "for whom?" If you observe the person's muscle tonus, skin color, and breathing pattern *before* you do an induction, you know what their normal state looks like. As you do the induction, when you observe changes in those parameters, you know that the person's state is altering.

In addition to watching for general signs of changes in someone's state of consciousness, you need to watch for signs of being in or out of rapport. The person will either make responses that are congruent or that are incongruent with what you are asking for, and this will be a good indication of the degree of rapport. Of course, as you lose rapport, the person will begin to return to their waking state.

Summary
A. Trance can be thought of as the amplification of responses and experience. If you describe an experience, talking about what *has to be there,* you will help the person amplify his/her response.
B. Matching builds rapport and is the basis for leading someone into an altered state. You can match any part of the person's behavioral output. It's particularly useful to match something like breathing rate which is always occurring, but is something the person isn't likely to be conscious of. If you match breathing rate with your speech tempo, you can simply slow down the rate of your speech and the other person's breathing will become slower. Another way to match is to verbalize what is present in the person's ongoing experience. "You are smiling as you look at me, you can hear my voice as I talk. . . ."
C. Smooth transitions make it possible for the person to easily go into an altered state. Connecting words like "as" "while" and "and" make your transitions graceful.
D. General signs of trance: first facial asymmetry, then more than usual facial symmetry. General muscle relaxation, small involuntary muscle movements, flushing, changes in breathing pattern.

II

Simple Inductions

This afternoon we're going to describe, demonstrate, and have you practice very systematically a variety of specific hypnotic induction techniques, so that you will begin to have choice in how you induce trance. What you did this morning is all you will need with some people, but you will not be successful with others if that is all you have in your repertoire.

Traditional hypnotists have done research which "proves" that only a certain percentage of people are hypnotizable. The way they proved that is by using exactly the same induction with everyone, so of course they are only successful with a certain percentage. If you have only one induction, it's going to work with some people and fail with others. Most traditional hypnotists don't even bother to add some of the basic pieces you used this morning, such as matching your voice tempo to the person's breathing. The wider the range of induction possibilities you have, the more people you will be successful with.

This morning we spent some time discussing what physiological signs accompany an altered state of consciousness. You were able to detect at least some of the distinctive changes in muscle tonus, breathing patterns, skin color, lower lip size, etc., in the person you were putting into an altered state. Those particular signs of an altered state are precisely what you will be watching and listening for this afternoon as you continue learning about inductions.

The basic principle of doing a hypnotic induction is to watch for the physiological signs of developing altered states, and to do anything

34

you can to amplify those signs. There are also specific ways of proceeding. There are generalizations—patterns that you can use which are *likely* to lead in the direction of altering someone's state. I remind you that all the generalizations we offer are lies: that is, they will not work for every person or at every time. They are good generalizations because they force you to go to sensory experience and notice what's going on. *Always* give up a generalization or a pattern in favor of what is actually being presented to you in the way of sensory feedback. We will be presenting these patterns to give you specific ways to proceed. As you proceed, if you see signs of trance developing in the other person, continue; what you are doing is working. If you don't see those signs developing, do *anything* else.

The first two methods I am going to demonstrate are similar to some of the methods you already used this morning. However, they are important and useful enough that I want to describe them in a slightly different way.

Verbal Pacing and Leading: 5-4-3-2-1 Exercise

This morning you did verbal pacing and leading when you made three sensory-based, verifiable statements, used a transition, and added a non-verifiable statement. You can make this method more elegant by making your beginning statements almost entirely externally-oriented, and then gradually increasing the number of non-verifiable internally-oriented statements you make. Milton Erickson often described trance as having an inward focus of attention. By gradually increasing the number of internally-oriented statements, you use pacing and leading to shift the person's attention inward.

So when you practice this method, start by making five statements: four which are sensory-based, and then one which is internally-oriented. Connect them with some transitional word like "and" or "as." "You are listening to the sound of my voice *and* you can notice the colors in the room *as* you feel your arm on the chair *and* you can begin to have a sense of contentment." Then you make three verifiable statements followed by two non-verifiable, then two and three, one and four, and at that point you should have a fairly nice trance state developing.

I would like you all to think for a moment: what would constitute an example of a non-sensory-based description that you could offer in conjunction with your verifiable statements? I want to make sure you understand what constitutes a non-sensory-based description of an internal experience.

Man: And you will become comfortable.

Woman: And you will experience the feeling of delight.

Woman: Satisfied.

"And you will be satisfied with the progress you are making."

Man: And you will feel some things being different.

Man: And you will remember pleasant memories.

"And you will remember a specific pleasant memory."

Man: Are you intentionally using the future tense?

Actually, I suggest that you use present progressive tense for now. "And you *are becoming* aware of the delightful experience, and you *are beginning* now to remember. . . ." "Now you *are becoming* aware of the sense of being able to learn about hypnosis."

Would you come up here, Barb? I'd like to demonstrate.

There are two things that the rest of you can attend to as I proceed. One is to keep track of the observable physiological changes that Barb goes through as she alters her consciousness. The other is to keep track of what I am doing verbally, because I am going to be using the pattern I've just been talking about. That way you can correlate what I am doing with her responses.

Now, Barb, with your eyes opened or closed—it's entirely a matter of your own comfort in this—I would like you to sit there and allow me to offer you some verbal descriptions. One thing you might consider doing is questioning whether or not the verbal descriptions I am offering you are accurate for your ongoing experience. For example, at this moment you are sitting there and you can hear the tone of my voice. And you can feel the warmth of your fingers being interlaced.

What just happened? I hope you can detect that, because Barb's response just now is an important beginning.

Man: She was nodding.

Yes she was, but there was something even more profound.

Man: She closed her eyes and opened them.

Well, her pupils dilated. The part that I think you could have seen even from the back row is the smoothing out of her facial muscles. You all know the phenomenon called the "blank stare"? You are talking to someone, and suddenly you have the feeling that you are all alone? There's a technical term for it in Northern California called "spacing out."

I said two things to Barb, both of which she could immediately

verify. As she verified that those two statements were true, and especially as she verified the second one, there was a sudden congruence
between what she was hearing and what she was feeling, which allowed
her to begin to change the way she was perceiving the world around
her. She began to go into an altered state. Let me go on a bit so you
have a chance to watch this.

As I said, Barb, you can do this with your eyes open or closed,
whichever one is more comfortable. And as you sit there, you can feel
the support that the chair offers you along your lower back, and you
can feel the place where the rungs are supporting your feet just in front
of your heels. And you can notice, as you sit there, the warmth where
your hands are resting on your legs and thighs, and a sense of growing
comfort. And the next time that your *eyes* begin to *close*, simply allow
them to *stay* there and enjoy a growing sense of comfort internally.
(Someone sneezes.) The sound of a sneeze washes through you, leaving
you even more comfortable. And as you sit there breathing in . . . and
out . . . you have a growing sense . . . of comfort. . . . Listen for
those particular sounds . . . and enjoy a growing sense . . . of security . . . for the purposes that we have here. . . .

At the moment, Barb, I'd like your unconscious mind to make a
choice . . . about giving you a sense of refreshment . . . and renewal
. . . as you sit there listening to the sound of my voice . . . as *well* as the
tinkling of the china . . . but with a sense of growing independence of
your surroundings . . . and a comfort . . . internal . . . and for the
purposes of what we have come here to do . . . as a demonstration
. . . you have already succeeded very well. . . .

And I am going to request of your unconscious mind . . . that it
cause . . . one . . . or both . . . of your hands and arms . . . to begin
to lift, if indeed . . . it is appropriate . . . in small . . . honest . . . unconscious movements. . . . And you can wonder . . . as you sit there
. . . breathing in . . . and out . . . whether or not . . . that particular
response will be the one selected by your unconscious mind
. . . *or* . . . equally useful . . . for the purposes we have here this
afternoon . . . would be for your unconscious . . . to give you a
sense . . . of comfort . . . and if more appropriate . . . to cause you
. . . with a sense of refreshment . . . to slowly drift back and rejoin
us . . . here . . . in this room . . . pleased with how quickly you could
learn . . . these initial phases . . . of altering your state of consciousness. . . .

In either case . . . I would like this opportunity . . . to ask your unconscious to prepare some material. . . . The carpenter who approaches . . . the construction of a building . . . has . . . as his basic . . . tools to begin with . . . boards . . . nails . . . and the tools he brings. . . . The boards and the nails . . . have no meaning . . . until they are assembled . . . in a particular form . . . and attached to one another. . . . So, too, with little marks on paper. . . . The particular marks on paper that we call the alphabet are constructed . . . by small . . . boards or sticks. . . . And it's a lot easier to see . . . clearly . . . the finished product . . . that the carpenter . . . can construct . . . a house . . . a garage . . . than it is to see that same form . . . while the boards . . . and the nails are still separated . . . one from the other. . . .

There are natural . . . ways . . . of perceiving . . . which can be learned. . . . From the air . . . an entire skyline . . . for example . . . the San Francisco waterfront . . . can be taken in with a single glance . . . and its meaning discerned. . . . And indeed . . . from an airplane it's much easier to see such things . . . and to grasp . . . the entire . . . meaning of the waterfront of San Francisco . . . than it is to wander down among the buildings. . . . The same is true in many other areas of our life. . . .

So whether your unconscious chooses . . . to have you return with a sense of refreshment . . . or causes you to go in deeper, so signal me by causing one or both hands and arms to lift. . . . It's a choice that I leave entirely to your unconscious. . . . I would request that whichever choice it makes, it begin to assemble those materials . . . that I have been referring to . . . so that your perceptions can be ordered . . . in a new and more efficient way. . . . (She opens her eyes and stretches.)

As usual, I spent only the first four or so utterances staying with the pattern I said I was going to use, and then just went into everything else I wanted to do. I began by making statements that could be immediately verified in Barb's experience. At any point in time, we all have available to us a potentially infinite amount of sensory-grounded experience. The artistry is in knowing what part of sensory experience to choose to mention. It's particularly useful to choose anything that you guess would be outside of her awareness *until you mention it*. I was fairly certain, for example, that she was aware of the tone of my voice. And indeed she was. That came as no surprise. However, she was less aware of the feeling of the rung of the chair and the support it offered to the heels of her feet. So when I mentioned that, you could see more

observable changes in her. She had to change her present consciousness in order to verify that what I said was true.

Two things happened by that maneuver. Number one, I gained credibility; what I said matched her experience. The second thing is that
since she wasn't attending to the sensation of her feet touching the rung
of the chair until I mentioned it, it was also a covert instruction to
change her present consciousness—in this case in the direction of
attending to a body sensation.

I made half a dozen remarks like that. Then there was a sudden shift
in the kind of verbalizations I offered Barb. What did I do?

Woman: Then you went into metaphor.

I did something else before that.

Man: You started leading.

Yes. First I was just pacing: making statements describing her experience. And then what kind of statements did I make?

Man: Suggestions to close her eyes.

I made suggestions about eye closure, but she was already doing
that. We call that an *incorporation*. She was doing something, so I
incorporated it into what I said.

Right after eye closure, I started making statements about internal
states that I wanted her to develop. I said things like "a growing sense
of comfort and security as you sit here." For me, the nonverbal signs
that she already offered—slower breathing, muscle relaxation, etc.—
have the name "comfort." They may not for Barb. The word "comfort"
has as many different meanings as there are people in this room. When
I use words like "comfort," I'm no longer talking in sensory-grounded
terms. I'm suggesting that such states develop in her—whatever those
words may mean to her.

I hope that you all have some appreciation for what the rest of my
statements were about. I have to explain that Barb had asked me
earlier for a particular kind of change with reference to an academic
skill that she wants. I told a series of metaphors directed toward
preparation for that change. You may be able to find some way of
making sense out of that, and you may not. She has a way of making
sense out of it, and that's the important thing.

Barb: I didn't at the time. It was just so many words. I just quit trying
to deal with it consciously.

Exactly. And that's one of the responses that I want. "It was so many
words that I just quit trying to make sense out of it. What the hell are

you talking about? Carpenters and the San Francisco skyline. And from a plane, it's different than it is walking around among the buildings."

In other words, the latter part was tailored to the request that she had made of me earlier. As I told the metaphors, her conscious mind did not understand. However, I received signals that her unconscious understood the reference and was beginning the preparations that I had requested of it. Are there any questions about what I did?

Man: You decided not to pursue the hand levitation?

No, I offered her a choice. I always do.

Man: Didn't you get some resistance to levitation and then give her an alternative?

There was no resistance. Her hand began to lift. The movements in her fingers and thumb were already there. Then I offered the second alternative, and her unconscious selected that one. If I had not offered the second choice, her hand would have continued to rise.

I made suggestions about hand and arm levitation and got twitches, which almost always precede the actual movement. At that point I remembered I was supposed to be demonstrating inductions, not trance phenomena. So I made the suggestion about her bringing herself out with a sense of refreshment and renewal and delight that she had achieved so much so quickly.

A good hypnotist is like a good government. The less you do to achieve the outcome effectively, the better you are at your job. My way of thinking metaphorically about what Barb and I did is that she allowed me to enter a loop with her in which I could feed back certain parts of her experience which allowed her to alter her state of consciousness radically. But the entire time, *she* was leading in the sense that I was being responsive to the changes in her, incorporating those, and then making a suggestion about where we ought to go next. She accepted all the suggestions I made to her. If she had indicated at any point that I was making a suggestion that was not appropriate for her, I would have offered alternatives.

Man: How would you know when a suggestion was inappropriate for her?

A reversal of all the growing signs of trance would indicate that. Any reversal of the muscle flaccidity, the breathing changes, the lower lip size changes, or skin color changes would have indicated to me that I had just proposed something that was not appropriate for her.

Man: I was wondering what you thought of her nervous laugh at the very beginning when you said her hands were experiencing warmth. She laughed but you ignored it.

That was when I interrupted and said "I hope you noticed that response." The response I was referring to was the muscle flaccidity, the pupil dilation and an immediate body sway. Immediately following my comments she laughed. She would not have laughed if I had gone on with the induction. Her laughter was a recognition that it was working. I had said only two sentences and it was already working and she detected a change. Is that true, Barb?

Barb: Yes.

So the laugh would never have emerged if I had gone on with the induction. Her response was so immediate and distinct that I wanted to make sure all of you noticed.

Woman: What happened to me when you did the induction is kind of strange. I was trying to watch you, because that was my job, and instead I went through the whole thing myself. I was really embarrassed because my hand was coming up and—

Well, you had lots of company. About thirty other people sitting out there did, too, so don't be too embarrassed.

Larry: Can you give us more words that you use for internal responses—things you were guessing she was feeling inside?

Well, I wasn't guessing. I was leading at that point. I was asking her to *create* those experiences. I didn't use the words "security" and "comfort" based on what I was seeing, because I don't know if the signs that she was offering me mean security and comfort for her. I just know those are general words that are often associated with muscle relaxation.

Larry: Right. I am trying to find out other words you would use for that.

There are lots. You can use words like ease, peace, serenity, calmness, or being centered. They are all just words. They don't have any intrinsic meaning. They are interpreted individually by each person for his or her own needs.

I'm insisting on making a clear distinction between sensory-grounded descriptions and non-sensory-grounded descriptions. The sensory-grounded descriptions allow me to get into synchrony with her. The non-sensory-grounded descriptions allow me to offer her very general procedures that she can use idiosyncratically. Her interpretation of these will be rich and meaningful and individual to her. I have no idea what they are, but that's fine. That's content, and that belongs to her. My job is to run the process.

This is a very simple word induction, and you can always fall back on it. It will work. It just takes longer than some of the other fancier ones. When you use it, remember to *connect* the statements about sensory-grounded experience to the statements about internally-oriented states. This is called "causal modeling." The simplest and weakest way to connect statements is to use the word "and." "You hear the sound of my voice *and* you feel the warmth where your hands are resting on your thighs *and* a growing sense of comfort *and*. . . ." In the induction I did with Barb, I started linking with the word "and," and then I moved to a stronger form of linkage. "The feeling of warmth and support *as* your body fits against the chair *will allow* you to grow even more comfortable."

There are three kinds of linkage. The simplest is "X *and* Y." The next stronger form is "*As* X, Y" "*As* you listen to the sound of my voice, you will become more comfortable," or "*When* I reach over and touch you on the knee, you will have a sense of dropping into an even more relaxed state." "*While* you are sitting there listening to the sound of my voice, your unconscious mind can prepare a particularly interesting recall of a pleasant childhood experience." The strongest form "X *causes* Y" uses words like "*cause*" or "*make*." "The lifting of your arm will *make* you drift off into a pleasant memory."

So the pattern is to say four things that are immediately verifiable, and then connect them with an "and" to an internally-oriented state that you are proposing. First you have the pacing and then the leading. As you proceed, you can gradually increase the number of internally-oriented statements, and you can gradually go from a weaker form of linkage to a stronger form.

Linkage can be very powerful. It's astounding how much linkage goes right by people's conscious minds, and yet has an impact. Once I literally had somebody go totally blind in a seminar. I was demonstrating something, and I said "All you need to be able to do is *see in order to do this*." I had linked seeing to being able to do the task. After I went through the demonstration, a woman raised her hand and said "I have a question." I asked her what the question was, and she answered "What do you do if you can't see anything?" I thought she meant she hadn't noticed the person change in my demonstration, so I said "You weren't able to see any responses?" She said "No, it's totally dark."

She wasn't worried at all, but I was thinking "Hey, wait a minute here!" I went over to her and said *"You don't have to learn this"* and poof! . . . her vision came back.

That woman's response was very unusual. For most people, the linkage will work the other way. Since they can see, they *will* be able to do the task. As long as you know what you're linking to what, you'll be able to deal with whatever impact it does have.

Nonverbal Pacing and Leading

All hypnosis can be usefully thought of as feedback. At this moment Bob is sitting in front of me. We are passing lots of information back and forth both verbally and nonverbally. Out of all the messages that we offer each other, some are conscious—that is, he and I know that we are offering them—and some are not.

One thing I can do with Bob's messages is to select those which I can identify as being outside of his awareness, and begin to feed those back by body mirroring. As I feed those back, one of two things will happen. His consciousness will alter and he will become aware of those things, or his unconscious responses will simply be amplified, so that more and more of his responses will be unconscious and fewer and fewer of them conscious.

After you have paced some unconscious response, you can begin to amplify or lead into some other response. I can pick out any portion of Bob's nonverbal behavior and do this. I can pace his pupil dilation by dilating my own pupils, and then, as I look at him, begin to defocus my eyes only as fast as he will follow me. Defocused eyes are a good indication of trance, because they accompany internal processing as opposed to focusing on something in the external world.

I can match his eyeblinks and then gradually blink my eyes more often and more slowly until I get him to shut his eyes. I can mirror his muscle tonus and then slowly relax my own muscles to assist him in relaxation. When you pace and lead nonverbally, there's no need for talk. You just mirror to get rapport, and then slowly put yourself into an altered state of consciousness, making sure that the other person is following you.

Pacing and leading is a meta-pattern. It's actually a part of *every* other induction we'll be teaching you. You can use nonverbal pacing and leading either by itself, or as a part of another induction. I recommend that at some point you practice *just* the nonverbal portion. Without words, just arrange yourself in a mirroring position. Then you can very slowly—noticing how fast the person follows you—put yourself into a deep trance. Be sure to have some way for you to come back out.

Overlapping Representational Systems

For those of you who don't know what representational systems are, let me explain briefly. We noticed some time ago that people specialize in the kind of information they process and pay attention to. If you divide experience into information in the different sensory channels, you have a visual chunk of experience, an auditory chunk, and a kinesthetic chunk. You also have olfactory (smell) and gustatory (taste) chunks, but those two channels don't generally take up very large portions of your experience unless you are cooking or eating. In our normal state, some of us are primarily aware of visual experience, some primarily auditory, and some primarily kinesthetic. We call these representational systems, because they are the systems that we use to represent our experience. The words we use when we talk about our experience are an indication of which sensory channel we are consciously using.

Now the interesting thing is that if you ask someone to describe her normal state of consciousness and then to describe what it's like to be in an altered state, she'll often use a different representational system. For example, someone might describe her normal state as "having a *clear, focused* sense of who I am" (visual words), and her altered state as being "*in touch* with the universe" (kinesthetic words).

This means that when you find out what state someone is in normally in terms of representational systems, you have an excellent indication of what would be an altered state for that person—*anything else.* If someone comes in who is really *in touch* with her feelings and has a *firm grasp* on her life, you might want to take her to an altered state where she is primarily aware of visual images. So if she came in and said "Well, I just *feel* like I want to go into a trance, because I'm *in touch* with having a lot of needs, and I get *irritated* sometimes, and I want to *feel relaxed* and *smooth out* some of the difficulties in my life" I would have a subtle indication that her awareness is mostly kinesthetic.

Jan, would you come up here a minute? Tell me something you like about your house.

Jan: Oh, I love the view. I've got a place overlooking the ocean—it's just beautiful.

She is offering me visual information, so I know I'm safe if I begin talking about visual information. That will pace her experience. Remember, the meta-pattern is pacing and leading: matching what the client is already doing and then leading to something else. That "something else" is to go to systems which she doesn't ordinarily use. That will be an altered state for her.

I'd probably begin by asking for a context that is visually pleasing. I already know Jan likes the view of the ocean. Do you like the beach?

Jan: Oh, yes!

I would like to invite you, with your eyes open or closed, to follow along with me as I offer you a description of the experience . . . of being at the ocean. . . . If you were actually able . . . to go to the ocean . . . on a day like today . . . one of the first things that you can become aware of . . . is that as you look up . . . you see clearly . . . the distinctive lighting of the sky. . . . You may be able to see some clouds floating across the sky . . . and as you look about . . . you can enjoy . . . the clarity of the air . . . and you glance down and see . . . the surface of the beach . . . and as you stand there . . . looking down at the beach you're standing on . . . you can see your feet . . . and you can feel . . . the feeling . . . of your feet . . . on the beach. . . .

And when you look out across . . . the ocean . . . you can see wave . . . after wave . . . after wave . . . rolling from the horizon . . . toward you . . . each one having a unique form . . . a particular curl . . . a particular color as it splashes. . . . And as you look out at the waves . . . moving in . . . you notice . . . the wind is blowing some of the spray off the top of each wave as the breaker hits the shore. . . . And as you watch that spray, you can feel . . . the moisture in the air . . . as the breeze blows on your face. . . . And if you were to now take . . . a couple of steps . . . into the water . . . and feel the coolness of the water swirling around your feet . . . and ankles . . . and you can really enjoy it. . . .

Now if you look up or down along the beach, you can see a familiar figure . . . someone you had not expected to find there . . . and you wave . . . and that person calls across to you . . . reminding you of another time and place . . . and something rather pleasant and surprising . . . that came from that experience . . . and enjoy the experience . . . and learn . . . from it . . . whatever might be useful for you. . . . And when you are prepared . . . and have enjoyed them . . . at your own rate . . . taking all the time you desire . . . come back. . . .

Now, what form of communication was I using?

Woman: You seemed to be using primarily visuals and a lot of going back and forth between those and kinesthetics. Did you reach a point where you decided to stay in kinesthetics?

I would have if I had continued the induction. When I go back and forth, I'm testing to find out if she can follow. Think of this as a verbal counterpart of breathing together. I breathe with her for a while and then I alter my breathing. If she follows, I now have rapport; I have the lead and can continue to develop whatever kind of experience is appropriate.

How did I know that she was able to follow me, by the way? After I said the first few things, I knew immediately that she was able to go along with me. How did I know that?

Man: Her head moved congruently with your instructions.

Yes. When I talked about looking up, her head moved up. When I talked about looking down, her head moved down. When I talked about looking out at the waves, she looked out at the waves. Her body responses indicated that she was having the experience I was suggesting. That is enough information to know that I have rapport. Now, the question is: do I still have rapport if I switch systems? Answer: try it and find out. So I had her look down at the beach. Then I said "And feel your feet against the sand."

Jan: I did.

Woman: So then when you get her into another system, do you tend to stay there?

Yes. Then I would talk mainly about the sensations in her body. As she steps into the water, she can feel the swirling of the water . . . and the moisture in the air . . . as the wind blows against her face.

I first develop a visual image about where she is and then find a point of *overlap* between the visual image and any other system. So, in this case, if she looks down at the beach and sees her feet against the sand, then she can feel the firmness of her feet upon the beach. If she looks out and sees the wind blowing spray off the top of the breaking waves, then she can feel the breeze against her face.

There is always a visual, an auditory, and a kinesthetic dimension to every experience. So you begin with whatever representational system the person offers you. That's pacing: joining the client's model. Then you can use a simple verbal formula which is "You see the clouds moving across the sky . . . and as you watch the clouds move, you feel the breeze against your face." Seeing the clouds moving suggests wind.

The point of overlap between the visual image of clouds moving, driven by the wind, and the kinesthetic system I want to lead her to is the feeling of the breeze upon her face. The verbal formula is "as X," which is the pace, "Y," the lead.

Woman: You only used auditory once that I was aware of. You said she could hear the friend calling to her. Is there a reason why you did not emphasize auditory?

I didn't need it. In this culture the auditory system is seldom well-developed except in musicians. There were lots of other places where I could have included auditory elements: the sound of the wind, the sound of the waves breaking against the shore.

I want to distinguish between induction and utilization. An induction of going visual-visual-visual, then overlapping to kinesthetic, and when she follows, continuing with kinesthetic, will radically alter her state of consciousness. Once that has happened, and I've got all those physiological signs that we were talking about earlier, then all I have to do is build a full experience again. Then I would include all three systems. I would have her walk up to the person, reach out, touch the person, look carefully at his or her face and notice what expression is there, and then listen to what the person has to tell her. Then I would use that fantasy with all three representational systems as the matrix for whatever changes she wants to achieve.

Woman: There was an auditory interruption. Somebody's tape recorder clicked loudly, and I was wondering why you didn't utilize that. It certainly interrupted you.

It interrupted me, but it didn't interrupt her. *She* didn't hear it. I knew that because she didn't respond. There was no change in her breathing, her skin color, or her muscle tonus. Since there was no response, it would have been absurd for me to mention it.

Woman: If she did hear the tape, how would you have included that in the induction?

"And there are disturbing noises, even at the beach."

Man: What about incorporating the swinging of her leg?

I could have. I could put her on a swing at the beach. That would have worked nicely. Utilizing the leg swing and some other pieces of her behavior would have been good choices to make. You don't have to use *all* the good choices every time that you do an induction, only enough of them to get the response that you want.

Jan: I can remember my leg going around, and at the time I knew why, but I don't now.

How could she recover that information, using the same principles of representational system overlap? . . . Jan, swing your leg again. Close your eyes and swing your leg again and notice what comes in visually. . . . A little bit faster.

Jan: Just people's faces.

My interpretation, when I think back about it now, was that she age-regressed as she was doing it—she became a little girl again at the beach. There is a difference between the way an adult swings her leg and the way a child swings her leg. The way she swings her leg now is relatively adult. The way she was doing it when she was in the altered state was more childlike. She was a little girl back at the beach. Do you have any idea how old you were at the beach?

Jan: The same age I am now.

She *said* she was the same age that she is now, but she also offered me nonverbal facial and tonal changes which are characteristic of age-regression. That's also how I would describe the way she was swinging her leg previously.

OK, any questions about this kind of induction?

Man: I don't remember how you first started. Did you ask her something?

Yes. I did something that I think is extremely useful. I said "Do you like to go to the beach?" and noticed her response. If I had just automatically assumed she liked to go to the beach, I couldn't have known if her entire family had drowned when she was three years old as she stood on the shore watching. In that case, a beach would not have been a good choice for a relaxing induction.

The principle is to discover what representational system a person typically uses in her normal state. Some people utilize all systems, and with them you could actually begin anywhere. In the context of stress—and therapy is one such context—people typically have become specialized. That's part of the way they got stuck and came to you for help. With respect to the presenting problem, they will be specialized in one representational system or another. Simply introducing the other two representational systems will often be adequate for them to come up with some new behavior for themselves. You can do that by using overlap.

Overlap will always be evident in what we do. Not only overlap from one representational system to another, but overlap from the outside to the inside. I know a man who said "I do inductions a hundred different ways." I was interested, so I had him demonstrate as many as he could think of. They were all *identical* from a formal point of view. On every induction he used the following sequence: outside visual, inside visual, outside kinesthetic, inside kinesthetic, outside auditory, inside auditory. Each of his inductions had different content, but that's the only *pattern* he used to do inductions. Even though he has only one sequence, he's a very effective hypnotist in terms of achieving the usual outcomes of a traditional hypnotist.

In the context of working here in the group, you could begin with any system unless you have a partner who is already severely specialized. However, I'd like you to take that initial step in order to go through exactly what you would actually do in practice: ask the person something about her previous experience, notice which predicates she uses, and use that system as a place to begin. Offer four or five descriptions in that system, and then find a point of overlap to lead her into another system.

Accessing a Previous Trance State

The easiest of all inductions is to ask your client if she has ever been in a trance before. If she has, you ask her to recount in great detail the sequence of events that occurred the last time she went into a trance. Ask her for the exact configuration of the room, the sound of the hypnotist's voice, and exactly what the hypnotist did to lead her into that profound trance. You will notice that she will relive the experience for you as she describes it. It's an example of automatic regression. In order for her to go back and get all the information in response to the specific questions you are asking, she will re-experience the trance state.

If she rushes over the experience too quickly, and you are not getting a full response, you can either indicate nonverbally for her to slow down, or ask her questions which require that she give you more detail. You can ask "Were you seated just as you are now?" "No, very differently." "Well, would you show me how?" The body position which she last associated with the altered state of consciousness will help her overlap back to that trance experience.

"Were you in a room like this?" "No, no. The walls were green." "Allow your eyes to close and form a mental image of the room you were in the last time you went. . . ." You divorce her from her present state, the present space-time coordinates, to give her more freedom to access all the information, and therefore to re-enter the trance state which was most effective for her in the past.

50

You can add other delivery techniques like embedded commands (see Appendix II) to your questions to reinforce their power. "Well, was he leaning to his right or to his left when your *eyes* first began to *close?*"

That really is the easiest of all inductions. Usually all you need to do is ask her to recount in detail the sequence of events that occurred when she last went into a deep trance. When she has accessed that trance state, you simply utilize it.

How many people here have ever had the experience of visiting Milton Erickson?

If you look around now, you can tell which of the people here have visited Milton, because as I ask that question, they access the trance experience of being with him.

Naturally Occurring Trance States

There's another really easy way to go after a trance state. Everybody has been in a somnambulistic trance; it's just a question of whether they have recognized it as such.

This morning we asked each of you to pick some state in your personal experience in which you have a limited focus of attention. The other two people in your group talked to you about that experience in order to amplify it. You can get the same kind of response without knowing anything about the person by choosing and describing somnambulistic trance states that naturally occur in our culture. What you do is very easy. You sit across from a person and say "Well, before we begin, let's talk about common kinds of experiences, because it is of use to me as a communicator to know what kind of personal history you have, as a way of drawing upon your resources to instruct you in this new matter of hypnosis." Then you describe five very powerful, commonly-occurring trance states. You will notice that as she attempts to understand your words and find examples of what you are talking about in her personal experience, she will go into an altered state.

What happens in your experience when I talk to you about the feelings you have on a long car trip? That's an example of not giving a direct suggestion to go into trance, but simply mentioning a situation where trance states occur naturally in our culture.

For example, I drove yesterday from . . . Santa Cruz, California, where I live . . . up and over the Santa Cruz mountains . . . and back down the other side . . . to the airport in San Jose. And as has happened so many times when I am driving . . . especially along a route which I know . . . a great deal about . . . I have driven it a number of times . . . the last thing I remember . . . before arriving at the airport . . . was turning onto Highway 17, the freeway that I took all the way across the Santa Cruz mountains to San Jose to catch the airplane. And I evidently drove quite safely . . . and during the drive . . . the monotony of the road . . . I assume . . . induced in me a sort of automatic . . . and unconscious response . . . which I could trust . . . to get me safely from where I began . . . to where I wanted to go. . . .

And that was a great deal . . . like another experience which I'm sure you and many people listening to me have shared . . . which is the experience of sitting in a lecture . . . where attendance is mandatory . . . but the person who is talking . . . is not a very exciting speaker . . . someone who is simply . . . talking in a way that induces a sense of . . . boredom . . . and offering you words without a great deal of attention to stimulating you. . . . And in such experiences I've noticed my mind tends to wander . . . to other places and times . . . which are less boring and somehow more stimulating than my present environment. . . .

Or the experience I've had in my life . . . of walking through the woods . . . on a quiet day. . . . Some of the prettiest areas in the part of the country that I live in . . . are the marvelous redwood forests. . . . I've heard people liken . . . the visual impact . . . of those redwood forests . . . to being in a cathedral . . . a large church of some kind . . . and the sense of majesty . . . and calm . . . serenity that they bring. . . . And as I walk through the redwood forests . . . one thing about redwood forests . . . is the fact that they are so homogeneous . . . that they do not support . . . much in the way of wildlife, especially birds . . . so often there is a majestic sort of silence associated . . . with . . . walks through the redwood forest . . . and although there is not a lot of variation . . . in the experience I have . . . as I do walk through them . . . I certainly have a sense of calm . . . and relaxation . . . which I deeply . . . appreciate.

What one thing do those three experiences have in common?

Woman: Relaxation, solitude.

Man: Serenity.

Woman: Repetition.

They are repetitious. They are monotonous. And if any of you were looking around as I was talking, you could see the physiological signs that you're learning to associate with trance developing in most of you.

So a very natural and covert way of leading a person from the state of consciousness she is in toward an altered state, is to tell a series of stories or little episodes as I did, which have in common only the kind of response that you want to elicit from that person. At that point it is entirely a question of how acute your own sensory apparatus is, so that you can notice whether you have achieved the kinds of responses you want. You tell as many stories as necessary to achieve the response. You can talk about riding in an elevator. Almost everybody goes into a trance in an elevator. They look up at the numbers and then their pupils dilate and they become immobilized. In elevators the only place it is culturally acceptable to look is at the numbers or at the walls or the floor.

Another example: What happens when you are driving along a street and you drive up to a red stop light? You *stop*. When the car stops moving, you stop moving.

What are other naturally occurring examples of trance states?

Woman: Watching a movie.

Man: Sitting in church.

Yes, although sitting in church is getting less universal. A lot of people haven't had that experience and won't be able to identify with it, but it's a good one for those who have.

Woman: Watching television.

Yes. If you want to pass information to your kids—if you'd like them to clean their rooms or something—get them while they're watching TV. They're going to be gone: living what's going on in the TV show. So you sit next to them and say—softly so you don't disrupt them—". . . and you have this overwhelming compulsion to. . . ."

Man: Chronic mental hospital patients watch television all day. I never thought of reaching them there.

You might try it that way.

When we were first learning hypnosis, Richard Bandler and I used to play a game with each other. We'd get a group of "naive subjects"— people who had never been officially induced into a trance. Then we would challenge ourselves to get them from the present state to a somnambulistic trance state in a minimum number of steps. One of the first things I always asked for was a meditative state. Meditation is a very altered state relative to normal consciousness. I would ask if I could be allowed the privilege of watching them go into the meditative state without interfering in any way. They would go into the meditative state—a dramatically altered state.

When they were there, I would say "With your permission, I will now offer a suggestion for you to move from this meditative state, leaving its integrity fully protected, to a state called a general somnambulistic trance, from which we can then begin to make the changes you have asked for." I make a clear distinction between trance and meditation, because if there is not a separation between what is called meditation and somnambulistic trance, every time they meditate they will go back into the trance state. I don't want to connect the two, unless I have a specific reason to.

If and when you do official ritualistic kinds of hypnosis, I suggest that you wait until you have already covertly succeeded in getting a couple of trance states with the client. Let me give you the most common example. Somebody comes in and demands that you do hypnosis with her for a presenting problem and you say "Of course. However, before we begin there are a couple of things I need to know." Then you induce a series of trances. You say something like "Well, the first thing to do is to check your ability to recall in detail information that I'm going to need for your case history." So you induce a trance by taking a case history. You ask "Now, where were you born?" and you have her describe in detail the house in which she lived, and the sounds it made, the feelings she had there, etc. And, of course, she is gone; she age-regresses in order to get the detailed information about her past. One description of trance is getting the person independent of her present time/space coordinates. This fits that definition. The only link between her and the present time/space coordinates is your voice. Along all other dimensions, she is somewhere else.

Regression is considered one of the "deep trance" phenomena by traditional hypnotists. It's actually something you get all the time. Gestalt therapists typically get deep trance phenomena automatically, much more easily than a hypnotist, and yet most of them would resist the label "hypnosis." All over the world people are looking at empty chairs and seeing their mothers or their fathers and talking to them and hearing responses. Those are positive auditory and visual hallucinations. They constitute deep trance phenomena. But it's not labeled that way, so there's no resistance involved.

By the way, just as a teaching device, let me make a point here. If you ever lecture on hypnosis, of course the group is going to be going in and out of a trance. The only way that the group can make sense of your descriptions of hypnosis and trance is to access their own experiences that fit those descriptions. Depending on how confident you are in your own personal power, you will get perhaps a hundred people in deep trance rather rapidly—or not, depending upon what outcome you want. There isn't an easier subject in the world to lecture about, because as you talk about it, it is happening.

You can also use your observation of people's responses to know whom to choose as a subject when you are doing groups. You choose one of the twenty percent of the group who have already been in and out of at least five somnambulistic trances during your fifty-minute presentation. By the end of this workshop you ought to have the sensory experience to know who's responding by going into a deep trance and taking in all the material at that level of consciousness; who's in a mixed state, responding consciously and unconsciously; and who's staying entirely conscious. To demonstrate teaching points, you should always be able to pick out exquisite demonstration subjects. If there's a particular response you want to demonstrate, you can talk about what you are going to do, instruct people in what responses are appropriate, and notice who develops those responses most rapidly. That person will be the subject to select.

Some of you here may be drifting off a little more rapidly than might be useful to you for the purpose of learning this material. You might consider stopping for a moment to silently drop inside and ask some part of you to maintain a state of consciousness which is most useful to you for learning purposes. It would be nice to have some blend of having the experience and also being able to keep conscious track of the patterns being used. Let's have a moment of silence while you make those arrangements. You can use the reframing format if you already know it. . . .

Exercise 4

I've just given you five specific induction techniques: (1) verbal pacing and leading, (2) nonverbal pacing and leading, (3) representational system overlap, (4) accessing a previous trance, and (5) describing commonly occurring trance situations. Get into groups of three, and each of you pick a technique that interests you, and which you haven't done systematically before. Person A will pick an induction and do it with B. B can just enjoy it.

Person C will use all of his conscious attention to notice what changes occur as B goes into trance. Pay attention to which statements and behaviors produce the most response, and whether there are any statements or behaviors that bring B back out of trance. C is going to be a "meta-person" to keep track of what's going on. As person C, if you notice that the hypnotist is talking too quickly, give her a hand gesture that indicates "Slow down." If the hypnotist's voice is too high and it seems irritating to B, give her some signal to lower her voice.

When you are A, after you have induced the trance, I want you to give B some general instructions for learning, and then for returning. When you've gotten good trance responses of the nature that Barb offered us here earlier, then simply sit there, take a couple of deep breaths, smile and mentally pat yourself on the back. Look at your observer, and give some minimal cue that you are satisfied that you have achieved a trance. Then match breathing with your subject and when you speak make your voice tempo match her breathing cycle. "And enjoy . . . those particular experiences . . . which your unconscious mind . . . can offer you at this point . . . a sense of wonder . . . and adventure . . . as you enter . . . new states of consciousness . . . gleaning from this experience . . . a sense of assurance . . . about your own capabilities . . . and flexibility . . . as a human being. . . . And after doing that fully . . . and deeply . . . your unconscious, slowly . . . with full respect . . . can bring you back to this state . . . giving you a sense of refreshment and renewal. . . . I will be attentive. . . . If at any point . . . you would be interested . . . in my assisting you . . . in getting back . . . indicate that with a hand movement."

Then sit there and watch. This will be an excellent opportunity for you to train your perceptions to notice the changes that a person demonstrates as she goes in and out of altered states. If you get a hand wave, then you can match her breathing as you say "I am going . . . to count backwards . . . from ten . . . to one . . . slowly. . . . When I reach 'one' . . . your eyes will open . . . and you will have a sense . . . of refreshment . . . and you will be . . . totally present here." Then count backwards with her breathing until you reach "one."

Take a few minutes for feedback when you're done. B can tell A about anything in the induction that was particularly helpful, or about anything that B found disruptive or got in the way of developing the altered state. C can add anything that she observed from the outside, especially relationships between A's suggestions and B's responses. This will be really useful feedback for A. After the feedback, switch positions and give both B and C a chance to try an induction.

So A is going to first induce a trance, then give general learning instructions, and finally give instructions to come back out of trance. Go ahead.

*　*　*　*　*

56

Discussion

Man: I have a question. When I was putting Lynn under, she began to demonstrate a lot of shaky movement in her left hand. Later, she said that that was connected to a nerve center in her cheek which had been operated on a long time ago for a cyst, and that supposedly there's still nerve damage. But at the time I didn't have the faintest idea what—if anything—to do with that.

The minimum response to anything that happens which you don't directly suggest as you are inducing an altered state of consciousness is to verbally incorporate it immediately: "Yes, and you continue to have those specific experiences and the body sensations connected with them." That validates the response and reassures the person that you are alert to the signals she is offering you, even though you may not understand what the signals represent.

"Organ language" is another really powerful pattern which I find useful in dealing with any phenomenon that is significant. By "significant" I mean there's no doubt that something unusual is going on—but I have no idea what it might represent.

"Now, the first time that a person . . . goes into an altered state of consciousness . . . it often *shakes* them *up* a little bit. . . . But they often find it *handy* . . . to come to *grips* with the part . . . of the problem . . . that may be attached to this particular syndrome in a way that . . . allows them to *put their finger on* changes . . . which they can really *grasp* the reality of." I included four or five allusions to the part of the body and to the activity that is being performed by that part of the body. If there are still any remnants of the person's conscious mind left around at that point in the trance, it typically won't understand those allusions. However, the unconscious mind typically will understand and take that as a validating message.

The two maneuvers I just offered you are ways of incorporating an obvious response that I didn't ask for, and validating it. It's my way of saying "OK, I recognize what you are doing, and it is perfectly all right with me for you to continue to do that." That kind of response is usually adequate.

Another slightly more powerful method you can use is to say " . . . and with each such movement you'll go deeper into trance." Then you typically get one of two things: either they go really deeply into trance, or they stop shaking.

You could also use the shaking as an access point to do some therapeutic work. "Those particular experiences . . . connected with those dramatic movements of your hand . . . at this point in time . . . will become available to you . . . only when you reach an adequately deep state of trance . . . for you to appreciate them . . . as experiences from your past . . . which may or may not have had negative repercussions then . . . but which you can now recognize with comfort . . . as something that you survived . . . and to draw from a review and a rehearing . . . of those particular experiences . . . ways in which you might protect yourself . . . in the present and in the future . . . learning from your own experience . . . which is the foundation of your present resources."

All that is "fluff" in the sense that it includes no content. But it is an appropriate and meaningful communication in the sense that you are telling her to do something with the experiences she is having in order to learn from them.

Woman: What do you do if the person doesn't come back out?

If you tell her to come back and she doesn't, that indicates that you've lost rapport. So you have to go back and get rapport. You might just pace her breathing for a while. Then ask her to gather up all the enjoyable, positive aspects of this experience, so that she can bring these back with her when she returns in a few moments. Count backwards slowly from ten to one, saying one number for every other breath that she takes. This will help insure rapport. Give instructions that when you reach "one" her eyes will flutter open as control is returned to her conscious mind, and she will be puzzled and delighted by the experience she has just had.

Woman: I've had clients who apparently go into physiological sleep. I have assumed that somehow the unconscious is still listening, but I'm not at all sure of that. There's no response to me at all.

OK. First of all, I don't believe the last statement: that they don't respond to you at all. I would suggest for your own learning purposes, that you use several simple nonverbal devices to find out if they are still responsive to you. The easiest way to do it would be to get in close enough that they can hear your breathing, and then breathe with them for several minutes. I assume that you have the internal flexibility not to simply fall asleep yourself. You can give yourself instructions that you are going to copy their breathing and even though that breathing is typically associated with physiological sleep, you are going to maintain a certain level of alertness. After a minute or two of breathing with them, change your breathing pattern very slightly, and they should follow at that point.

You can get rapport without running the risk of going to sleep by putting your hand on their shoulders and varying the pressure of your touch with the rhythm of their breathing. You can increase the pressure when they exhale, and decrease the pressure when they inhale. We call this "cross-over" pacing, because you pace with a different sensory channel. Do this for two or three minutes, and then change your pressure pattern slightly, noticing whether their breathing follows you.

Woman: What if they don't follow?

If they don't, then they are in a physiological sleep state, and you need to spend more time building rapport. You can still do it, but it takes more time.

We made up something called "sleep therapy" once when we were working at a mental hospital where people had access to their clients twenty-four hours a day. We had been there several times; this was our third visit. The staff members were delighted with the responses they were getting using our patterns, and dealing very effectively with all their patients *except* the anorexics. They were having trouble with the anorexics.

Anorexics are people who consider themselves grossly overweight. The perception of the rest of the world is that they are about to starve to death. They are extremely skinny, to the point that their health is threatened.

One of the things that we instructed the staff to do with the anorexics—which wiped out this last stronghold of unresponsive patients—was what we called "sleep therapy." If you live with someone for whom this is acceptable, you can try it out yourself.

Go into the place where she is sleeping and use one of the two techniques I just mentioned to you to get rapport. Breathe with her for three or four minutes to get rapport. Since she is in a severely altered state, it takes some time to get rapport. Or instead of breathing with her, you can touch her and use pressure differences. You could get rapport auditorily by singing or humming little soft notes with her breathing movements. You can use any repetitive pattern that you can control in your own output to match her breathing cycle. Then very carefully and very slowly change what you are doing, to find out if you can lead her. Don't change your breathing radically, because part of a person's ability to be alseep and to stay asleep without interruption depends on her maintaining that breathing pattern. Unless you want to wake her up, it would be inappropriate for you to change her breathing radically.

You then proceed to set up finger signals—something that we'll teach you tomorrow. "As you continue to sleep deeply and rest yourself completely, you can respond to certain questions that I ask you by lifting one finger for 'yes' and another for 'no.'" The person is in a severely altered state in which her normal conscious resources are not available, and therefore not in your way. You can now begin to access information directly by getting yes/no signals, or propose changes and new behaviors. You can do all the work in that state without interrupting her sleep.

Woman: And what if her breathing doesn't change when I change mine? Does it mean she is indeed in a physiological sleep state?

No. You can gain rapport with people who are in a physiological state of sleep. The difference is that you have to spend more time following them before you attempt to lead. If you attempt to lead and you do not get the response, take that as a statement that you didn't pace long enough; go back and pace longer.

People who are asleep do respond, but more slowly and less overtly. The same is true of people in an anesthetic sleep state during operations. Many doctors think that their patients are completely out when they are on the operating table. It's just not true. People accept posthypnotic suggestions under anesthesia faster than they will just about any other way. Just because their eyes are closed and their conscious minds are zonked, doesn't mean their ears don't work.

Once I worked with a woman who was living a very wild and rowdy life. Some of the things she was doing were destructive to her, so I was trying to get her to change. I worked with her for a while and couldn't make sense out of what she was doing. Finally I turned to her and said emphatically "Look, you absolutely have got to stop living wildly like this. It's not doing you any good, and it's just a waste of time. And what makes you do it?" Immediately her nostrils flared dramatically, and she said "Oh, I'm really dizzy!" I asked "What do you smell?" She sniffed again and said "It smells like a hospital." I asked "What about a hospital?" She replied "You know that ether smell?"

It turned out that some time earlier she'd had an operation. She'd been anesthetized, and since the doctor "knew" that *she* wasn't there, he talked freely. He looked at her insides and said "It looks terrible. I don't think she's going to make it for very long."

She did make it. Sometimes it's nice to be wrong! However, somehow or other she got the idea that the doctor's statement meant that she wasn't going to make it *after* the operation, not that she wasn't going to make it *through* the operation. The statement was ambiguous; the doctor hadn't specified "If you make it through the operation, everything will be fine." His statement didn't get sorted out in any meaningful way; she just responded to it. She came out of the operation thinking that she wasn't going to live very long, so it didn't concern her that some of the things she was doing were self-destructive.

Martha: When we did the exercise, and I was going into a trance, some part of me wondered "Am I really in?"

Right. And now we are talking about the whole interesting area called "convincers." The thing that convinces Martha about the experience of hypnosis will be different than what convinces Bill or someone else.

Martha's Partner: I'm really curious about that. Her eyes dilated and closed, but later she said that she had an internal dialogue going on the whole time. So that's not a somnambulistic trance state, right?

Different people have different understandings of somnambulistic trance. There isn't any way I know of defining it for all people. Generally people are convinced that they are in a trance when they experience something very different from their normal state. One person's normal state may be another person's trance. For a person whose consciousness has been specialized into kinesthetics, the convincer will probably be a set of visual images that are vivid, colorful, and stabilized. A person who hasn't had a body sensation in thirty years will probably be convinced by an experience of detailed and strong kinesthetic sensations.

Man: I heard you say earlier that if someone has been in a somnambulistic trance, she will not have any conscious memory of it.

Right. Typically when you alter a person's consciousness that radically, when she comes back somebody in the audience will ask "Were you in a trance?" and she'll say "Oh, no! I knew what was going on the whole time." If you then mention some specific activities she carried out, she will say "I didn't do that! You're kidding!" That is, she has complete amnesia for a large segment of that trance experience. To assist that person in being subjectively satisfied that she was in a trance, I often set up a post-hypnotic suggestion that I will trigger by kinesthetic cueing. I'll have it be something obvious and inexplicable like taking one shoe off. That way she will notice that something has happened for which she has no explanation.

You can also find out in advance what a person's "complex equivalence" for trance is: what specific sensory experiences would constitute proof to her that she was in a trance. Then you can develop that kind of experience for the person.

Actually, for the purpose of personal change, it's irrelevant whether the person believes that she has been in trance or not. If you can achieve an altered state and use it to help the person make appropriate changes, that's all that matters.

When you have thoroughly learned about hypnosis, you will find that you will never again have to do any "official" trance inductions that your clients will recognize as such. You will be able to induce altered states naturally, and you will be able to utilize them to achieve changes without the person consciously realizing that anything like "hypnosis" has ever occurred.

Anchoring Trance States

For those of you who are not familiar with the term "anchoring," we want to give you an idea of what it is and how you can use it. Anchoring is already written up in detail in our book, *Frogs into Princes* (Chapter II), so we won't repeat that information to you now. However, we do want to talk about anchoring as it relates to hypnosis.

Every experience includes multiple components: visual, auditory, kinesthetic, olfactory, and gustatory. Anchoring refers to the tendency for any one element of an experience to bring back the entire experience. You have all had the experience of walking down the street and smelling something, and then suddenly you are back in another time and place. The smell serves as a "reminder" of some other experience. That's an anchor. Couples often have a song that they call "our song." That's an anchor too. Every time they hear that song, they re-experience the feelings they had for each other when they first called it "our song."

Many of the inductions you just did made use of anchoring. When you helped your partner access a previous trance experience, you were making use of anchors that were already set up in that person's experience. If you asked your partner to assume the same body posture she had during a trance experience, to hear the sound of the hypnotist's voice, or do anything else paired with trance, you were using naturally occurring anchors.

If a person can tell you what her experience of trance is in sensory-based terms, you can use anchoring to construct that state for her. All you need to do is to break down her experience of trance into its component visual, auditory, and kinesthetic parts.

If you start with visual, you can ask "How would you look to other people if you were in deep trance? Show me with your body here. I'll mirror you so that you have feedback about what you're doing, and you can adjust your body until what you see looks right." When she tells you it's right, you anchor her with a touch or a sound.

Next you find out if she would be making internal images, and if so, what kind. If her eyes are open in deep trance, ask her what she would be seeing on the outside. As she accesses the answer, you anchor her state.

Then you go on to feelings. "How would you feel if you were in a deep trance? How would you be breathing? Show me exactly how relaxed you would be." When she demonstrates how she would feel, you anchor that state.

That leaves the auditory component of "deep trance" to be anchored. You could ask her if she would be aware of the voice of a hypnotist, and what that would sound like. Then find out if she would have any internal dialogue or sounds in deep trance.

As you systematically go through her visual, kinesthetic, and auditory experience of trance, both internal and external, you can anchor each component of "trance" with either the same anchor or with different anchors. If you use different anchors for the different components, you can then trigger all the anchors simultaneously to "remind" her of what trance is like. That's another way to use anchoring to induce a trance. By using anchoring in this way, you can even build an experience that the person has never had previously. You simply anchor the component parts of the experience together.

Once you've induced a trance state, you can set up anchors so that you can quickly reinduce a trance whenever you want to. Whenever I do hypnotic inductions, I always change my voice tone, movement style, posture, and facial expression so that one set of my behaviors is associated with trance, and another set is associated with a normal state of consciousness. Once I have induced an altered state, this gives me the ability to reinduce one quickly simply by beginning my "trance" behaviors. Those behaviors will serve as unconscious signals to go into a trance. The "reinduction signals" that hypnotists use are a special case of this kind of anchoring.

Effective communicators in many fields are already using this kind of anchoring without knowing it. On Sunday morning I turned on the television and watched one of the preachers. This preacher talked very loudly for a while, and then all of a sudden he said "Now I want you to stop, and (softly) close your eyes." His voice tone and volume changed entirely, and people in his congregation closed their eyes and demonstrated the same behavior that I see in people who meditate, people in deep trance, people who sit on trains and airplanes and buses, passengers in cars, jury members, patients in group psychotherapy, or psychiatrists who are taking notes about what a client is saying. That preacher had paired one tone of voice with his usual talking, and another tone of voice with the altered state he called "prayer." He could use that tone of voice to quickly induce an altered state in his entire congregation.

If you change your tone of voice slowly when you notice somebody going into an altered state, the change in your tone of voice will become paired with going into an altered state. If you maintain that changed tone of voice when she reaches a state that you want to keep her in, she will tend to stay there. Your voice tone anchors that altered state.

If a client walks in the door of your office, and you seat him and immediately do a trance induction using your normal tone of voice, normal posture, and normal movement style, you will be in trouble the next time you want to talk to his concious mind. The experience he has of you and your office will be a "reminder" to go into a trance. The next time he walks into your office, when you seat him and begin to talk, he will automatically begin to go into a trance.

Early in my career as a hypnotist I had a lot of problems with clients dropping into a trance when I just wanted to talk to them. I wasn't yet making a systematic distinction in my own behavior. If you don't make distinctions, your normal behavior will be a reinduction signal, whether you want it to be or not.

If you make a distinction in your behavior between when you talk to a client at the unconscious level, and when you communicate at the conscious level, that gives you systematic choices about whether or not to keep his conscious resources around. If you have a private practice, you can use two chairs: one for trance states, and the other when you want to communicate with his conscious mind. Soon just indicating which chair to sit in will serve as an entire induction.

Analogue Marking

A special kind of anchoring is particularly useful when you want to elicit hypnotic responses. It's called analogue marking, and involves marking out certain words nonverbally as you're talking to someone. I can mark out these words as separate messages with my voice tone, a gesture, a certain expression, or perhaps a touch.

I might talk to you about people who are really able to *relax*—people who can allow themselves to *be comforted* by the situation they find themselves in. Or I could tell you a story about a friend of mine who is able to *learn easily* to *go into a deep trance.* As I said that last sentence, I was marking out "*learn easily*" and "*go into a deep trance*" with a slightly different tone of voice and with a wave of my right hand. They constitute separate messages within the obvious message, that your unconscious *will identify* and *will respond to appropriately.*

At this point I have connected a certain tone of voice and a certain gesture with the words *relaxation* and *trance* for many of you. Now, all I need to do is use that tone of voice more and more often, and your unconscious *knows what to do.* That voice tone conveys the message much more effectively than telling you to *go into a trance,* because it bypasses your conscious mind.

All of this is anchoring. A word like "relax" is itself an anchor—a label for something in your experience. In order to understand what I mean when I say the word "relax," you have to go inside and access your personal experiences related to that word. You have a fragment of the experience as a way of understanding the word itself. And as you are *feeling comfortable,* I connect that experience with a certain voice tone. Now my voice tone also becomes an anchor for that response.

You can use any discriminable aspect of your behavior to do this. Milton Erickson would sometimes move his head to the right or the left when he wanted to mark something out for special attention. The same voice will sound slightly different when coming from a different location in space. The difference may not be enough for you to notice consciously, but it will be enough for you to respond to unconsciously, even if you have your eyes closed.

By the way, analogue marking isn't something new. Your clients already do it, and if you listen to what they mark out for you, you can learn a lot. When I was running a private practice, I got really bored after a while, so I sent a letter to all the psychiatrists I knew, asking them to refer me their most outrageous and difficult clients. They sent me fascinating people.

One psychiatrist sent me a woman who would wake up in the middle of the night sweating profusely and vibrating, and no one could figure out what was wrong with her. She was terrified because this occurred quite frequently, and she had been in therapy for several years without any reduction in her symptoms. The psychiatrist was giving her pills to try to control her symptoms. He even hooked her up to an EEG machine for hours at a time, waiting for one of these fits to occur so he could measure it. Of course the fits would never happen until he took her off the machine. He'd hook her back up again, and then she'd sit there for hours longer, and again nothing would happen.

This woman was quite conservative and from a wealthy area of town. When she came to see me she was terrified, because her psychiatrist had told her I was a weirdo who did strange things. But she wanted to change desperately, so she came to me anyway.

She was sitting in my office looking very timid when I walked in. I sat down, looked straight at her and said "You've been in therapy too long. So your conscious mind obviously has failed utterly to deal with this problem and the conscious minds of your therapists have failed utterly to deal with this problem. I want *only* your unconscious mind to tell me *exactly* what I need to know to change you—nothing more and nothing less—and I don't want your conscious mind to intrude unhelpfully. Begin speaking *now*!"

That's a strange set of instructions, isn't it? I had no idea if she would be able to deal with those instructions on any level, but she answered in a really interesting way. She looked back at me and said "Well, I don't know. I'll be sitting in my room at night and I'll switch off the *electric* light, I'll lie down in my bed . . . and, you know, it's really very *shock*ing because I've been in *treatment* for years now, but I still wake up scared and covered with sweat."

If you listen to that communication, it's pretty straightforward. The words that she marked out were "*electric shock treatment.*" That gave me the information I needed. Her present psychiatrist didn't know it, but in the past another psychiatrist had given her electric shock treatment.

Some time ago her husband had become wealthy and moved her from a neighborhood where she lived around people whom she loved and enjoyed, to a very fancy house on a hill where there were no other human beings. Then he went off to work and left her there alone. She was bored and lonely, so she began to daydream to entertain herself. She was seeing a psychiatrist, and her psychiatrist "knew" that daydreaming was "escaping reality" and that escaping reality was bad. So he gave her electric shock treatment to cure her. Every time she began to daydream, her husband put her in the car and took her down to the hospital where the doctors hooked her up to the electric shock machine and zapped her. They did this 25 times, and after 25 times she stopped daydreaming.

However, she still dreamed at night. She tried not to dream, but as soon as she began to dream, she began to experience electric shock. It had become an anchored response. She had all the physiological indications of it. When I went to school, this was called classical conditioning. However, her psychiatrist didn't believe in classical conditioning, so this never occurred to him.

This is an example of well-intentioned psychotherapy that created a problem. The people who gave her the shock treatments really believed they were doing her a favor. They believed daydreaming was escaping reality, and therefore bad. So rather than channeling her fantasies in a useful direction, they gave her electric shock treatment.

Exercise 5

I'd like to have you all practice using analogue marking to get a response from someone else. I want you all to pair up and first pick some observable response to get from your partner. Pick something simple, like scratching her nose, uncrossing her legs, standing up, getting you some coffee—whatever you want. Then start talking to her about anything, and weave instructions to do the response you selected into your conversation. You can include the instructions one word or phrase at a time, marking them out tonally or visually, so that your partner can respond to them as one message.

You see, with what we've discovered so far about hypnosis, we've only begun to *scratch* the surface, and no one really *knows* what we'll learn next. I hope it can be an *uplifting* experience. But you've got to *hand* it *to* those who are *fac*ing the possibilities. . . . Now already there are lots of people in this room lifting their hands to their faces and scratching their noses. It can be that simple.

Often when you do hypnosis, the responses you'll go for in another person won't be quite as obvious as the ones I'm suggesting that you choose for this exercise. For now I want you to choose something that's so obvious you will know whether or not it's occurred.

If your partner is aware of what response you are trying to elicit, she may incorporate the movement you are asking for into another movement that she consciously makes. That's fine. Just notice whether you get the response you are after. If you don't, embed another set of instructions for the same response into your conversation and mark it out.

*　*　*　*　*

Discussion: Negative Commands and Polarities

Michael: How can I gracefully set up a verification of a suggestion I make to someone to stop doing something? Let's say someone bumps into me a lot, and I deliver the message "Don't do that again."

If you say "Do not do that again," he'll do it again and again because you told him to. *If you phrase any suggestion with a negative in front of it, that will happen.* If you say "Don't think of blue," he'll think of blue.

Michael: All right. "You will not interrupt me again."

Then he will interrupt you again. You are giving him a hypnotic command to interrupt you again. If you say "Go away!" he is likely to go away, and you will have an immediate test: either he will leave or he won't.

Michael: Assuming you are able to phrase it so that there's no problem—I mean phrase the suggestion properly—

Yes. Assuming that you have phrased it properly, he will either carry it out or he won't. If it is something that you can't detect, then you won't have a way of knowing in that context. If you say "feel good" you won't know if he is carrying it out except by the subtle responses that he makes.

If I were you, I would very explicitly teach myself to phrase things positively, because you just went through three negative suggestions in a row. *No single pattern that I know of gets in the way of communicators more often than using negation. Negation only exists in language and does not exist in experience.* For instance, how do you experience the following sentence: "The dog is not chasing the cat."

Man: I saw a dog chasing a cat and then I saw a big black "X" across the picture.

Woman: I saw a dog chasing a cat, and then they stopped and stood still.

Right. You have to first represent whatever is negated. If I were you, Michael, I would spend a week learning to phrase everything you say positively, without negation. Learn to specify what you *do* want instead of what you *don't* want.

Typically clients come in with a long list of what they don't want, and usually they have been telling everyone around them what they don't want. That effectively programs their friends to respond in ways that bring unpleasantness and dissatisfaction. "Now I don't want you to get upset by what I'm going to tell you." "Don't get angry at what Billy did."

Of course you can use the same pattern to get a useful outcome

"Don't get too comfortable." "I wouldn't ask you to relax."

Negation is particularly effective to use with anyone who has what we call a "polarity response." A polarity response simply means an opposite response. If I say to David "You are becoming more relaxed" and he tightens up, that's a polarity response.

Sometimes people call this "resistance" and assume you can't work with such clients. People with lots of polarity responses are very responsive; they're just responsive in the reverse direction from what you instruct them. All I have to do to utilize this is tell them *not* to do all the things I want them to do. They will be caught in a polarity response and do them all. "You are listening to the sound of my voice, and I don't want you to close your eyes." "I don't want you to have a growing sense of comfort and relaxation." So that's a context in which negative commands are very useful.

Another way to handle polarities is to use tag questions. "You are beginning to relax, *are you not?*" A tag question is simply a negation in the form of a question added on at the end of a sentence. "That makes sense, *doesn't it?*" "You do want to learn about tag questions, *don't you?*"

Charles: How do we pick up on whether someone has a polarity response or not?

Think about it this way, Charles. If somebody is processing information and has a polarity response, you will be able to notice radical shifts in the sequence of expressions on his face. If somebody's process is to visualize himself doing something and then tell himself it's not a good idea, you will see radical shifts as he switches from one content to another internally. These radical shifts are different than the natural transitions in the usual sequences of expression. That's my main way of knowing.

Another way of knowing is that you will get lots of reversals behaviorally. The classic example is the person who goes "Yes, *but* . . ." First he agrees, and then he disagrees. There are lots of other ways of finding out. One way is to just give someone a direct suggestion. You look at somebody and say "blink" and find out whether he blinks immediately, stops blinking, or just sits there. Those are all very different responses to a direct command.

You can also make a statement and observe the response, and then repackage the same statement with a negation and see if his response reverses. "You can understand that." "No, I suppose you can't understand that." If you get disagreement to both sentences, you know his response is independent of the content of the sentences.

I've talked about using negation and tag questions. You can have an even greater impact if you add the use of embedded commands. Take the statement "And I don't want you to *become more relaxed* as you listen to the sound of my voice." If I change the tempo, pitch, or timbre qualities of my voice when I say "Become more relaxed," that instruction is marked out analogically for special attention at the unconscious level.

You can use embedded commands with or without negation. "As you sit there you can begin to *relax*. . . . Don't *close your eyes* only as fast as your unconscious mind allows you to *remember a pleasant time* from your past when you didn't *feel* too *comfortable*. If you analogically *mark out* the *instructions* you want someone to follow, you will gracefully have a powerful impact.

III

Advanced Inductions

Leverage Inductions and Pattern Interruption

Now I want to add still more possibilities to your repertoire of induction techniques. Al, may I borrow your arm for a moment? (He raises Al's arm and holds it by the wrist, jiggling it slightly until it remains up when he lets go. As he is doing this, he is talking.)

Now what I would like, if it is acceptable to you, is for you to simply allow that arm to drift down, no faster than you can find . . . a comfortable . . . place . . . and time . . . in your past . . . when you could go away . . . and refresh yourself for a moment or two . . . so that your arm should drift down . . . no faster than your eyes . . . close . . . with honest, unconscious movements . . . so that when your hand . . . slowly comes to rest . . . on your thigh . . . after its slow movement . . . down . . . you return . . . with a sense of relaxation . . . which wasn't present . . . before. . . . You are doing it very well. . . . Take your time. . . . (Al's hand touches his thigh and he opens his eyes and smiles.) Thank you.

(John Grinder approaches David and looks at his name tag.)

David? My name is—(He reaches out to shake hands with David. As David's hand comes up, John reaches out with his left hand, holds David's wrist lightly, lifts it up near his face, and points to David's right palm with his right forefinger.) Look at your hand. Would you consider carefully all the color changes and shadows that occur in your hand. Study the lines and creases with interest as you allow your arm to begin to drift down slowly. And I might offer you the same suggestion

70

that I offered Al, and that is . . . as your arm begins to drift down . . . with honest unconscious movements . . . your eyes will begin to feel heavy . . . and will close. . . . You will see clearly . . . just prior to your hand . . . finishing its downward movement . . . something of interest to you . . . that you haven't seen . . . for years. . . . Take your time. . . . Enjoy it. . . . As soon as your hand comes to rest . . . on mine . . . at that particular moment . . . you will have . . . a sense of completion . . . and amusement . . . having remembered to forget . . . what that memory was. . . . And as you know . . . from having been here before . . . (David's hand touches John's right hand and John completes the handshake. John's voice tone, which has shifted during the induction, returns to "normal" and he continues.)—John Grinder, and I have enjoyed meeting you very much. I don't know how you got the information to come to the seminar, but I am glad that you did.

These are called leverage inductions. There are many phenomena that are believed by the general population to be indicators of altered states of consciousness. Catalepsy is one such phenomenon. Hand and arm catalepsy is usually an indication that something unusual is going on. People don't typically sit around with their hand and arm suspended in the air. If you can create that experience, it gives you credibility as a hypnotist, and you can use that experience as leverage to achieve other altered states.

I asked Al "May I borrow your arm for a moment?" How do you make sense out of a question like that? He accepted that as a meaningful utterance, and allowed me to lift his arm. I gave it a little jiggle, and when I released it, his arm was cataleptic. Now the leverage part is done. By my communication I've put Al in an unusual situation: his hand and arm are hanging there, cataleptic in space. In order to utilize that in the context of a hypnotic induction, I then attach the kind of response I would like him to develop—moving in the direction of a hypnotic trance—as a way for him to escape from the leverage position. I ask him to allow his hand and arm to go down with honest unconscious movements, only as rapidly as his eyes close and he remembers an experience. I also suggest that when his hand comes to rest on his thigh, he will come back to a normal state of consciousness, amused by the entire process.

Cathy: How do you know if his arm is cataleptic?

I can feel it. As I hold it up and jiggle it slightly, it will become lighter and then stay up by itself. Kitty, close your eyes for a second. Cathy, reach over and lift ler left arm. Pick it up and notice how it feels. Kitty, now I would like you to form an image of a place where you took a vacation once that was particularly pleasant. Nod your head when you have it. Now, I want you to examine in detail all of the objects in your visual environment. And I would like you to begin to describe out loud all the details of form and color that you can see there in your vacation spot.

Kitty: I'm in this sequoia forest.

What specifically do you see there?

Kitty: Many trees and deep shadows.

OK. Cathy, put your finger under her wrist. Ask her for more and more detail, and each time that she begins to talk, move your finger up and down a little to find out whether she is holding it or not. When she begins to hold it, you will know that you have got an unconscious response in her arm. Whenever she is fully involved in seeing and describing those images, she will be unaware of her arm. Doing that will teach you to feel the difference between somebody consciously holding his arm and someone unconsciously holding it. By the way, if the person is consciously holding his arm, go ahead and utilize it as if he weren't doing it consciously.

A variation on this is what we call the dreaming arm. It's a kind of leverage induction. It's a really nice technique that everyone should know, especially if you work with children. Kids *love* the dreaming arm.

The first thing I do with a kid is get his interest. I ask "Do you know about your dreaming arm?" He might think I'm being a little strange, so I'll start laughing at him and say "You don't know about the dreaming arm? I know about it. I might tell you, but you'd probably tell everybody else." That really gets kids going. Soon the kid is saying "I won't tell anybody. I promise. Please tell me!" So I'll respond "Oh, you probably don't really want to know." This is what Milton Erickson called "building response potential."

From that point on it's really easy. You ask "What's your favorite TV program or movie?" Nowadays it's always the "Bionic Man" or "Star Wars." Then you say "Can you remember the very first scene when Steve Austin is running along and the music is playing?" As he remembers the movie or TV show, you watch his eyes to see which way he accesses. (See Appendix I) If he looks up to his right, you lift up his right arm. If he looks up to his left, you lift his left arm. The arm will easily become cataleptic, because that arm is controlled by the same brain hemisphere that he is using to process information in response to your question.

If a person looks up to his left, he is accessing remembered images which are stored in the right hemisphere of the brain. When you lift the left hand, which is also operated by the right hemisphere, he won't notice what you are doing with his arm—*if* you do it gently so that you don't interrupt his images. His left arm will be automatically cataleptic, because his consciousness is entirely occupied by the images. The person typically won't have a representation of your raising his arm because all his attention is on the images.

You can also ask about music, especially if you know the person is very auditory. "When was the last time you heard a really interesting musical group?" You just lift the arm on the same side that he looks toward as he accesses.

Once you've got arm catalepsy, you just say "All right. Now close your eyes and watch the whole show in detail, with sound, remembering the most important thing is your favorite part, so you can tell me about it later. And your arm will go down only as fast as you see the whole show."

That has worked on every kid I have ever been around, except one who was the child of a hypnotist and had been programmed for years to be unhypnotizable. This child had worked with about twenty-five great hypnotists and had managed to defeat them all. Rather than bothering to attempt to play that game with her, I just congratulated her. I told her she was unhypnotizable and couldn't possibly go into a trance. Of course, then she had to try to defeat that statement, and she started to go into a trance!

After you've raised the arm and it is cataleptic, you can do the same thing you do with any leverage induction. You can say "I'm not going to ask you to put your arm down any **faster** than your unconscious mind can present you with a replay of that entire movie so that you can enjoy it now . . . watching and listening to each scene, one by one . . . in great detail . . . and it can be so pleasant to see parts that you'd forgotten you remember . . . now. . . ."

Woman: Which arm is the right one to use if they just defocus and look straight ahead?

The easiest response would be to lift both arms. There are only two. The one that falls wasn't the one.

Woman: Is it possible to look in one direction and have the other arm be cataleptic?

Yes, it's possible to do most anything. However, the explanation I am offering you gives you a principle—a way of deciding which one to use in order to be *more* effective.

Now let's go back and discuss the handshake interruption that I did with David. This is an example of the class of inductions called pattern interruption. If you can identify *any* rigid pattern a human being has—either as an individual or as part of the culture—all you need to do is to begin that pattern and then interrupt it. You will have the same situation of leverage that you have with arm catalepsy. The classic example is the handshake interruption.

A handshake is an automatic, single unit of behavior in a person's consciousness. If you and I shake hands and we ask somebody "What did we do?" he'll say "You shook hands." That verbal coding suggests that it's a single unit of behavior, and in fact it is. (He repeatedly reaches out his hand to Sue, then stops.) Even though Sue knows now that I am just playing each time I reach my hand out to her, that visual input stimulates her to extend her hand because it is part of a single unit of behavior that she has programmed in herself. If she had to consciously think about what my extended hand meant and then consciously respond, it would be extremely inefficient and clumsy.

Each of us has thousands of such automatic programs. All you have to do is notice which ones are really automatic in the person, and then interrupt one of those. As I extend my arm to make the handshake, she will extend hers. Then I interrupt by catching her wrist with my left hand and moving her hand slightly up. She will be momentarily caught without a program because there isn't any next step. If you interrupt a single unit of behavior, a person doesn't have any next step to go to. The person has never had to go from the middle of a handshake to anything else. You are now at a leverage point. All you do is supply the appropriate instruction, which they will typically follow. In this case, it could be "Allow your arm to float down, but only as quickly as you sink deeply into a trance. . . ."

Sue: Can you give me a distinction between leverage and pattern interruption?

The distinction is more in the way you organize your perceptions than in the actual experience. Leverages create a situation in which a person is put in the unusual position of already exhibiting some trance phenomenon, for example, catalepsy. Then you use verbal linkage to attach that present behavior to whatever else you want to develop.

An interruption involves putting a person in a situation where he is engaging in a single unit of behavior, for example, a handshake. You interrupt that single unit of behavior, and he is stuck, at least momentarily. As far as I know, no one in this room has ever gone from the middle of a handshake to some other piece of behavior, because handshakes don't have middles. Handshakes did have middles when we were about three or four years old and we went through a complex perceptual-motor program of learning how to shake hands with adults. At one time there were pieces to that behavior, just as there were pieces to walking at one point in your life. However, those are now such well-coded and well-practiced unconscious behaviors, that they don't have middles anymore. If you can catch a person in the middle of something that doesn't have a middle, they are stopped. At that point, you can supply instructions about how to proceed from that impossible position to the response that you want to develop.

The distinction between leverage and pattern interruption is a perceptual distinction on the hypnotist's part. In leverage you create some unusual behavior by your maneuvers and then you attach the response you want to develop to this behavior, as a way for them to get out of that leverage position. Pattern interruption means finding a single unit of repetitive behavior in the client and then interrupting it in the middle. Since it has the status of a single unit in consciousness, they have no programs for going from the middle of it to anything else. I will then supply the program.

When I walked over to Al and said "May I borrow your arm?" I didn't wait for a conscious response; I just reached over and lifted his arm. He could have taken it down and said "No." That's a possibility. That kind of response isn't possible with interruption, and that's one distinction between interruption and leverage. With leverage, I create a situation in which I surprise a person by getting him into an unusual situation such as catalepsy. With an interruption, he doesn't exercise any choice, because it is a single unit of behavior; suddenly he is in the middle of it, and it's not going on to the end.

Kevin: It seems to me that one of the presuppositions that we have in this room is that sooner or later one goes into a trance. That is different in the external world. In other words, if I meet somebody on the street and go to interrupt the handshake, it's going to be a little bit more difficult.

I agree there are different presuppositions going on here than in the outside world. I would guess it would be much *easier* there. In here you are alerted that there will be some unusual things happening. Alerting your conscious mind in that way makes my task as a hypnotist more difficult. If you are alerted to the fact that we are going to do something like hypnosis here, it gives you choices about whether you are going to participate or not. I'll guarantee that if you walk out into the hotel lobby and extend your hand congruently and interrupt the handshake, the person will be totally stopped.

You can experiment with other patterns as well. The next time someone greets you and says "Hi, how are you?" try saying "*Terrible*, just *awful*. I'm afraid I may *die*!" and see what they do. In this culture the usual ritualized response to that greeting is "Fine." Most people don't have ways of responding to any other answer, and will experience an interruption. This is particularly true in a business or professional context.

For most smokers, the act of taking out a cigarette and lighting it is a totally unconscious single unit of behavior. If you interrupt that by removing the cigarette from their hands, you will get the same kind of response.

It is much easier to do this with people who aren't alerted to the fact that you are working on hypnotic patterning than it is in a group like this. If some of you are skeptical about that, please entertain yourself by practicing it here effectively, and then go out and test for yourself whether or not it is easier or more difficult with clients and strangers.

Man: What would you say once you got somebody's hand up who wasn't expecting it at all? If you were just on the street and walked up to somebody and interrupted a handshake, how would you proceed?

Well, what are you trying to do? What is your outcome? The answer is that you supply verbalizations for the outcome you want to develop, as a way for that person to escape from the impossible situation you put him in.

Man: Well, say you were just experimenting with a person.

Well, assuming that we set aside the issue of whether it is appropriate to go out and experiment on the unwitting public, as opposed to someone who comes to you and requests assistance, then what I would do is say "And allow your hand to go down until it contacts mine, at which point you will grasp it and shake hands as if nothing unusual had happened." So his hand goes down and you wait until it gets near yours. Then you grab it and say "Yeah, it's a pleasure." That way he will tend to be amnesic for the experience, and you won't encounter any negative response after you've completed the handshake.

Woman: Why will he be amnesic?

Well, because it's a single unit of behavior. What could happen inside of a handshake? If you offer these kinds of suggestions, and then complete the handshake as if nothing had happened, his consciousness will probably be simply that he met somebody.

Man: I've seen Groucho Marx on old reruns of his program, and often he did something similar. He would reach out to shake hands, and when the other person's hand came up, he'd pull his back. As soon as the other person would pull his hand back, he'd put his out again.

Woman: I would presume that people would come out of it almost instantly after you get their hands, and they would wonder what in the world was happening.

They will, *if* you do nothing but interrupt the handshake. That's the point of supplying verbal instructions about what you want to occur next. People can find a way out of an impossible situation, like an interrupted handshake, given enough time. I believe everybody's capable of that. I've tested that, and the length of time has ranged from about ten seconds, when the person recovers and says "That was weird," to five or ten minutes, where people have stood there until they found a way out of that impossible situation.

David: Was it important in your mind for me to not remember what happened while I was in that state?

No. It wasn't important to me.

David: Because I did remember it, but I also felt that in no way did that take away from what was happening.

Ron: Is it interruption when you expect to hear somebody and you don't, either like Milton Erickson's mumbling or when someone's voice drops and becomes inaudible?

The answer is in feedback. That would be an interruption for some people and not for others. Everybody is interrupted by a handshake interruption, but some people have a lot of ways to recover from unanticipated auditory experiences. You will discover that with people who are sophisticated auditorily, it won't have the interruptive effect. For people who are attending to you auditorily at that moment and don't have a lot of sophistication, it will.

For example, have you noticed how this TV monitor? . . .

Now, the different times at which people laughed is a pretty good indication of how long each of you takes to recover from impossible auditory situations. That was a sentence fragment; it wasn't a sentence. So if you felt that waiting for a completion. . . . That is the interruption phenomenon.

78

Man: Is this the same pattern Milton Erickson used when he actually did shake hands with a woman, and then led her into a trance?

No. That was kinesthetic ambiguity. That's a different kind of interruption. If I reach out and I shake your hand normally, at the end of a certain period of time we're supposed to release. If I fail to release, or if, as Erickson did, I begin to release but release ambiguously, in such a way that you don't know exactly when I make the last touch, you'll be suspended without a next program. If you read Erickson's account of that, what he did was release his hand with varying touches so that the woman wasn't sure when he actually broke the contact. The last thing Erickson did before releasing completely was to make a slight push upward at the wrist, which got catalepsy. It's the same principle as holding up someone's arm and jiggling it until his muscles take over and hold the arm up.

Norma: What about incongruence as a pattern interruption?

That's an excellent way to do it. Funny that Norma would be the one to mention that. I know from other contacts with Norma that she has a really exquisitely refined strategy for congruency checks. That's a very important strategy for anybody who is a professional communicator to have. It does, however, leave her open to certain manipulations. If you present some material congruently and suddenly . . . (He continues gesturing and mouthing words, but without sound.) If you continue to present it as if nothing had happened but you simply cut out one channel, in this case auditory, she almost falls forward off the chair. The congruency check strategy she is using as she listens and watches somebody communicate demands that movement of the lips be associated with some sound so that she can make a congruency check. If there is no sound, it really interrupts her program.

If you know about the class of information we call "strategies" (See the book *Neuro-Linguistic Programming Volume I*) you have access to a really elegant way of doing pattern interruption. If you interrupt someone's key strategy, you get a more profound interruption. Those interruptions really hold.

Man: You could also feed people numbers that they're used to getting in certain chunks, like the social security number, in chunks they're not used to. The social security number is usually given in chunks of three, two, and four numbers.

Yes, or you can use telephone numbers. Seven eight two four . . . three six seven. You can tell what strategy the person uses by their response. If they use a tonal pattern for storing telephone numbers, presenting the numbers chunked differently will totally interrupt them. If they do it purely visually, typically it won't have nearly as much effect.

Pattern interruption can be used in any competitive sport. You can notice that every time you make a certain move, you get a certain response. Then you can interrupt that pattern to gain an advantage.

My wife, Judy, is really good with saber. She will set up a movement pattern and run the pattern half a dozen times to discover what regular response her opponent makes. When she knows what response she's going to get to this pattern, she figures out what response to that response will succeed in her making a hit. Or she'll begin the gesture and then interrupt it. Her opponent will have already committed himself to some response to Judy's gesture, and she can then utilize that. Boxers do this too. They set up a pattern and then interrupt it.

If you've watched Bjorn Borg play tennis, you know that he wastes no energy. He organizes his consciousness in a very narrow band. It doesn't matter whether the crowd is going crazy cheering or booing; he doesn't hear any of that. There is no difference in his response whether he misses or makes an easy shot. He simply turns around and reanchors himself—he twirls the handle of his racket as he walks back to begin the next play. He wastes no energy at all; he's entirely concentrated on essentials. That concentration protects him from psychological maneuvers by opponents. If you can interrupt somebody else's altered state—the one that they need to perform well—then they will play poorly, and you may be able to beat them.

There are lots of applications of the principle of pattern interruption. Anything "unexpected" will get you that response. During that period when a person goes "on hold" because you have just done something wholly irrelevant or unexpected, that's the time to offer them clear suggestions about what response you want next.

You have to practice these techniques until you are personally powerful and congruent in carrying them out. You need to act in all of your behavior—verbal and nonverbal—as if this is going to happen, and it happens. As soon as you can present yourself fully congruently in making the maneuver, your job is to detect what response you get. You've got to have feedback. None of the generalizations that we offer you will *always* work. They always have to be adjusted to the feedback that you get.

Overload

About twenty-five years ago, George Miller summarized a huge amount of both human and animal perceptual research in his classic paper "The Magic Number 7 ± 2." Human beings have the capacity to consciously attend to about seven "chunks" of information at one time. Beyond that number, a person becomes overloaded and starts to make mistakes. If I tell you a sequence of seven numbers, you can probably hold that in consciousness without error. If I give you a sequence of nine numbers, you will find it much more difficult to recall them correctly, and will start to make mistakes. Each number is a "chunk" of information. However, if you—or I   divide the nine digits into three groups of three, you will be able to recall the nine numbers much more easily. Now there are only three chunks of three digits each. By grouping information in larger chunks, it becomes possible to deal with more information with the same 7 ± 2 chunks of conscious attention. You can consciously attend to seven leaves, seven twigs, seven branches, seven trees, or seven forests. How much you can attend to depends upon the size of the chunk of information that you are dealing with.

Whatever chunk size you choose, when you are paying conscious attention to 7 ± 2 chunks of information, anything else will not be processed consciously. Anything beyond 7 ± 2 chunks of information becomes overload and will be processed unconsciously.

An example of this happened in another workshop. I asked for someone who had a way of remembering names that worked exquisitely. A woman named Carla had one, so I had her come up to the front. Ann Teachworth was sitting in the audience, and I said to Carla "Do you happen to know this woman over here?" and I pointed to Ann. Carla said "No." When Carla was introduced to someone her pupils dilated and she made an internal image of the person's name on her forehead. Then every time she saw her again, her pupils would dilate slightly and she would see the name written there on her forehead. That was the way she always knew someone's name, and it worked very well. Since I know what she does, I know where in the sequence of Carla's experience she will be unable to consciously represent any additional input: when her attention is oriented inward and all of her 7 ± 2 chunks of attention are occupied with visualizing the person's name on her forehead.

I said to Carla "Look at the woman over there. Her name is Ann . . ." I paused, saw her pupils dilate, and then said "Teachworth."

She heard "Ann" and visually wrote it on Ann's forehead. Then I asked her "What's that woman's name?" Her pupils dilated again and she said "Ann." I said "Do you know what her last name is?" She said "No, you didn't tell me." When your timing and your sensory experience are refined enough that you know when a person's attention is inwardly oriented and when it's not, you can introduce anything you want. When someone is oriented inward, she will respond appropriately to your suggestions because you bypass her conscious mind. There's no way for her to filter or defend against such suggestions.

At that point I said "Her name is Ann Teachworth" and Carla said "Oh! Now I remember." That was an elegant demonstration that although she didn't have it available in conscious awareness because it didn't go through her name-remembering process, it was there. She recognized Ann's last name when she heard it, so it had been processed and remembered unconsciously.

Whenever a person's conscious processing is overloaded, you can pass information directly to the unconscious, and the person will respond to that information. The easiest way to overload someone's attention is by having her pay attention to a complex internal experience.

I used an overload technique the second time I ever officially induced a trance. I'll demonstrate. Would you come up for a second, Bill, and stand here?

"OK, would you close your eyes? Now what I would like you to do is to softly, out loud, begin to count backwards from two hundred by threes. And as you do that, I'm going to put my hands on your shoulders and turn you around in circles. If at any point you discover it is more comfortable for you to simply drop into a nice deep trance, do so with the full realization that you are in good hands."

By doing this, I create an overload by occupying all of his representational systems. He's using visualization as a way of helping himself count backwards. Auditorily he's saying the numbers to himself. I disorient him kinesthetically by turning him in circles. He's now overloading himself with things to attend to, so I don't have to.

I could just as well have said "Now turn slowly in a circle." However, if I turn him with my hands on his shoulders, I get a lot of tactile feedback about when he's changing states and what kind of state he's going into. I also give him something else to attend to kinesthetically: the feeling of my hands on his shoulders.

To make sure that overload works, you make sure that all systems are engaged. If he's busy visualizing and counting off the numbers while he's being disoriented kinesthetically, I can offer suggestions which will go right past his consciousness into the unconscious. If I say something that distracts him from the task, I will immediately know it, because he's counting out loud. There's a built-in feedback mechanism in this traditional method. If he stops counting, I know he's either dropped into a deep trance, or he's shaken off the disorientation and is consciously listening to the suggestions I am attempting to pass to the unconscious. Then I'll either insist that he continue to count, or I'll notice that he is in deep trance, stop fooling around, and go to work.

This is a really traditional trance induction, by the way. I read this particular method in a book years ago, and having had no experience of it, just followed the instructions as if I knew what I was doing. It was only some years later that I figured out what the principle was, so that I could generalize from that specific method to overloading someone in a variety of ways. The way we teach in these workshops is designed to do exactly the same thing, because we are interested in passing most of the messages to you at the unconscious level.

You can use *any* complicated task to occupy a person and distract his consciousness while you disorient him. Then you offer a very direct, immediate, and easy-to-follow instruction like "If at any point it is easier for you to simply *drop into a deep trance,* then *do so* and enjoy it with the full realization you are secure in your present position. . . ."

Here's another variation. I take Jack's hand here, and I want to overload him. So I say "All you have to do is sit here comfortably. I'm going to touch different fingers and your thumb, and I'm going to name the one I'm touching. Your job is to simply decide whether I'm doing this correctly or incorrectly."

Then I begin touching and labeling. "Forefinger, middle finger, ring finger, little finger, thumb. Middle finger, forefinger, ring finger, thumb." (He touches the little finger.)

Each time I make a "mistake" he will do what he just did: his pupils dilated and there was a hesitation in his breathing. He had to take some time to compute. It took him longer to decide that I had made a "mistake" than it took him to decide earlier that I was correct.

If I were to continue, I would gradually become more and more "incorrect." Soon he would be overwhelmed by the complexity, and in defense, he would go into a deep trance. At that point I would say "As I touch your ring finger this time"—and I would touch the wrong finger—"you are more relaxed." I would continue to overload, and go on to introduce additional suggestions about the specific kinds of overt responses I want—those that indicate he is going into a trance.

I am giving the person input in all three channels simultaneously and demanding that he make a judgement about whether the auditory input matches the visual and kinesthetic input. He will soon give up, and essentially say "OK, tell me what you want me to do."

Instead of overloading all representational systems, you can give the person such a complex task in one or two systems that it occupies all of his 7 ± 2 chunks of conscious attention. You can ask the person to count backwards from a thousand by one-thirds, visualizing each one of the fractions with a different color for the top of the fraction, the bar, and the bottom of the fraction. Each successive fraction has to have a new color for the bar and for each number. Then you can add suggestions like "With each number you will go deeper." These are all ways of manipulating a person in such a way that you are overloading his input channels and thus his ability to make sense out of what you are doing.

Woman: Is the double induction that you describe in the book *Patterns II* an example of overload?

Yes, the double induction is a special case of what I've just been doing. That's where you use two people to overload one person. It works really quickly. You get a lot of overload, you get it quickly, and you get a very powerful response. We first began doing double inductions accidentally in workshops and noticed what a powerful response we got. So we started employing it in our private practice just to find out how we could use it.

About six months later Carlos Castaneda's book *Journey to Ixtlan* was published. Near the end of the book is a really vivid description of a double induction. Don Juan is talking into one ear, and Don Genaro is talking into the other ear simultaneously. The descriptions we had gotten from people that we had done double inductions with before I read the book matched the description that Carlos gave perfectly— feeling split down the center of his body, and so forth.

You can tell from the description in the book that Carlos is what we call a "derived kino." He takes images and words and pays most attention to the feelings that he derives from them. With such a person, the double auditory input really does cause a sensation of kinesthetic splitting. Each message will be processed by the opposite hemisphere, and the derived feelings will be experienced in the same half of the body as the auditory input. The difference in the auditory input to the two ears will be represented differently in the two halves of the body. The differences in those two kinesthetic representations will be most evident at the mid-line, giving an experience of being split or divided.

Leverage inductions, pattern interruption, and overload are all similar in that they give you ways of getting a wedge in the other person's experience to start the process. You use those methods to break the state of consciousness he walks in with, in favor of a more fluid state. Once you have overloaded, interrupted, or created a leverage situation, you simply become more directive, and link that situation with what you want to develop. "And as whatever is going on continues, you will find your eyes becoming drowsy and beginning to close and develop a deeply relaxed state." You proceed to develop a trance, and then go on to use the trance state as a context for the change work that you want to accomplish.

Personal Power

Another induction method is just straight personal power. You just congruently tell somebody to go into a trance. If they go into a trance, fine. If they don't, you wait until they do. Of course, all the other patterns—nonverbal mirroring, etc.—are available to you at the same time. If you tell someone to go into a trance, and your behavior is absolutely one hundred percent congruent that they are going to go into a trance, they will. You have to be completely congruent for this maneuver to work. If you are congruent in your expectations, you will elicit the appropriate response.

There are additional maneuvers you can add that allow you to be more effective. If the person replies "I really want to, but I'm not able to" you say "Of course, *you* aren't able to. I'm waiting for *him*." So you dismiss the conscious response in favor of waiting for something else to emerge. If he objects, and you don't respond but just wait expectantly, he is likely to go back and try to go into trance again, until he gets it right.

A meta-strategy for creating congruency in yourself is to remember that you can fail only if you set a time limit on yourself. Most people think they have failed if they don't get a deep trance instantly. That's only a signal that you have to do more, or try something different.

If you have any personal hesitations or incongruencies about what you allow yourself to do, a way to create congruency in yourself is to use the language pattern called "quotes." You can say "Let me tell you about the last time I went to Phoenix to see Milton Erickson. I walked into Milton's office, and then Milton came rolling into the room in his wheelchair, and he looked at me and said 'Go into a trance!' " When you use quotes, you set a frame around your behavior that says "This is not me; this is a report of an experience I had." However, of course, you deliver any induction you want to with full force. If you get the trance response, great; you utilize it. If you don't get the response, and you are unwilling to continue until you do, then you can always dismiss it. "That's what Milton said to me; of course I wouldn't do that myself."

The pattern of quotes is a really nice way to try on new behavior that you are unsure of. You can allow yourself to know what it would be like if you were able to do it, by actually doing it as if you were someone else.

Stacking Realities

Another induction procedure is called "stacking realities." I guess the easiest way to explain a stacked reality is to tell you about doing a group in Michigan once. I was sitting there in Weber's Inn, talking to a group of people about metaphor. And as I began to talk to them about metaphor, it reminded me of a story that Milton Erickson had told me about a group that he had done once at the University of Chicago, in which there were a large number of people sitting around just like this in a sort of semi-circle, and he was up at the front. Now, as he sat there talking to this group of people at the University of Chicago, the story that seemed most appropriate at that point in time was a story that his father had told him about his grandfather who came from Sweden. His grandfather Sven was running a dairy in Sweden, and he found that the cows settled down better if he talked to them in a calm, soothing voice about whatever was on his mind. . . .

What I've done is to embed story inside of story inside of story until I overload your conscious capacity to keep track of which statement refers to which thing. Even in a sophisticated group of people like this, if I were to go on with the story now and deliver induction messages inside of the story, it would be difficult for you to know which of the realities I was referring to. Am I talking about Grandfather Sven talking to the cows, Erickson talking to a group in Chicago, Erickson's father telling him a story, or is it me talking to you? While your conscious mind is trying to figure that out, your unconscious will be responding.

Let's take an example that is more related to therapy. Let's say a woman comes to see me and says "I have this presenting problem X." I invite her to notice the wind moving the tops of the redwood trees as she looks out of the office window, and begin to relate to her a story about a young woman who had once come to me and sat in that very chair and had watched . . . closely . . . the tops of the same redwoods waving . . . not pushed, of course, by the same wind . . . back and forth . . . and that young woman had fallen into a deep reverie, and even as she was listening to the tone of my voice, she remembered a dream in which she had gone to the country to visit someone . . . someone special who had made her feel particularly comfortable. . . .

I've just included the beginning of a hypnotic induction inside of the stacked reality. With the stacked reality I overload the person's conscious ability to keep track of what level of reality I'm now operating on. The result then is a confusion, but typically a much more gentle confusion than you get with sensory overload. One way to increase this effect is to incorporate aspects of present reality into the story. The redwoods exist in present reality as well as in the story, so if I talk about the redwoods, it is easy to go back and forth between the two realities. Soon a client gives up trying to keep track of which reality I'm talking about.

Inside of any of those realities, I can then embed a process instruction to make changes. "And as I talked to that young woman who had come to visit me . . . even as she had her dream . . . the contents of which I didn't know, nor did I need to . . . it was only important that *she* did . . . and the changes which are attendant upon such dreams . . . would manifest themselves in a graceful way in her future behavior. Even as I watched her in her dream . . . I remembered something that had happened once when I visited an old friend of mine in Phoenix, Arizona."

Now I'm doing two things: I'm stacking realities so it's impossible for her to keep track, and I'm giving her instructions about what she should do while I continue—namely to have a dream which changes her behavior in a graceful way, etc. If there happens to be another person in the office, I'm all set up to do a direct induction. I'll look at the second person and say "And Milton looked at me, and he said 'Sleeepp' . . . only as long as you need to . . . to enjoy . . . perfectly . . . making a change which will surprise and delight you . . . the contents of which will not be available until you notice it . . . in your actual behavior . . . sometime within the next twenty-four hours . . . because it's always delightful to be surprised by your unconscious . . . and so Milton then said to that person that he *could* of course

. . . at any point . . . where it was useful . . . and when his unconscious mind was satisfied . . . that it had identified a particular change . . . which would be of use to him . . . he could simply. . . with a sense of refreshment . . . slowly return . . . to the level of reality which was most appropriate for him in *learning important things*. . . . "

In all of this, I'm presupposing several very important things: (1) personal power: I am congruent in doing whatever I am doing, and (2) rapport: I have tuned myself to the person well enough that they come to trust me as an agent of change.

When you have achieved that, then you can always embed a direct command for a hypnotic response, including a deep trance. The stacked reality gives you an opportunity to create rapport and evaluate the responses you get. Stacked reality overloads more gently than the other kinds of confusion and overload techniques. It also gives you the occasion, since anything can happen in a story, of incorporating an entire induction and utilization. Of course you would need to take more time than I just took to do it smoothly.

The stacked reality can have several functions. It not only gives me an excuse for presenting something in a story which otherwise might be resisted by the person's conscious mind, it can also trigger me into the appropriate behavior, voice tone shifts, etc., for inducing a trance. As I talk about Erickson and I hear myself using the same voice tone that he uses, it makes all my experience with Erickson immediately available to me at the unconscious level. I can't think of a better model for doing hypnotic inductions than Milton Erickson.

A project I might suggest to some of you who would like to work together, is to build a very general, open metaphor designed for a trance induction. Build a set of stacked realities inside which you can embed a very general hypnotic induction. By an open metaphor, I mean that you know in general where you are going. You know where you are going to begin; you know the cast of characters. There are going to be some general interactions, and you are pretty sure about the general outcome you are headed toward. However, you leave the stories open enough that you can incorporate any response that occurs. You always have the choice of shifting to another "reality" if you're not getting the response you want.

Using stacked realities provides an ambiguous frame for what you're doing. Within that frame you can use any or all of the other techniques and maneuvers that we are teaching you.

Exercise 6

I have just demonstrated five more kinds of inductions: (1) Leverage Inductions; (2) Pattern Interruption; (3) Overload; (4) Personal Power, and (5) Stacking Realities. In a moment I'm going to ask you to get into small groups and try them out with each other.

Let me recommend that you do yourself a favor and select something *new* to try out. You already know how to do what you know how to do. Some people come to our seminars and learn to do what they already know well, all over again. I recommend that you select either an induction method that you are totally unfamiliar with, or one that you have heard about but haven't practiced. When you do that, you will increase your repertoire. The more ways you have to achieve a particular outcome, the more successful you will be with a wider range of people. Some methods are very effective with some people, but not with others. If you have many ways of inducing a trance, you will find that everyone is hypnotizable.

I want you to get into groups of three again. A will pick a method of induction that is new for her, and use it to induce a trance in B. The third person, C, is going to observe B's responses that indicate a change in state. There will be changes in pupil dilation, skin color, breathing, muscle tonus, etc. C's job is to detect those changes.

A, after you have induced a trance, I want you to add four other steps:

1) Set up some obvious signal that will indicate to you when the person is stabilized at an appropriate level of trance. "Continue . . . deepening . . . your trance . . . to the point that you find most relaxing . . . and then you can indicate . . . that you have now reached the point where you desire to stabilize . . . by a simple, honest, and unconscious nodding of the head or . . . a lifting of the right or the left arm . . . a few inches off of your thigh. . . . "

2) When he gets there, offer him some very general set of instructions for learning. "Now, I would be delighted . . . to notice . . . how well your unconscious mind chooses some particularly positive experience . . . which you have not thought about in years . . . and allows you the pleasure of once again seeing . . . and hearing . . . and recovering the feelings . . . to your delight . . . of that lost experience . . . which involved . . . very positive sorts of experiences on your part."

Or you can say "I would like your unconscious mind to present you with an image or a feeling or a sound . . . of something that you would particularly enjoy creating for yourself . . . as an experience . . . sometime within the next few days . . . as a way of preparing yourself to carry out . . . the learnings you are making . . . in this workshop." It doesn't matter what the content is. Stay out of content. Make general suggestions that he do something inside of that trance state so that he has an experience which unequivocally indicates to him that he was in a new state of consciousness. Some of you may have a specific request about what you want to do when you get into trance. You might mention that to the others in your group before you start.

While you're giving a general learning instruction, you might add things like "And with each breath, you continue to get . . . deeper or stabilize yourself at the most comfortable level of trance . . . for you and for the purposes that you have." Don't include any content; let him choose the content. Just give him general instructions to make unconscious choices and learnings.

3) Whatever general suggestions you give, add some statement that provides you with feedback. "And when your unconscious mind has completed offering you that experience, simply indicate that it has by allowing one or both arms to float up with honest, unconscious movements, or by causing your eyes to suddenly flutter open as you have a sense of refreshment and delight that you have accomplished what it was that you were after." This builds in a signal for him to let you know he has completed the little piece of work that he was going to do in the altered state.

4) When you get that signal, you need to build a way for him to get back out of trance. "Now I am going to count slowly backwards from ten to one" or "I'm going to reach over in a moment and touch you on the shoulder." This tells him what is about to happen, and gives him some time to prepare himself. "And when I reach 'one' your eyes will flutter open, and you will awake feeling delighted by your experience, refreshed and renewed by what just happened, and ready to begin again learning something new."

As an alternative, you could lift his arm, which will be cataleptic, and say "And your unconscious mind can allow that arm to go down no faster than you drift back to this particular reality, bringing with you any sense of accomplishment, any sense of refreshment and renewal from this experience." Or "When I touch you on the shoulder, you'll feel a sudden surge of quiet energy which will give you a tingling sense of well-being as your eyes flutter open and you reorient to this place and time."

Any questions?

Woman: You gave us too much!

I gave you a lot. You'll be surprised at how much you'll remember as you go through, step-by-step, inducing a trance, giving general learning instructions, and bringing him back. OK. Go ahead.

* * * * *

Incorporation and Dealing with Abreactions

There is another very important general pattern that I want to talk about called *incorporation.* If something significant occurs, whether it's something internal—a profound response develops in the client— or something external—suddenly a door slams or someone walks by and bumps the chair that the client is sitting in—the least effective thing to do is pretend it didn't happen. You will then lose credibility and rapport with the client, because he needs to know that you are alert enough to notice what his experience is. When something happens, your next verbalization should immediately incorporate it.

In one of your practice groups, Cathy talked about hearing the buzz of the background conversation as she was going into a trance. What does that suggest to you metaphorically?

Woman: Bees.

Sure. You can incorporate the buzzing sound by saying "And the buzz of the conversation in the room can remind you of a pleasantly warm summer day. You hear the sound of the honeybees as you lie in the cool grass, feeling the warmth of the sunshine on your face." That's one way you can incorporate.

Woman: What if the person had a phobia of bees?

If you are watching you will know immediately from his response if he has a phobia of bees.

Woman: What would you do if that happened, though?

You immediately incorporate that: "And you can know that those bees are bees that come from another time and place, and that you are sitting comfortably here in this room." You take him out of the situation where it is dangerous for him and reorient him to the present time and place. Or you can make him a bee. Have him buzz around a little bit himself. To bee or not to be.

There's no way of knowing ahead of time if a metaphor that you are going to use, or a particular maneuver you are going to try, is going to trigger a phobia or some other traumatic experience. You have to use feedback to know if the maneuver you are making is appropriate. As long as you are constantly observing the client, you will know immediately if something unpleasant happens.

The other major way to incorporate is the following: "And that loud slam of the door you just heard will allow you to be even more comfortable as you sit here listening to the sound of my voice." You begin by simply stating what happened, and then connect that to the response you want to develop.

After the last exercise a man came up to me and said that as he was going through this experience, he felt himself going into a trance, and then he suddenly felt his body jar and pulled himself back. Now he had a *reason why* he did that; he said it was as if he didn't want to go any deeper. His response would have been very different if the person who had been talking to him had noticed those involuntary movements and had said to him "Sometimes as you begin to go into an altered state, your body begins to jar itself slightly, just like sometimes when you're very tired, and you're going to sleep, just before you drop off your body begins to twitch involuntarily. It's only an indication that you're just about to go really deeply into an altered state." You see, there's nothing in human experience which necessarily means anything, so you can make it mean whatever you want.

Now what about strong internal responses? All of you who operate as hypnotists need to have ways of taking care of abreactions: intense unpleasant responses that sometimes occur as a person goes into a trance. Let me put this into perspective. One of the unconscious motivations that causes people to specialize in one state of consciousness to the relative exclusion of others, is that they have stored massive amounts of unpleasant or incongruent experience in a representational system that is excluded from consciousness. If you are going to specialize in certain states of consciousness, one way to protect yourself from experiences which are painful for you to consider is to put them into the system that is out of consciousness. Then you get at least temporary relief at the conscious level. The unconscious mind holds back material that would be potentially overwhelming to the conscious mind. This is appropriate, and is one of the functions of the unconscious.

So if you alter someone's state and make available an unconscious system, it may be that the material most immediately available will be junk. In gestalt terms, it's unfinished business. In TA terms, it's material for redecision. Painful memories have been re-experienced so frequently in the history of official hypnosis that this phenomenon has been officially labeled "abreaction." My understanding is that an abreaction is simply the most natural response to suddenly uncovering a system which contains material from the past that is painful or overwhelming.

Now what if someone has an "abreaction?" Let's say he bursts into tears. Being quite alert at the sensory level, you notice this. Now what do you do?

Jack: Wouldn't you do the same thing you just talked about doing for external interruptions? I'd start by pacing what I observed happening.

Absolutely. That's exactly what I would do as well. First you pace. You say "You are having feelings of discomfort and they are *very* uncomfortable." You have accepted his response. He doesn't have to fight with you about the validity of his own experience. You've given him a verbal pacing statement of what his experience is. "And you are crying . . . and those tears are representative of pain and discomfort from your past . . . and you are *very* uncomfortable. . . . As you remember . . . these particular feelings and they again come into your body . . . I would like you to consider the following. . . . Each of us, in our own personal history has had many, many experiences, some of which we label as unpleasant. . . . Those unpleasant experiences often form the basis . . . for later abilities . . . and skills . . . which people who have never been challenged by such experiences . . . fail to develop. . . . How pleasant it is . . . to experience discomfort from the past . . . with the full realization . . . that you survived those experiences, and that they form a rounded set of experiences from which you can generate more adequate behavior in the present."

So after pacing I did what we call a "content reframe." What I just said changed the *meaning* of what was occurring. Rather than just being unpleasant experiences, the memories are now the basis for knowledge and skills.

Man: After you pace, could you put that part of him in front of him and have him observe what happened in the past?

Excellent. "I want you to *see yourself* at that particular age and have a sense of curiosity about what specifically happened . . . with your eyes and ears now open to what occurred and a sense of comfort in knowing that you survived it." That would create a dissociation from the unpleasant feeling as well as a content reframe. That's the basis for the NLP technique for curing phobias, described in detail in *Frogs into Princes*.

Man: The person that I was doing the exercise with got into something very quickly. His eyes started doing lots of rapid eye movement, his head was moving back and forth, his arm started to move, and I saw a lot of tension in his jaw. I was really confused. I didn't know whether or not this was an unpleasant experience, resistance to being hypnotized, or something else. I'd like some suggestions.

This brings up the importance of making the distinction between interpretations and sensory-grounded experience. "Increased tension in the muscles along the jaw line" and "head moving back and forth" are sensory-grounded descriptions, in contrast to the last two things that you mentioned. "Unpleasant experience" and "resistance to being hypnotized" are in the realm of hallucinations and guesses. Hallucinating is fine—in fact it is an important part of the art. However I really insist that you all make a clear distinction between when you are using sensory-grounded descriptions and when you are hallucinating.

Rather than spending your time internally trying to figure out what interpretation is appropriate, you can simply begin to verbalize sensory-grounded descriptions of what you can see and hear. You can describe muscle tension, tears, body posture, or breathing, etc. That will maintain rapport by pacing and matching their experience.

You have the choice of saying something like "And what a strong experience that was, and you were a bit surprised, were you not?" Or "And these signals which you have offered me on the outside have a powerful connection with the rich internal experience that you are presently having."

Often when a person first goes into a trance, his muscles relax, and you will notice an increase of moisture in his eyes, or a few tears. Don't hallucinate. It may mean that he is really sad, or it may mean that he is just relaxing. For you to decide which it is would be to impose your own belief and value system. Stay out of the content, and simply mention the obvious. "And as that tear trickles down your cheek, you have a growing sense of comfort and security, knowing that you are fully protected." There's no necessary connection between the tear going down the cheek and comfort. However, as long as you begin with an immediately verifiable sensory-grounded description—the tear going down—and then connect it with the response you would like to develop, you utilize what occurs to lead the person where you want him to go.

Joan: I inadvertently used a very powerful word for my partner. I asked him to think of his hands as being "disembodied." He immediately went into this thing of carrying around a very heavy disembodied arm. When that word came out of my mouth, I realized that it was wrong, but I didn't know how to correct it.

Well, first of all, reorganize your own representation. There was nothing to correct. You see, there are no mistakes in communication, Joan. There are only responses or outcomes that you get by your communication. The response that you got wasn't the one that you wanted. That doesn't make it a mistake; it just makes it the next step in getting the response that you do want.

You noticed that when you mentioned the words "disembodied arm" you got a violent response. Given the principle of incorporation, what do you do? You immediately say "And that really upsets you." That is one choice. Notice that it's not a sensory-grounded statement. I am making a guess that the name of the experience that I've just elicited would fit into the general, vague category called "upset."

If you don't trust yourself to make those guesses, then you stay completely general. "And you really have a *response* to *that*. And there are many responses that you might learn to make to that particular item." You don't even know what he was responding to, so you say "that particular item." Or "You might consider how your close friend would respond to that idea in a way which is different from the way that you just did." Again, you are incorporating.

If you want to stay very general, you say "You have a very powerful response." That will always pace appropriately. You aren't even saying if the experience is positive or negative—only that it exists. If you stay very general you will always be right.

If you guess that the person is experiencing something unpleasant, after you pace you can say "And how pleasant it is to remember the unpleasant experiences of the past and have the sense of satisfaction of having survived those things so that they need never happen again." Or "And how unpleasant certain experiences are. . . . Knowing that such unpleasant experiences form the foundation . . . for present strengths . . . it is quite pleasant (voice tone shift) . . . to remember how unpleasant . . . some of our previous experiences have been."

This is called content reframing. (See the book *Reframing*.) You are taking a response and you are putting it in a bigger context in which the response and the experience itself now become a positive foundation upon which other responses can be built. You have accepted the behavior absolutely. That's there; you don't tamper with it. And then you put it in a frame that says to use it constructively.

You can also take measures in advance to insure that whatever material intially emerges will be pleasant, so that you associate positive experiences with altered states of consciousness.Then later you can learn to deal with the other unpleasant stuff that may be there.

An easy way to avoid the abreaction difficulty is to look meaningfully at the client before you begin and say "Your unconscious mind has protected you—which is its prerogative and its duty—during your entire life, from material from your personal history that might be painful or overwhelming if it were to become conscious. I call upon your unconscious mind to continue to perform that function as it has in the past. And as you alter your consciousness, the first experiences that you have will be designed specifically to remember and uncover and enjoy once again some positive and delightful part of your past. The unpleasant material which is also located in that system can be sorted out and set to the side in a safe place for the time being. Once you have some facility with altered states, unpleasant material can be dealt with in a comfortable and powerful way, because the so-called negative experiences in our past often form the foundation for the very powerful resources that we have in the present, when seen, heard and felt in a new way."

If you do this, you will get the very positive rapport that you need with the other person's unconscious, because you are validating one of its most important functions—protection—and you are requesting that it continue to carry out that function as you work with it. You will also have made a special request: that the material that comes up be material that creates a very positive desire on the part of the conscious mind to continue to explore this new dimension of experience.

By the way, there's nothing wrong with abreactions. I'm just saying that it makes sense to find some very powerful pleasant experiences when you begin trance work. A lot of people believe that pain has to be associated with change. If the two become anchored together, people will resist change, because they don't like pain. It's not that they don't like change; it's that they don't like pain. If you make a clear distinction between change and pain, then people can change much more easily. You make your life much easier as an agent of change, because there's no necessary connection between pain and change.

Stan: In other words you are saying that this is mental judo, except that in judo you are always using what the person is doing against them. In this case you would use it *for* them.

Yes. Stan, would you put your hands together above your head?

Now, would you push with your right hand? Shirley, would you do that for me too? Put your hands together above your head and push with your right hand.

Now, in both cases, when I asked them to press with their right hand, *they also pressed with their left*! This is a kinesthetic metaphor for what's often called "resistance." You can push against people, and if you do, you will get resistance which you will then have to work with directly. *Or,* you can recognize that every response is the best choice that a person has available to them in that context. Rather than push back against it, which will cause an expenditure of energy and time and effort on both people's part and doesn't guarantee any useful response, you can accept it and turn it around.

The same difference appears if you compare American boxing and Oriental martial arts. In the Oriental martial arts you never oppose the force from another person; you take the force and utilize it to move in the trajectory that you want to move anyway. What I just had you do is a very precise kinesthetic metaphor for the difference between some traditional direct-command forms of hypnosis and the kind of patterning that we're teaching you here.

Man: When you notice an abreaction, do you ever ask the client to supply the content?

I don't. Asking for content is a traditional psychotherapeutic choice. I don't need content, so I don't ask for it. It slows me down. But each person has needs for feedback, and a belief system about what is appropriate and important. Your clients may have been trained by you or other psychotherapists to believe that they have to talk about the content of their experience. If either one of those conditions is true about the interaction, then you ought to involve content in it to satisfy those needs.

Man: Did Milton Erickson ever ask for content?

I think Erickson's done *everything*. I'm sure that at some point with some clients, he has gotten lots of content. I've also seen him do pure process, content-free therapy, so I know he had the full range. If you can do pure process work without any content, you already know how to work with content. That gives you the full range of choices about how to proceed.

This afternoon you've done two exercises out of the ten methods we've talked about. You did them very well, and were able to induce relatively nice trances. You won't *know* any of these other eight induction techniques until you do them. Make yourself a little promise for your own evolution as a human being. I'm only a hypnotist, so this is only a suggestion. As a communicator you owe it to yourself to have lots of choices about securing various outcomes. Make arrangements with friends and / or colleagues, or use your private practice to practice privately, and systematically go through the other ways of getting the same outsome. If you have ten ways to induce a trance, you'll always get it. Using a meta-strategy called "finesse," you can begin one type of induction, and if the response is not emerging quickly enough to suit your needs or the client's needs, you very smoothly go on to the next class of inductions and do one of those. If the response still isn't developing rapidly enough, you go on to the next one. The client's experience will be that you are smoothly going through a number of communications with him. He will never know that you tried one method, decided it wasn't working quickly enough, and went on to another.

Benediction

We have attempted to engage your attention today, and to indicate that there are worlds upon worlds of possibilities that each one of you brought here with you, that we would like to help you find the resources to get access to. Today we have covered a significant number of the patterns that we consider important in successful hypnotic communication and successful communication in general. We have gone through a series of induction techniques, and we ask that you add those techniques to your present unconscious repertoire as alternative ways of accomplishing things that you already know how to accomplish by other methods.

If you felt that we were moving too fast today, covering more material than you could assimilate at the conscious level, let me reassure you that you are absolutely right. That's a deliberate part of the technique that we have evolved in doing this kind of instruction, understanding that your unconscious mind will represent for you anything that you missed consciously. We thank your unconscious mind for its attention, and ask that your unconscious mind make use of a naturally occurring set of states that is going to happen later on for you tonight.

Sometime this evening you are going to go to sleep. During sleep and dreaming, natural integrative processes go on all the time in very dramatic and interesting ways. Sometimes you remember the content of such dreams; sometimes you do not. That's irrelevant with respect to the integrative function that dreaming has. I call upon your unconscious minds, during the natural integrative processes of dreaming and sleep tonight, to make use of that opportunity to sort through the experiences of today. Your unconscious can select and represent those portions of what we or someone else did that were effective in eliciting certain responses that you would like to add to your repertoire.

So your unconscious can sort through the experiences of today, both the ones you are aware of and the ones that were going on outside of your awareness, and store in some useful form whatever it believes would be useful additions to your repertoire, so that in the days and weeks and months to come, you can discover yourself evolving your own behavior, coming up with new choices appropriate for your needs in context, and doing things that you learned here without even knowing about it.

At the same time that you are having these bizarre and unusual dreams, we call upon your unconscious to ensure that you sleep soundly and that you will awaken rested and refreshed, and join us here to being the seminar tomorrow morning in this room.

Thank you for your attention today.

IV

Utilization

Process Instructions

The topic this morning is utilization. Once you have achieved an altered state, how do you utilize it in a useful way? Today I'm assuming that you already have attention and rapport, and I'm assuming that you've already done an induction and your client is sitting there in an altered state.

The major positive attribute of an altered state of consciousness is that you don't have to fight with a person's belief system. The unconscious mind is willing to try anything, as far as I can tell, if it is organized and instructed in an appropriate way. The conscious mind is continually making judgements about what is possible and what is not possible, rather than simply trying some behavior to find out whether it is possible or not. The conscious mind with its limited belief system is typically extremely limited in terms of what it is willing to try, relative to what the unconscious is willing to try. The unconscious typically doesn't have those kinds of restrictions.

If a person arrives in your office and says "I can't do this and I want to" a useful assumption to make is that she has already done everything she is capable of to try to make that change with the resources she can get to consciously, and has failed utterly. So the least interesting part of the person to communicate with will be her conscious mind. One way to avoid fighting with someone or having "resistance" is simply to get the conscious mind out of the way and go directly to the "boss."

A question many of you have been asking since this workshop began

99

is "What do I do once I get someone in a trance?" The simplest way to utilize any induction is to give the person a content-free set of instructions that essentially says "learn something," "change now." We call these "process instructions" because they are very specific about the *process* the person is to go through to change and solve problems, but very *un*specific about the *content*. The *what* is left ambiguous, but the *how* is specified. Following many of the inductions we did earlier, we gave a brief process instruction. The benediction we gave you at the end of the day yesterday was essentially a process instruction. In that benediction we instructed you all to review your experience, pick out the useful pieces, and use them in the future. Notice that the content was left out. We didn't say *which* experiences to pick, exactly *when* to use those experiences, or *what* to use them for. All those specific details are left to the unconscious mind of the listener.

There are several advantages to presenting instructions in this way. One big advantage is that you don't have to know what you are talking about. You don't have to know details about another person's life in order to give a set of content-free process instructions that will be useful. If someone comes in with a problem, you can give process instructions to "Search through your personal history at the unconscious level, taking time to identify a particular resource that could be of use to you now in dealing with this difficulty." You do not specify what the "resource" will be, only that the person will find one. You don't specify the "problem" and you don't even need to know what it is!

A second advantage is that process instructions engage and occupy the listener in a very active way, because the listener has to fill in the content that you leave out. A third advantage is that the other person's integrity is completely respected. You are never going to introduce inappropriate content for her, because you are not introducing any content at all.

For those of you who know the Meta-Model, it may help you to know that the verbal patterns of hypnosis, including process instructions, are the *inverse* of the Meta-Model. The Meta-Model is a way of precisely specifying experience. Using the Meta-Model, if a client comes in and says "I'm scared" my response is "Of what?" I ask this in order to get more specific content information about what's missing.

If I'm giving process instructions, I am deliberately *un*specific. I leave pieces out in order to give the client the maximum opportunity to fill in the missing pieces in the way most meaningful to her or him.

You can recall examples of this in what we did following many of the inductions we demonstrated earlier. We said things like "And you can allow your unconscious to present you with some memory from the past that you can enjoy. . . ." I hope that you have a general sense of what process instructions are. (If you want to learn the specific language patterns you can use to build process instructions, see Appendix II.)

One language pattern, *presuppositions,* is so important I want to mention it here. Jane, would you come here a minute? Do you know that there have been times in your life when you've been in a deep trance state?

Jane: I'm not sure. I think I'm in one now.

Today would you prefer that I do a verbal or nonverbal induction to take you into a deep trance?

Jane: Verbal.

All right. Would you prefer to do it now or would you like for me to describe to everyone else what I am going to do before I begin?

Jane: Describe it first.

What was the technique I just used with Jane?

Man: Giving her choices.

I was giving her choices. However, what was common about all the choices I was offering her?

Man: That she would go into an altered state.

Yes. They presupposed the outcome that I was interested in. "Would you prefer I do a verbal or nonverbal induction to put you into a deep trance?" It doesn't matter which one she says. She has now accepted a world where very shortly she is going to find herself in a trance. "Would you prefer that I induce the trance now, or shall I explain what I am going to do first to the rest of the audience?" Again, the presupposition is that she is going into a trance; the question is whether she'll go now or in a few moments. I create what Erickson calls an illusion of choice—a false sense of alternatives. That is, she really can choose between verbal or nonverbal, and now or after I finish the explanation. However, *all of the alternatives that I am offering her have in common the response that I want,* namely a trance. If you were watching, you know that she began to go into a trance before I had a chance to do anything. In a way I agree with Jane. She was in an altered state when she arrived up here and sat down.

Example 1: Now I'm going to continue and give you a simple example of a process instruction. I'm going to continue to use presuppositions, as well as the other hypnotic language patterns.

Jane, would you form a really vivid mental image of a particular place that you find restful, maybe a place where you once took an extremely pleasurable vacation. And I trust that your unconscious mind can make a distinction between . . . (He faces Jane.) when I direct my words to you, specifically . . . (He turns his head to the audience.) and when I direct my words elsewhere. . . . And I request of your unconscious mind . . . that it take only those portions of what I offer . . . directed toward you, which are appropriate . . . for your needs . . . and respond to those in a way . . . tailored to your particularly appropriate desires for the task at hand.

And while you are there . . . Jane . . . enjoying that particular place and time . . . I would very much appreciate it if your unconscious mind . . . would select . . . a fragment . . . of a particularly amusing . . . experience . . . perhaps one . . . that you had forgotten about . . . so that in a few moments, with your permission . . . when I reach over and . . . touch you on the right shoulder . . . you suddenly . . . remember something of interest and amusing pleasure . . . that you haven't thought about in years. . . . (He touches her shoulder.) En . . . joy. . . . (Jane smiles broadly; audience laughs.) Really enjoy it! Our past experiences . . . are a source of constant amusement. And once you've enjoyed it . . . fully . . . go ahead and allow yourself to settle into a comfortable state. . . . When you have that sense of refreshment . . . please drift back and rejoin us here . . . so that your conscious mind . . . as well as your unconscious mind . . . can be engaged in the learning process. . . . (He changes to normal speaking voice.) Thank you, Jane.

Is it clear how I just used process instructions with Jane? I asked her to think first of a restful place, and then to think of a pleasurable experience from the past. If I had simply said it that way, however, I wouldn't have gotten the intense response you just observed in Jane's change in expression. As we said at the beginning, hypnosis can be thought of simply as an amplifier of experience.

Example 2: Now I'm going to get a little more complicated. Let's pretend that I just walked up to Liz here, and said "Hello, my name is Richard Bandler" and extended my hand. (He does this as he says it.) As her hand comes up, I've already got an unconscious response. Now I need a way to amplify it and utilize it. I might take her wrist and turn her palm toward her face and say "Look at your hand." That gives her a program to replace the one I've just interrupted.

"Watch the changing focus . . . of your eyes . . . as you see the tops of your lids slowly move down . . . over . . . eyes . . . only as fast as you become aware of that need to blink. Take all the time you need, and allow your hand to go down only as fast . . . as you become completely relaxed . . . in your own special way. And it isn't important how fast that hand goes down. It's only important that it goes down . . . at the same rate . . . and speed . . . that the other hand *begins* . . . to *lift up*.

Because there's something that you want to learn about . . . and it isn't really important that anyone but you knows what that special learning is, because your unconscious mind has known . . . all along . . . and if you're going to learn about it, it will be important . . . *slow down!* . . . to learn about it in a balanced way. . . . And your unconscious mind knows what kind of balance will be necessary. . . . That's right. . . .

It's *so* useful and it's really *so* important . . . to allow your unconscious mind . . . to give you . . . the opportunity . . . and ask it for your own meanings . . . to make changes and to have a learning experience . . . and new understandings . . . which you can use . . . for yourself . . . in some way . . . which will be . . . beneficial to you as an individual human being. . . .

Now, I don't know . . . whether or not . . . you could begin to dream a dream . . . which has within it the solution that your unconscious knows . . . will give you what you want. But I do know that if and when you *do begin that dream,* it won't make any sense at all. And it's not important that you understand. . . . It's only important that you learn . . . and you learn . . . exactly what you need to know. . . .

Every night . . . Liz . . . you engage in the natural process of dreaming. . . . Some of those dreams you're aware of . . . and some you're not aware of. . . . That's right. . . . And I'm going to reach down now. . . . I'm going to lift up your arm . . . and I'm not going to tell you to put it down . . . any faster . . . than you take *all* the time that's necessary . . . to begin to build a conscious understanding . . . of what it means . . . to use your unconscious creatively. And when your hand touches your thigh, you will slowly awaken . . . and you will take that new understanding with you. In the meantime . . . there'll be no need to listen to anything . . . else. . . . But it is so pleasant to eavesdrop in a way that you learn. . . . "

Now, can you tell which of her movements were conscious movements, and which ones were not? If you're going to work with altered states, it's very important to be able to discern that. In the beginning, there were many, many movements that she made with her body. Some of those were movements that she made in relationship to her own conscious responses to what was going on, and many of them were not.

Woman: When she turned on the chair, that seemed like it was a conscious movement.

OK. When her left hand lifted up off of her thigh, was that a conscious movement?

Man: I would say no.

What leads you to say that? What about the movement was different?

Man: It was flowing. It seemed smooth.

Can you be even more specific about exactly what you observed? When she moved her feet, she made a perfectly smooth movement, but it was a very, very conscious movement. Liz, did you know your *hand* was going to *lift up*? . . .

Liz: I'm not sure of that. (Her hand lifts in a gesture, responding to the embedded command.)

It just did! Her hand lifting just now was a very unconscious movement. One of the characteristics of unconscious movement that you can notice is that at the beginning, the movement is often very small and hesitant.

Pick up your hand—deliberately pick up your hand. When you pick up your hand consciously, do you begin with your wrist? . . . No, you don't begin with your wrist. You begin with your elbow, or possibly your shoulder. Martial arts masters begin with their belly—their center. That's really different than starting to lift at the wrist.

Even if she were to begin with her elbow, the quality of movement is very different when it's unconscious. I would have the tendency to call it jerky movement. It's a more graceful kind of movement in one sense, but it's more hesitant; there are lots of pauses. Conscious movement is more like a whole program, and as it begins, you can see where it's going to end. It's all one piece.

There's a real difference between the kind of movement that you get when a person is in an altered state, as compared to a familiar state. There's a real difference between the way her hand lifted up off her thigh when I gave her the instructions in trance, and when I asked her to lift her hand deliberately. If she decided in her mind "I want a Kleenex" and reached for one, it would look very different than if I instructed her to do it in trance.

It's really important to recognize these differences if you want to know what state your client is experiencing. When I lifted up her hand and I told her to allow it to go down and so on, it began to move down very slowly with small pauses, like a leaf from a tree. That was really good unconscious movement. Then it began to go down more smoothly and faster. Her conscious mind had interceded. Her arm began to have weight again. I said *"Slow down!"* and it looked as if her arm hit something, or as if it were on the end of a string. It stopped as if a string held it there, and then it went down with the same kind of movement as before. Being able to discern the difference between the two kinds of movement allowed me to be able to amplify one and diminish the other. That allowed me to boost her more and more into an altered state.

Now, what about the handshake movement? When I come over here and I put out my hand, what kind of movement does she respond with? When people engage in automatic unconscious programs like shaking hands, or perhaps taking out a pack of cigarettes, their movement usually looks more like conscious movement in that as it begins, you can see where it's going to end. It has a definite direction. There are still ways to distinguish this kind of movement from conscious movement, and if you watch examples of both you will know what I mean. When people engage in automatic programs like shaking hands, they perform the motor activity smoothly and easily, but without focusing their attention on their movement. It looks automatic.

OK. What I just did with Liz was another example of a process instruction, with some other things added. First I spent a little time developing a trance state, amplifying unconscious responses. Then I began to instruct her to have "new understandings" and to use them in a "beneficial way." I didn't say what the new understandings were, or even what they were about, and I didn't mention what the beneficial way would be. I didn't mention that because I had no idea what they were. I left that entirely up to her unconscious mind.

Then I asked her to dream a dream in which she will learn what it means to use her unconscious creatively. Again, I'm not saying anything that means anything in and of itself. I'm allowing her to make the most appropriate meaning out of it for *her*. And then I equate completing that task with allowing her hand to come down.

When you give process instructions, you use a lot of words like "understanding," "resource," and "curiosity." We call these kinds of words *nominalizations*. They are actually *process* words that are used as nouns. If you turn a word like "understanding" back into a verb "You will understand. . . . " you realize that a lot of information is deleted. You will understand *what*? If someone uses nominalizations when they're speaking to you, it forces you to go inside and access meaning. If a client says to you "Well, I'm looking for *satisfaction,*" you can turn satisfaction back into a verb and ask "You are trying to satisfy yourself how?" or "You would like to satisfy yourself about what?" But if you don't do that, then you have to fill in the missing pieces yourself. That's what most therapists do with what their clients say. They hallucinate what the person means. If all I say is "I'm looking for *support*" you have to go inside and get your ideas of what it means for someone to support someone else.

Each time I select verbal patterns that do not refer directly to sensory experience, I'm calling upon you to be active in the process of understanding them. Each time you do that, you're doing a process which we've named, incomprehensibly, "transderivational search." People take the words that you offer and relate them to their own personal experience. As a hypnotist I use the fact that people do that naturally. I begin to generate language that is stuffed full of nominalizations. I have *no* idea what the meaning of those nominalizations is, but my client will fill in what's most relevant for her. (See Appendix II for more details.)

Woman: Several times during the process instruction you said "That's right." What was your purpose in saying that?

Saying "That's right" is one of the simplest ways to amplify whatever response is occurring. For example, if I'm giving her process instructions to make some learning, and I see rapid eye movement or other changes indicating that she is processing material internally, saying "that's right" is an instruction for her to do more of it. It's a pace of *any* experience, and allows me to amplify her response without having to describe it.

Example 3: Let's play a little more. Ann, let me ask you to do something. Close your eyes. First, I want you to make a clear, rich, focused, visual image of a wall, and on the wall I want you to have doors. Do the doors look different to you, or do they look the same?

Ann: Yes, there's a difference.

There's a difference. OK. Now, the door that's farthest to the right will take you someplace that will be very *familiar.* Just keep looking at those doors. And the door that's farthest to the left will take you somewhere that will *seem* totally different, but when you get to the end, you will discover you've already been there before. Now, there's another door there, is there not? Now, *feel* yourself walk up to that third door and put your hand on the door knob, but *do not open that door.*

Ann: I'm just really . . . not feeling a door knob. It's a swinging door.

You haven't looked around. Search it very carefully. It may open in a way that you've never had a door open before. . . . Do you discover anything unusual about this door? . . .

Ann: Yes.

Go ahead and try in vain to push it open. . . . Search the door more . . . until you find some unusual characteristic . . . which has meaning for you as a person . . . to allow you to really get the door open . . . in a way that it's never opened before. . . .

Ann: Well, I did it.

Now, very slowly . . . I want you to step through, but before you push the door all the way open, I want you to realize . . . that you are going to enter an experience . . . which will have the following characteristics: There will be elements . . . that will make no sense whatsoever . . . and you will have no words for those elements. But they will be the most important of all . . . and they will have the most meaningful relationship to changing you . . . as a human being . . . in ways that you don't fully understand. And as you notice those elements, pay close attention to them. There will be certain *other* elements which will surprise you delightfully . . . like when you turn around, there's no door there anymore. . . .

Now I want you to observe your environment . . . with clarity . . . and with depth . . . because there's something . . . there . . . that you haven't seen yet. Something that will have personal significance for you. And as your eyes drift up and down . . . around your environment, you won't know what it is until after you pass it. . . . That's right. Now, when you go back, however, it's not quite the same. But when you *do go back*, you can use that as an opportunity . . . and as a reminder . . . of something that you've needed to know for quite some time.

Now, while you're doing this consciously, I know . . . at the unconscious level you are doing something else . . . and that something else is much more important than what your conscious mind is engaged in . . . because at the *un*conscious level . . . you're beginning to build a foundation . . . on that one object. A foundation which will be a solid structure . . . on which to build new . . . and more satisfying future behaviors.

And while your conscious mind continues to explore your environment . . . and to wonder, really wonder . . . what the unconscious mind is going to do . . . that structure is being built all the while . . . as you continue to engage in this process. That solid foundation . . . will serve as the same basis . . . as the foundation you built . . . the very first time you stood on your own two feet . . . because before that you'd only had the experience of crawling . . . until someone lifted you up . . . and for only an instant . . . you balanced on your own two feet . . . with their support. . . . But even then . . . you were building an unconscious foundation . . . which would later serve . . . as the basis . . . for your own walking . . . and running . . . standing and sitting.

And that object . . . is the beginning of a foundation . . . for a whole new set of experiences . . . and I know . . . that your unconscious mind can build that foundation quickly . . . *or* it could build it slowly, but in either case it must *build* it *thoroughly* . . . so that it doesn't collapse at a later time. . . . Because the choices that you want in your future behavior . . . must have all the necessary ingredients available . . . at the unconscious level. . . . And in order to be available, they will have to have a solid structure of understanding . . . and the necessary elements . . . to make that behavior available . . . to you as a human being.

Now you're faced with a dilemma . . . at this moment in time, that you hadn't consciously realized . . . but you're beginning to realize it now. . . . Either . . . you go back and find the door and walk out . . . leaving something unfinished . . . or you allow your own unconscious processes to finish it for you. Or you stay where you are . . . and leave the world . . . outside you . . . to itself . . . and take all the time that's necessary . . . to build a structure . . . which will have all the ingredients . . . that will be necessary for you to have the future development . . . that you have been informed . . . would be beneficial to you . . . as a human being. . . .

And that decision . . . has got to come from you . . . and your own unconscious processes. . . . There's no need for it to come from anywhere else. . . . While you sit there . . . your unconscious processes . . . have kept your heart beating . . . have kept you breathing . . . have kept the blood flowing through your veins, and have done a hundred thousand other things that your conscious mind is not even remotely aware of. . . . The importance of this . . . is realizing that you can trust your own unconscious processes . . . to take care of you. When you walk down a busy street . . . and your mind is lost in thought, you automatically . . . stop at a red light . . . and even though you are engaged in internal activity, when the light changes . . . you *know* that it's time to proceed ahead. . . .

And you can always trust those unconscious processes . . . to do something . . . which is beneficial . . . and useful . . . if given the proper impetus to do so. And it's not really important *why* it didn't happen in the past. It's only important to know . . . that it's possible in the future.

Once a long time ago, before I had ever done any therapy, I sat observing a man in a restaurant. One of the interesting things about this man . . . is that he was completely drunk . . . and yet . . . each time a fly landed on his hand, he involuntarily twitched . . . and the fly would move off his hand. He repeated this process . . . again . . . and again . . . and again . . . and even though his conscious mind . . . did not know what was going on, his unconscious activity was organized . . . and methodical . . . and protective. . . .

When you're driving down a highway, sometimes the roads are icy; sometimes they're not. Sometimes you are concentrating on what you're doing . . . and other times your mind is elsewhere. And when your mind goes somewhere else, one of the most important things you can learn from that experience . . . is that if something suddenly needs your conscious attention, you're suddenly there. . . .

Now I want you, Ann, to take all the time that you need . . . to solidify all those learnings and understandings . . . for yourself . . . in a way which will be most useful for you as a human being. And it isn't really very important . . . whether your conscious mind knows that occurs. It's only important that your unconscious mind . . . *begins immediately* to demonstrate to you . . . in new behaviors . . . its vast potential to make changes in your ongoing behavior . . . now and in the future.

Now, in a moment I'm going to come back and talk to you. And I'm going to ask you questions . . . and some of them you will answer willingly . . . and some of them you may not want to answer. There will be no need to answer them. Before I do that I am going to speak to other people . . . and you will always know when I am speaking to them . . . because I will direct my voice elsewhere. So you can take your own time and do what you know you need to do . . . and what you *don't* understand that you need to do. That's right. And be as conscious as you need to be in that process. . . .

Now let's talk about what I did with Ann. There was no content in any of those instructions. At the process level there was an explicit set of instructions which said basically two things: 1) engage your unconscious; and 2) solve your own problems.

Notice that as we teach you utilization methods, we're still using the tools we taught you earlier. I started by *pacing* everything that I could see about the way she was, and then as she would slowly begin to change, I would *lead* her along by slowly changing my output channels. For instance, I gauged the tempo of my voice . . . to her breathing so that as . . . I began to . . . slow my . . . tempo down . . . her breathing would slow down. I was watching all of the behavioral cues we mentioned earlier: her skin tone, her skin color, her breathing, her pulse rate, the movements of her eyelids, and so on. These nonverbal cues give me feedback. I know what people look like when they go into deeper and deeper altered states—states that are accompanied by physical relaxation.

Ann, are you consciously aware that this kind of experience has an impact on you?

Ann: Yes.

So I established lots of pacing mechanisms and set up feedback loops. I made myself an elaborate biofeedback machine for her. I watched the changes in her skin color, and as her skin color changed I *very slowly* began to change from my normal tone of voice to a very different tone of voice. Initially I changed my voice tone and tempo at the same rate that she changed. Then by changing my voice even more in the same direction, I could lead her further and further into an altered state.

While I was doing this nonverbally, I was also giving her verbal instructions, both at the conscious and unconscious level. Some of these verbalizations were particularly designed to give me feedback about whether or not she was with me. I talked about the drunk twitching when a fly landed on his hand, and then watched to find out whether or not her hand would twitch. And it did.

Ann: But did you use my resistance to—

There can be no resistance.

Ann: All right. When you told me to visualize the three doors, I visualized two doors at the top and one like an archway. When you started giving me instructions about the first two, after the first few words were out, I knew I was going to take that third door no matter what you said. Did you know that?

Of course. That was part of the program. The question is, *how* did it turn out that you would only take that door?

Ann: Well, I'm asking. How were you aware that I was not going to take that first door?

What was the difference in my descriptions of the three doors—above and beyond the words I used to describe them? . . . I said (low tonality, expressing slight disgust) "There's a door that you can go in and everything inside will seem *familiar*." Listen to that tone of voice! Does it make sense to you now that I would know which door you were going to go through?

However, if when I said "There's one door and you can go through it and everything on the other side will be *familiar*" your face lit up, color came into it, and you sighed, then I would know something different. The rest of my communication would have been adjusted to that.

Ann: How would you have structured your communication differently if I had chosen the first door?

Well "chosen" is not a word that I'm willing to accept. If you had *responded* to that door, if unconsciously I had gotten indications that what you needed to do was to have an experience with what was familiar, I would have had you go in the door expecting everything to be familiar.

If I start with an opening like that, I can still do anything I want! Then I can have it transform into something *un*familiar. "As you reach for what you thought was there, you are surprised to find that. . . . " "Have you ever cracked open an egg and had a little bunny rabbit fall out?"

What I'm trying to do is give a set of instructions that allows Ann to make unconscious changes. So the most important rule is to respect her unconscious responses. That requires that I'm able to do only one thing—know which responses are conscious and which ones are unconscious.

Did you notice how I structured the experience of the third door? What did I tell her to do with that door? I told her to "try *in vain*" to open it. If I say "I tried to open the door" that's very different than "I tried *in vain* to open the door." If I say "I tried to open the door" I can try again. It may even make sense to try again. But if I say "I tried in vain to open the door" there's no possibility. One has the possibility; the other doesn't.

Now why did I do that? . . . If she's going to go in a door which has unfamiliar things behind it, the best way to begin is to make the door have a response which is unfamiliar—to have a door that opens in an unusual way. That makes the door itself and the experience she's about to have congruent with each other.

I structure my language carefully. For instance, if I say to you (He turns to a woman in the audience.) "Now you can try to lift your hand" there's an implication that you won't be able to, but there's still a possibility that you might. But if I say "You can try in vain to not lift your hand. . . . It's a far-reaching experience. . . . And then you begin to wonder which hand *won't* lift first . . . because you thought it was *that* one."

Now, if you notice, this woman is completely immobilized. That's a trance phenomenon, by the way. And it's utilization of "resistance" by including lots of negations. I gave her something to respond to, found out how she responded to it *un*consciously, and amplified the unconscious response. Her unconscious response was immobility, and the way to increase her immobility was to ask her to move more and more. The more I asked her to move, the more immobile she became. *The point is, that response of "resistance" is as predictable as anything else,* as long as you have the sensory experience to notice which response is unconscious.

The main ingredient you need to be able to function as a communicator is sensory experience. If you can make the distinction between what is conscious and unconscious, and *amplify* the unconscious responses, you will alter someone's state of consciousness. One way to do this is to ask, as Fritz Perls did "What are you aware of?" If she says "Well, I'm conscious of talking to myself and tightness in my jaw" then you say "But you weren't aware of the warmth where your hand touches your face, and the feeling of your feet on the floor, and your elbows against your thigh, and your breathing, your chest rising and falling." That is all you need to do. That person will start to go into an altered state because you are directing her awareness to places where it would not normally go. That's one way to amplify unconscious responses.

It doesn't matter if the conscious mind is involved in the process. In fact, it's more useful to engage the conscious mind in something of relative unimportance—like *which* of three doors it's going to go through. Who cares which door it goes through? What's important is that we alter her state of consciousness. Once we've done that, then we can begin to create experiences by which she accesses unconscious resources. She's *still* consciously concerned with which door she went in, and why, and it really didn't matter, because as soon as she gets inside the door, I can put anything I want in there! The important thing is that *in experience* she goes through a door. That experience is leaving her usual state of consciousness and entering one that is altered with respect to her normal state of awareness. Once she is through that door, I give her unconscious a process instruction—a program for positive change.

I gave her this program using very unspecified language, for the reasons we discussed earlier. It's very important to understand when to use unspecific language, and when not to use it. When you give process instructions, make your language very unspecified. However, if you want someone to do something very specific, like bake a particular cake or cure a phobia, it will be important to give that person very specific instructions, so they can understand how to do it. If you want someone to bake a cake and you tell him to "take all the appropriate ingredients from your refrigerator, mixing them together in the most satisfying way . . . " you probably won't get the cake you wanted.

Often I hear people using the unspecific language we use for process instructions when they are trying to communicate something specific to another person. And they have no idea that the other person has no way of understanding them, because of the words they are using. For example, in therapy, people talk about how important it is to have high self-esteem, or a positive self-image rather than a negative one. But they don't talk about exactly how you build those things, or how you know when you have them.

Sally: It happens in comparing their personal experience.

What are they comparing with what?

Sally: They are comparing their child emotions with their adult understanding of what they think is happening in the present.

OK, and when they compare those, what do they do with the comparison?

Sally: They then have an improvement in their own self-image—their own self-esteem.

How?

Sally: By seeing. You see, sometimes a person has a feeling of badness about herself because it is incorporated in a memory. So as you take the present experience or knowledge in the person, and you look back at that, then at the same time you're helping that person in the session. She can then rework things so she has a different—

Let me ask you something. Do you understand that there is nothing

114

in the description you are giving me that allows me to know what you are saying? This is not a criticism of your understanding, because I think you know what you're talking about. But you aren't talking to me in a way that will lead me to understand.

Sally: Maybe it's the knowledge base that I have. Our communication is a little bit different.

Well, it's not that, because I even know what you want to tell me. I know because people have told me many times. However, the discrepancy between *how* you're telling me and the way you would *need* to tell me in order to communicate what you want me to know, is an important distinction for what we're learning here.

You see, the kinds of descriptions you are using will be exactly what works in hypnosis. If I want you to make something up, to go off on your own and hallucinate, then I use the kind of non-specific linguistic structures that you were just using.

However, if I want you to do something specific, I have to tell you something specific. If I want to give you information about doing something, I've got to make sure that you know every detail about how to do it. You see, if I wanted you to use a particular mental program that I believed would raise your self-esteem, I might say "OK. I want you to pick a specific unpleasant memory from your past—a memory in which you realized that you did the worst you could possibly have done. . . . And as you look at that memory and feel the feelings you had back then, what you don't yet realize is that without unpleasant memories like that one, you wouldn't have learned anything of importance in your whole life. If you'd never experienced the pain of a burn, you wouldn't be smart enough to avoid fires."

That instruction is at least somewhat specific. It tells you to take some unpleasant memory, feel the feelings, and then reevaluate the memory in a specific way. While that instruction doesn't tell you detailed content, it *does* specify the kind of memory you are to think of and what you are to do with it.

If I don't care *how* you make a change, I unspecify my language even more and use lots of nominalizations. Close your eyes for a minute and try something. I want you to go inside and pick two, three, or four pleasant past memories which may *seem* unrelated . . . but your unconscious never chooses anything in a random fashion . . . because there's a learning of importance for you as a person. . . . Now I know in your past, there's a wealth of experience . . . and that each and every one of those experiences . . . constitutes the basis for building a learning . . . or understanding for yourself . . . that is relevant to you . . . only as an adult . . . that wasn't relevant to you as a child . . . but it can serve as the basis . . . for building something that you learned.

Now take a few moments to let that relearning begin to take shape . . . to crystallize. . . . You might be beginning to see an image . . . which is not clear . . . and which you do not understand. . . . And the more you look at it . . . the more you realize how much you don't understand . . . and as you watch at the unconscious level . . . you can be *building that learning* in a way . . . which is significant. . . . The significance of your building that learning . . . is something that consciously . . . you can appreciate only when it's complete . . . and then you'll realize . . . suddenly. . . the ideas . . . and understandings about how to make changes in yourself . . . can begin to flow . . . into your conscious mind. . . . But those ideas have nothing to do with that new learning . . . because when one of those ideas comes into your mind . . . if it's truly an unconscious one . . . it will have to have a giggle attached to it. . . .

Now, the way I just communicated with Sally is very much like the way she communicated with me. However, there's a big difference between *trying to get the conscious mind to understand something* and *trying to get the unconscious mind to do something.* The description that she made is the kind of description I might make to a client when I want her to *do* something, but it's not what I'm apt to give a clinician when I want him to *understand* something.

It's always easier to see these things from outside the field than from inside it. That's true in almost everything. A friend of mine who is a prominent technology physicist told me about a time when he'd been working on a very complicated problem. He'd probably been awake for a month, diligently working on this problem.

His mother had been staying at his house and taking care of his kids while he was locked away in his laboratory. She came into the lab and brought him a cup of coffee and asked "How's it going?" He said "Oh, it's going fine." She asked "What exactly are you doing?" and he explained the complicated problem to her. She listened and said "I don't understand it. I would have just done this" and she gave him the answer that he needed. She had never even gone to high school, but her answer is now the basis for one of the most sophisticated digital computers that has come on the market.

When you're inside a field, you're programmed to see certain things at the expense of others. Of course that gives you capabilities, but it also gives you limitations. When I entered the field of therapy, people said "All you need to do to be a good therapist is to be fully in touch with the needs of people. You help them to raise their self-esteem and their image of themselves so that they can have better and richer lives." I said "How do you do that? How do you raise self-esteem?" And they said "By making people see things the way they really are." I disagree with that; I think it's by creating more *useful* self-deceptions than the ones they already have. I don't know how things "really are."

The point is that there are many words that *sound* meaningful but aren't. Nominalizations always sound meaningful, but that doesn't mean that they are. If you want to get someone's unconscious to *do* something, nominalizations are exactly the kind of words that you can use effectively to do that.

Let me give you a general way to think about making up process instructions, because in addition to copying the kind of instructions we've been demonstrating here, you can make up your own. To make up process instructions, first think of any sequence that will lead to learning. One such sequence is to 1) pick some important experience from your past, 2) review and rehear what occurred then thoroughly enough to learn something new/additional from that experience, and 3) ask your unconscious to use the new learning in appropriate situations in the future.

If you're going to learn something, you need to have a *way* to learn it, and you need to have a way to determine when and where to use the new learning. So make up a sequence that includes those components. Once you have a general idea of what steps you want to include, you can deliver the instructions using hypnotic language patterns, allowing the client enough time to respond.

Generative Change: Hypnotic Dreaming

Next I want to give you a strategy for inducing generative change, both for those of you who want to make personal changes and those of you who do therapy. Generative change *doesn't* mean you want to quit smoking, lose weight, or get over your problems. I call those "remedial changes." Generative change means you'd like to be able to do something more exquisitely, or you'd like to learn something new. It's not that you want to change something you do badly, but that you want to improve something that you already do well.

When I started doing therapy and my sixth or seventh client walked in, I had an amazing experience. He started out in the usual way. He said "There are certain changes I'd like to make." I asked "What are they?" He said "I would like to be able to meet people and get them to like me." Since I was programmed to respond in a certain way, I asked "Do you have trouble doing that now?" He said "No, I'm really great at it."

I stopped. All of my presuppositions were being violated. I asked him "Then what's the problem?" "There's no problem" he said "I just do it so well, and I enjoy it so much, I'd like to be able to do it twice as well." I looked down into my therapy bag of tricks, and nothing was there! Most therapies aren't designed for that kind of situation.

Don't restrict yourself to fixing things that are broken. If you do something well, wonderful! You might enjoy doing it twice as well. There's no restriction on making that kind of change. Usually if you make enough generative changes, you will inadvertently wipe out lots of remedial problems. If you concentrate on making yourself better in an area where you are already good, very often other "problems" will be taken care of spontaneously.

I'd like to have you try out an interesting strategy for generative change that makes use of hypnotic dreaming. As far as I can tell, hypnotic dreaming doesn't differ very much from regular dreaming, except that during hypnotic dreaming you are not snoring.

There are lots of formats to use dreams to alter your reality. The first thing you'll always do is figure out what outcome you're after. You might want to be able to do X better, or for your client to be able to do X better. Let's say your client already can do X, but you want her to be able to do it better.

Then you ask yourself "What kinds of things would allow somebody to do anything better?" Be really general in responding to this. Remember, this is hypnosis, and you are in the Land of Nominalizations.

Woman: Improved perceptions.

Man: Energy.

Be careful about using the word "energy." You have to be very careful about using certain idioms that are widely used in other contexts. The energy crisis has produced a tremendous number of hypnotic messages about energy conservation. If you use energy as a metaphor for having more personal oomph, sometimes you can get into trouble, because you will have to counter massive publicity. There are advertisements now on radio and television for the entire nation to conserve energy and become lethargic.

A well-known therapist uses a metaphor for personal growth called

118

"yeasting." I discovered in one of her seminars that some of the women in the group developed yeast infections! This, by the way, is one of the primary things that old-school hypnotists discovered. They discovered that there's a sense in which all language is computed literally, particularly in a trance state. Any phrase that has an idiomatic meaning gets computed two ways. The phrase "kick the bucket" has an idiomatic meaning that someone has died, and also a literal meaning. Both meanings are computed whenever you use an idiom.

If you frequently say "My children are a real headache" I can guarantee that you will begin to get headaches. People who have a lot of back trouble talk about everything as being a pain in the back, or about carrying the world on their shoulders. We've already talked about this class of language. It's called "organ language" and it's very powerful.

What else will lead to doing something better?

Woman: Knowledge. Practice.

OK. Some kind of new idea will, and practicing something will. If they already do something well, they may have already practiced it enough. If they haven't, practice is something that could lead to improvement.

What we are doing is beginning to build an equation. I know most of you don't like the word equation, but you will begin to. The more you try to not like it, the more appealing and mysterious it might become. . . .

What I just did is always a good equation. Remember, this is one of the ways you can deal with abreactions. It's the same equation. "It's so pleasant to learn from unpleasantness. And the more unpleasant it becomes, the more pleasant learnings you will have." This means the more they go into the negative state, the more they will come out of it. "The more X, the more Y" is a very useful equation for you to keep in mind.

This morning we're going to build an equation that uses dreaming. We can say that anything that produces one of these things—a new idea, practice, or improved perceptions—implies doing something better. That's the same equation I just talked about. We still need something that will produce the new idea, etc., and we'll use dreaming to do that.

Exercise 7

In a moment I want you to make generative changes with each other.

Do this in pairs so you can all do it fairly quickly. Person B, I want you to choose some particular behavior that you already do well, and would like to do even better. Person A, I want you to do any induction you choose with B, until you get a fairly deep trance state. Then reach over and say "I am now lifting up your arm, and I'm not going to tell you to put it down any faster than you begin to dream a dream. . . . During this dream . . . odd and diffuse things will begin to happen. . . . But you know that unconsciously . . . something is building up . . . which is going to crystallize . . . into an idea . . . which will produce in you . . . a change in your perceptions . . . which will allow you to be able to do X . . . even better than you ever suspected. . . .

Because there is something about X . . . that you have overlooked . . . and your unconscious knows how to *go back* . . . and *look again*. . . . What does it mean to overlook something? . . . Overlooking means you looked too high . . . so now you can go back . . . and shift your gaze . . . past experiences . . . at the unconscious level, when you were in *that* particular experience . . . only this time . . . your unconscious can look at it in a new way . . . and find out . . . what it was in the times you did it absolutely exquisitely . . . that was different . . . from the times you only did it . . . sort of exquisitely. . . .

Discerning that difference . . . it can present you that difference in a mysterious dream . . . so you will continue to dream that dream . . . a very colorful dream . . . and enjoy it immensely and wonder . . . really wonder . . . what it is you are about to learn . . . and the idea will *not* come to you any faster . . . than your hand moves slowly down . . . and touches your knee . . . such that when it *does that*, that idea will crystallize in your mind . . . and you will wonder how you could have been so foolish as to overlook it all along." . . .

This is another example of a process instruction. I said to have a dream and learn something from it. However, I also added specific instructions about *how* the unconscious is going to learn it. I said "Go back, review your past experiences, extract the difference between when you do really well and when you do only a mediocre job, and present this new perception in a dream."

However, if I were to just say those things directly, I wouldn't be as effective. It wouldn't work as well, because it wouldn't have the color or the punch. It also wouldn't have the artful vagueness that allows the unconscious to respond in a way that's natural to it. Dreaming is a very natural means for the unconscious to present material in a way that the conscious mind doesn't understand, and then to have it slowly evolve into something which is more meaningful consciously.

Man: What can I do if I want to come up with a solution to a problem that has so many factors I can't compute them all consciously?

What would be a way of going about that? Let's do it this way. Let's go back to the dream. This is one of my favorite instructions. Let's have him dream six dreams, and each one will be the same dream, but will have a different content and different characters. However, he won't understand the first dream at all, because there will be too many things going on in that dream. He won't really understand the second dream either, but unconsciously, with each dream, he will begin to collect and distill the meanings and understandings of all the factors involved into a more and more coherent package. In this manner, by the sixth dream even his conscious mind will be able to understand what is going on. The first dream will be totally confusing. The second dream will be a little less confusing. The third dream will be even less confusing than that. The fourth one will begin to become clear, but he won't quite grasp it. And the fifth one will feel like it is on the tip of his tongue. But in the sixth one, the meaning will suddenly burst fully into consciousness. This is a pretty direct way of going after it   indirectly. It's a great instruction.

Now I want you to pair up and try one of these utilization methods. You've been practicing inductions quite a bit already, so don't spend much time on that. Just tell your partner to close her eyes and relax and pretend that she is in hypnosis. That's always a quick induction. Then either give her a process instruction, or give her an instruction to use hypnotic dreaming to learn something. If you give her a process instruction, make it a more involved one than you used when you practiced inductions previously. Give her a sequence of steps that can lead to learning. Use everything else you've learned up to this point too. If something unexpected occurs, you can incorporate it into what you are doing, and what you want to have happen. OK. Go ahead.

* * * * *

Clean-up Routines

Dorothy: What do you do if the person is in a trance and the hour is up before you've finished working with her? What if she's right in the middle of something?

You need to have a way of dealing with that kind of situation in many contexts. I call such methods "clean-up routines." You might be a family therapist, with mother here, daddy here, and baby Joan over there. They've all just gotten into a disagreement, and it's two minutes before the arrival of your next client. In any situation like this, you ought to have two-minute "tape-loops"—absolutely meaningless content-wise and absolutely meaningful process-wise—to put everything together.

"We've worked very, very hard and a lot of things have been stirred up at the unconscious level that are extremely useful in a positive way. Over the next days and weeks, you will notice understanding emerging from your unconscious. As a result of beginning to put things together here, you will notice changes, alterations in your behavior that will delightfully surprise you. And now, as you gather all the parts of yourself that have expressed themselves today, once again into yourself, you can sense the energy that they represent made available to your unconscious mind, to continue these processes which we have begun here, in a meaningful way. . . . "

This is another example of a process instruction. You stay entirely at the process level and say "Put yourself back together." You include post-hypnotic suggestions that their behavior will continue to change as a result of many of the things that you stirred up. The instructions essentially say "Continue this process even though I won't be here." You can suggest that her unconscious will continue to search for an optimal solution which it will reach sometime before she awakes the next morning.

"During the afternoon, as your unconscious mind continues to work hard to find and test the various possible solutions, in order to find the one which most uniquely fits your needs as a total organism, leaving you free at the conscious level to go about the rest of your day in safety and perform adequately any tasks that you intend to. So as your unconscious mind continues this work, your conscious mind will attend to the tasks of the day and your own safety." Doing this kind of thing is important as a close. It's an integration; it's reassembling the person.

I remember once when I first started doing gestalt therapy, I was working with one person as a demonstration in a group. I didn't have the faintest idea of what I was doing, and as far as I could tell, nothing happened. So at the end I said "Now Irv, we've worked hard here today, and we've stirred up a lot of things inside you. So I want you to be particularly alert and sensitive to those behavioral changes which

122

will occur over the next two-week period until we get together again, which are the direct result of the marvelous work that you've done here today. And don't be too surprised to discover how radical these changes are—but appropriate to your particular needs." That's saying nothing, but it will work. It's a post-hypnotic suggesion.

If you're doing trance work as a part of an exercise in this workshop, and you want to end things quickly because we've called you back, first spend a few moments pacing your partner's breathing. Then you can say "Now I would like the opportunity to join you once again. . . . Allow yourself to finish . . . those important and meaningful things . . . that have been made available to you . . . during this process. . . . Draw from your experience any . . . sense of refreshment . . . and renewal available . . . and return here . . . at your own rate . . . rejoining me here in the room . . . to begin the next phase of this seminar."

That's a cleanup that is particularly appropriate for what you are doing in this workshop. The principles I used to construct it are the same ones I used to make up the other examples I just gave you.

Building Generalizations: A Hypnotic Utilization
The next question we want to pose to you is "How do you take a series of experiences and build a learning from them?" If I gave you a magic wand that would allow you to tap someone on the head five times and give him five experiences, what five experiences could you use to change somebody? Pick one client that you have and decide how you would like him to be different. Think about it more specifically than "having higher self-esteem." What would be really different about him in sensory experience? How would he act differently? . . . Now, what experience would he need in order for him to act that way?

You see, having experiences in a sequence is what served as the basis for you and everyone else to build old generalizations. No matter what content your generalizations have, the processes people use to create generalizations are similar. People who have phobias have generalizations about elevators, closets, water, or something else being dangerous. You all have generalizations about learning that are having an impact on how you are learning hypnosis right now. Some of you might have a generalization that you can do anything that you try. That generalization may be based on several examples of having succeeded in the past. Some people form generalizations based on only one experience; most phobias are created that way. Other people require more examples of the same thing before they form a generalization.

When you want to change someone, you can give him experiences to get him to make a new and more useful generalization—one that would make his life more positive. Of course, the first thing you need to decide is what generalization you would like to build. How could you determine that?

Man: Ask him what he admires in somebody else.

Yes, you could do that, and then you'll find out what he *thinks* he could benefit from. I don't do it that way. I figure that if what he wants would be a good choice, he would have learned it already.

I don't buy into the "you shouldn't impose upon people" philosophy, because I think you end up doing it anyway without knowing it. I keep meeting people who are the result of that kind of imposition. When I ran a private practice, over half of the people who came to me were there primarily because they had been screwed up by therapists—often "non-directive" therapists. The therapists didn't know they were doing it. They were intending to help their clients in some way, and instead they screwed them up.

For example, some therapists teach their clients about self-esteem, and then they can feel bad about not having it. That happens over and over. Most people never felt bad *about* feeling bad when they first went to a therapist. They just felt bad. But when they were taught about self-esteem, then they felt bad about feeling bad, and they were worse off! When you give people concepts, you have to be careful to do it in a way that takes them somewhere useful.

Some therapists teach their clients to accept all their limitations so they can be happy. Sometimes that works really well. However, if they come in with hysterical paralysis, that probably won't be a very good way of working with them.

Man: What do you mean by "happy?"

I'm not talking about philosophy here; I'm talking about the subjective experience of enjoying something. It's a subjective, kinesthetic experience in which people have the absence of pain, and they have stimulation of the nervous system in such a way that they describe themselves as liking what they're getting rather than being in a state of desire. You see, if people come in to therapy whining and moaning and complaining, it seems to me that they're not happy.

If you as a clinician don't have your own life together, it's going to be really hard to figure out a basis on which to do something to help somebody else. When I did an ongoing training program, one of the most rigorous parts of the program was that my students had to get their own personal lives together—right away! Because if I found out they were having long, meaningful conversations all night with their wives and things weren't working out, and they felt like they had to have affairs, I canned them right out of the program. They knew I would do it, so they made sure they got their lives together.

It is of paramount importance to me for people to be able to take care of themselves. I'm not talking about being able to survive, but taking themselves to places that are enjoyable. I make jokes about my next book being titled "OK is Not Good Enough." I don't consider the paradigm of repair a good paradigm. The paradigm of repair in psychotherapy, where people come in unhappy and broken and you fix them, is only part of the picture. It makes more sense to me that we build models based on notions of generativity.

People are just beginning to do this in the area of physical health. For a long time, medicine used a model based totally on repair. However, the only *really* amazing thing that medicine has done is to invent innoculations. The fact that people can be injected with vaccines against polio which prevent them from getting it is a miracle. It's the finest thing medicine has ever done, and it's certainly not based on repairing what's gone wrong.

If you're generative, you modify things so they're better than they were when you started. You utilize the natural propensities of the system to make the system even *more* effective. That's the way I think about everything. I want to work with what's there in such a way that it's better than it needs to be—not just adequate.

My personal criterion for doing successful work is whether people are happier. Those are just my own ethics. You can work towards unhappiness if you want. You see, whatever you do, you set up target states. If you're a lawyer, you don't work toward happiness, you work toward conviction: toward getting people convinced of things. If you're a clinician, hopefully you set up happiness and competence as target states.

A lot of therapists set up *understanding* as a target state. Clinicians have been very successful at building paradigms that give people understanding, so that people understand exactly what's wrong with them. They end up with clients who really understand, but they still can't cope with the world, and they can't make themselves happy. Other therapists have referred me dozens of clients who would sit down and give me a long, detailed explanation about where their problems came from, why they have them, and how they affect their lives. I'd say to them "Well, that's really interesting, but what do you want?" They'd say "I want to change it!" So I'd say "Then why did you tell me all of that stuff?" They'd respond "Well, don't you need to know that?" I'd say "No, I don't have to know about that." They'd be flabbergasted, because they had just spent five years and $50,000 finding out why they were screwed up!

Husbands and wives often make each other unhappy because they set "being right" as a target state. So they end up being right, but everybody ends up being unhappy as a result.

We want to teach you to build learnings in the context of hypnosis. You can use these techniques to get any outcome you want. If you want to you can make people unhappy, you can make them ill, or you can give people hysterical paralysis or phobias. Those things don't seem eminently fruitful to me. However, if that's what you want to do, it's an ethical choice that you'll have to make.

The question I'm asking you is "What experiences could you give somebody that would result in building a useful generalization?" It's a practical question.

Man: If he already has a troublesome generalization, you could give him a counterexample.

Yes, that would work. I believe that learning can happen in a number of ways. One of the best ways to teach the conscious mind something is to provide it with a counterexample to what it believes. There's a nice example of this in our book *Magic I*. In one of our groups a woman who couldn't say "no" lay down on the floor and began to cry hysterically. She exclaimed that she was helpless and people walked all over her. I asked her "What do you mean 'people walk all over you'?" Then I started to walk across the room towards her to stomp all over her. Having been in enough of my groups, she was smart enough to get out of the way.

She said that she lived with two other women, and they constantly made her do everything and ran her life. I said "Well, why don't you do something primitive like turn around and say 'Don't do that'?"

Saying that got one of the most intense nonverbal responses I have ever seen in a person. She turned paler than she already was and said "I can't do that." I said "What do you mean you can't do that?" She said "Well, I can't tell them 'no.'" I asked "What would happen if you told them you wouldn't do the dishes or you wouldn't do something else?" She said "Oh, it's just impossible."

She ended up telling us a traditional story that would please a psychiatrist. She had learned not to say "no" when she was a little girl. One day she was about to go to the store with her mother, when her father said "Why don't you stay home with me?" She said "No, I'm going to go with mommy." She went with mommy, and when they came back to the apartment, her father was lying on the floor covered with blood. His hand was about two inches from the telephone. He had been an alcoholic, and had just died.

After that, she just never said "no." That meant she probably didn't keep her virginity too long. She was a homosexual, which I thought was interesting. That one experience with her father was enough for her to build the generalization that if she said "no," somebody was going to die.

I put her in a "double-bind" by telling her that I wanted her to go say "no" to someone on the other side of the room. She said "No, I won't do that." And I said "Did I die?" She said "What?" And I said "You just said 'no' to me. Am I dead?" She went through another set of visible changes and then said "Well, you're special."

I had given her an *experience* of a counterexample to her generalization that if she said "no" people would die. At that point she could say "no" to me and know I would live, but she still couldn't say "no" to anybody else. So I had other people come up and tell her to say "no." I had to build a broader base of experience on which she could do something else.

This took a long time. You see, there's something terrible about knowing you're wrong, but not knowing what you're supposed to do differently. I didn't know how to do hypnosis then. Had I known how to do hypnosis, I could have changed her generalization much more easily, gracefully, and without all the struggle and pain.

Let me pose another possibility for building generalizations. Any time you define something as being *new*, you can just build new generalizations for it. If you define something as new, you can build a generalization without destroying or changing one that's already there. Give me an example of when that would be useful.

Man: Don't you do that with children?

I hope so. But I want you to give me a specific example.

Man: If you're teaching someone to multiply and he doesn't know anything about it, then you can give him a generalization about learning multiplication without breaking an old one.

Right.

Judy: I disagree with that. I think that when you teach addition, you don't have any generalizations to break. In teaching my children multiplication, I teach them that it's based on addition. It's sort of like addition, but it's just a little bit different. So in that example I think you *do* have generalizations to break.

Sometimes hypnotic communication flies right by, doesn't it? Judy just said in essence "When I teach my children multiplication, I do in fact have to break generalizations, *because I teach them that it's like addition.*" Now, I agree with her reasoning. The reason that she has to break generalizations is that she thinks multiplication and addition are related to one another and she teaches her children that they are. They *are* related to one another, but no more or less than addition is related to subtraction or division or exponents or anything else. If she taught multiplication as a totally new thing, she wouldn't have to break an old generalization.

Man: This workshop on hypnosis is an example. I wasn't aware that I knew anything about hypnosis until I came in here. For me it's totally new learning, so I'm not breaking any generalizations about living—being—growing. Since I assumed there were no old ones to begin with, I'm just making new ones.

I'm suggesting to you that there are at least two ways of building new generalizations. One way is to break an old one, and the other way is to simply build a new one. You see, one nice thing about people is that they can have incompatible generalizations within themselves. There's nothing that prevents them from being able to do that. There's a whole form of therapy based on trying to get rid of all your incompatible generalizations so you can be one-dimensional. According to that system, to be authentic is to be totally consistent.

There's no need to break old generalizations or get a person to be completely consistent. It can be simpler to define something as being new, so that the person has no generalizations and therefore no limitations. That doesn't mean the person will know what to do, but it does mean he won't have any interference once he finds out.

The nice thing is that you can define anything that exists as something new. You see, if you have a generalization that you can't get along with your mate, you can go for something besides "getting along." You can build a totally new kind of relationship that's different than anything that you ever had before, because now you're going to understand something that you didn't really know about before. Before you were trying to survive. You were trying to get your way or be right. You never stopped and thought about what it would be like if both you and your mate did everything you could do to make your partner make you feel good.

If I can build a new outcome for you, and then teach you specifics about how to get there, either consciously or unconsciously, your other limitations can make it easier for you to get there. They won't get in the way of your new generalization; instead they'll get in the way of your doing all the other things that you used to do and which didn't work. So the limitations that somebody has can become assets.

Another way you can build generalizations unconsciously is to build learnings that encompass everything. In Greek society there was an occult group based on something called mathematics. Mathematics is now considered a science, but not long ago people who did mathematics were considered sorcerers, and thought of themselves that way. It was like practicing magic or some religion. Mathematicians at that time discovered that there were two sets of numbers. First they discovered positive numbers, and then they discovered subtraction, and with subtraction came negative numbers. This caused a division in mathematics. Some mathematicians thought that everything was addition. There were others who believed that the right way to think about numbers was subtraction. Those two groups had wars about who was right.

Then someone came along and said "Hey, we can put both of these principles into the same schema and call it algebra." The idea of algebra didn't require breaking any generalizations or violating anything. It only required being inclusive; it required getting a larger picture.

I used to go to lots of psychotherapy groups to find out what group leaders did. At one seminar they locked us all in a room and told us we were all jerks. They said the reason we were jerks was that we felt bad about ourselves. They said that since we sometimes felt stupid and helpless, or didn't feel like we were worthwhile, we were dummies. This was true because we had another choice. That choice was to feel good about ourselves.

They went through a rigorous procedure of torturing us for days and days, and somehow this was supposed to make us feel better about ourselves. What they didn't teach us is that feeling good or bad about yourself is really part of something bigger called *feedback*. You see, if you feel bad about yourself, but that doesn't lead you into changing your behavior so you can feel good about yourself, it's not very useful. If you feel good about yourself, but you're doing things that hurt other people and you don't get feedback about that, that's not useful either. Just because you feel good about yourself doesn't mean that you're doing good things; and doing good things doesn't mean that you're going to feel good later on.

One of the things that has amazed me more than anything else in my experience with human beings, is that people who are supposed to be in love, fight. And when they fight they do things that could really affect their relationship negatively over a long period of time. Usually it's because they forget what they are doing with each other. They forget that they are together to be intimate. It slips their minds, and they start arguing over where they're going to go on vacations, how to bring up the kids, who should take out the garbage, and other wierd little things. And they are really effective at making each other feel bad. They have forgotten something that would tie meaningfulness to the whole experience.

Now I want to give you a more official example of hypnosis, because too many of you are not looking around the room and noticing what's going on in here. So I'd like to take somebody out of the audience and put him up here. There are certain advantages to sitting in this chair, because you get to watch 100 people go in and out of altered states, and *they* only get to watch one. Is there somebody in the audience who would volunteer?

OK. What's your name?

Woman: Linda.

OK, Linda. Are you married? (Yes.) Can you think of anything that your husband does that makes you feel some way that you don't like? You don't have to talk about what it is, but I'd like for you to think of some idiosyncratic behavior of his—perhaps some tone of voice, some gesture, some set of movements—that makes you feel unpleasant. If he didn't do that behavior, you wouldn't have to feel unpleasant, but if he kept it and your response to it was really positive, it would make your life a lot easier. So he could do exactly what he does, but rather than feeling bad, you could still enjoy yourself—perhaps even feel very pleasant. . . .

OK. Take a few moments. Close your eyes and look at times and places where you've seen him do those things. And when you look at him in those situations, I want you to be very sure . . . that you can discern which of his hands moves the most. . . . In each memory notice specifically how he's dressed . . . and approximately what time of day it was. . . .

It's not that these facts are important in and of themselves . . . because what's important here . . . is not necessarily . . . going to be . . . facts at all. . . . Because in your past you've had the experience . . . where what you thought was an absolute fact . . . became the opposite of what you came to believe later on. . . . That's the nature of time. . . . Time changes everything. . . . In fact, without time . . . nothing at all changes. . . . Light wouldn't exist without motion . . . and motion doesn't exist without time. . . .

Right now, I want you to take the time to go way, way back into your own childhood, and find there some past, pleasant memories that you haven't thought about for a long time. . . . Because many things happened to you . . . in your own childhood . . . things that were fun . . . things that were important. . . . Right now, the most important thing . . . is that your unconscious mind . . . *begin to learn . . . to separate out* . . . one thing from another . . . to begin to work active- ly . . . and sort through those childhood memories . . . to find one that is just . . . pleasant . . . enough. . . .

And I want you . . . that's right . . . to enjoy that process . . . . When you *find that pleasant memory* . . . I want you to experience those feelings. . . . Get inside that memory. . . . Notice the smells and sounds and the tastes . . . of what goes on. . . . Because inside that memory . . . is enjoyment for your conscious mind. . . . And inside that memory . . . is the foundation that your unconscious mind . . . can use to build an entirely new learning. . . .

Now, inside that memory . . . that pleasant memory . . . something is occurring. . . . Do you know what the name of that something is? . . . That's right. . . . Remember that name. . . . That's a set of words . . . that you can *remember* later on. Now, when you went through life . . . you went from one memory to another. Only they weren't even memories yet, they were just experiences. . . . And as you moved from one experience to another . . . you'd have an enjoyable one . . . but as time went on, your enjoyment would change to some- thing else . . . because there were also experiences which were very, very unpleasant . . . some which really scared you . . . some which you fought your way through . . . and from which you learned a lot about living. . . . That's right. . . .

And as you got through those experiences, you said to yourself "Never again." . . . And as time went on . . . those unpleasant experiences faded into the past . . . and they became the basis . . . of powerful learnings . . . about how to cope with the world in a way that was effective. . . . They were useful. . . . However, they're not nearly as useful . . . as what happens when you say the name . . . of that pleasant memory. . . . Say that name to yourself . . . and as you do . . . you can go back there again. . . . That's right. . . . Go back inside that memory . . . the pleasant one . . . and find the enjoyment. . . . That's right. . . . Because you forgot to do something. . . . Lots of people forget. . . .

When you go from a pleasant experience to an unpleasant one, you don't use the pleasantness as a way of coping. . . . On the other hand when you leave an unpleasant experience and go to a pleasant one, somehow or other it's so easy to take the unpleasantness with you. . . . It seems foolish somehow, but yet it's easier that way. And if you take some time . . . take a deep breath . . . and let that unpleasant memory really fade . . . and then move forward . . . and go back into that pleasant memory . . . that enjoyable memory . . . and when you're in that memory this time . . . you tell yourself . . . "I'll never forget this again. . . ," Because some things . . . are a resource . . . that you want to take with you . . . to be at your beck and call. . . . And some things are a burden . . . and they're *no longer needed*. . . .

A long time ago . . . my aunt told me . . . that whenever something bad happened . . . I should never forget it because if I would ever forget it, it would happen again. . . . If I had taken her advice, I would have spent a long time trying to remember a lot of bad things. . . . But if you have a bad experience and you say to yourself "Never again" . . . you can trust that your unconscious will allow you to know what to avoid in the future. . . . And if you say "A few moments ago I forgot to take that pleasant memory with me, and I felt all those bad feelings, and I'm *never* going to do *that again*" . . . you can *go back into* that *enjoyment* . . . go into that pleasant memory . . . and perhaps remember another one that's even more pleasant. . . . Find one that may even have a giggle under it or a giggle over it . . . perhaps one that has tenderness . . . perhaps one that just has a lot of fun. . . . Because you went through your childhood . . . you became a teenager . . . and now you're an adult. . . . You made it, so to speak. But since you've made it . . . that's no reason for you to give up all the good things. . . . It's much more effective to take them with you. . . .

See what is the most pleasant memory your unconscious mind can find. . . . You can consciously look for memories, but unconsciously you know how to sort through memories much faster . . . and much more effectively. . . . Your unconscious knows much more about your own experience than I do . . . and it can sort through memories at a high rate . . . until it finds one that it thinks your conscious mind would never have thought about, which is pleasant in a very unique way. . . . It can find more than one if it chooses. . . . It might show you a piece of one . . . a fragment of another; it might show you a whole sequence of pleasant memories. . . .

And as it *does so* . . . you might not realize it . . . but you're doing the same thing you did . . . every day of your childhood for the first four years and every day thereafter. . . . You're sorting through memories and experience, trying to make sense of them . . . in a way that's useful. . . . And if you find that thread . . . that allows you to have a good feeling . . . then very, very slowly I want you to feel the palms of your hands . . . begin to touch one another, slowly . . . the warmth and texture. . . .

And as they come together I want you to *keep those good feelings* . . . and I want you to see your husband doing that special idiosyn-cratic behavior . . . that in the past you didn't like . . . and I want you to see him do it . . . and keep those good feelings . . . and know how good it can feel to have somebody special in the world. . . . That's right. . . . The most unique experience that a person can have . . . is to have someone who is special for them.

You see, one of the things that you may have noticed . . . is that if you've ever been in a room with a woman and her young baby . . . and when she looks at that baby and you see her face . . . there's something very special there . . . and very meaningful there. . . . And that special quality is something that's more important. . . .

Now . . . in my years of working with people . . . I've seen many people who forgot. . . . I've seen mothers who come in and yell at their children in front of me—they scold them, they strike them, they make them feel bad. . . . They've forgotten *that special feeling,* and they think what they're talking about is more important. . . . That's a ter-rible waste. . . .

When you see your husband doing that idiosyncratic behavior, you will have palms on your hands . . . and if you feel that good feeling inside you, that pleasant thread of enjoyment, not only will you have palms, but you'll have someone special in them. . . .

Now, I don't know . . . if you feel that you can afford . . . to do otherwise . . . but I know that as I go through life, it's important to me . . . to be able to appreciate and to enjoy all the qualities . . . that make a special person unique . . . and individual . . . not just some of them, because what you're learning here is not just a way . . . that your unconscious can assist you in taking one piece of behavior and making it tolerable . . . but a way in which your unconscious can begin to *appreciate* every idiosyncratic piece of behavior. . . .

I remember when I was young . . . I didn't like the crust on bread . . . . And when I'd get a sandwich, the first thing I'd do is peel the crust off and feed it to the dog. . . . I had to be very covert about this because my mother believed that the crust on Wonder Bread was nourishing. My mother was very naive. Now as time went on, I discovered that not all breads tasted like rubber; I discovered that there were some breads on which the crust really did taste good. There was San Francisco French bread, certain kinds of rye bread, and certainly cinnamon toasts of odd, interesting fashions. And I discovered that as time went on my *tastes* . . . *changed* . . . from one thing to another . . . and as your *tastes change* and you learn to appreciate something . . . that you didn't before . . . it makes you aware . . . and more alert . . . to just exactly what it is . . . that makes something important.

Now above and beyond all of this . . . there's something else going on here . . . which is that you've begun . . . a process . . . which can continue for many years . . . about learning to use your unconscious resources . . . to go deeper into a trance if you wish to . . . or just to communicate . . . with the unconscious portions of yourself . . . for the purpose of learning . . . and change. . . .

Now, one of the things that will help you . . . is to realize . . the significance of one foot as opposed to the other. If you very slowly begin to move your right foot, you can wake yourself up . . . but if you hold that right foot still . . . and begin to move your left foot, some-thing else will happen. . . . Try it. . . . Now isn't that interesting . . . . Now why don't you use that right foot . . . and under your own control and steerage bring yourself right back here to the Grand Ballroom. OK, thank you. You can go sit down now.

What I just did with Linda can be thought of in many different ways, because it includes a lot. Some of it was quite explicit and straightfor-ward, and some of it was not. At the simplest level it's a process instruction. It included hypnotic language patterns and guided Linda through a sequence that will lead to learning.

You can also think about what I did as reanchoring. I accessed positive experiences and attached them to situations in which she used to be irritated with her husband. I instructed her to do that verbally, but the verbal part of my behavior was probably the least important part in getting the response from her. I was also anchoring tonally: I used one tone of voice to anchor her positive memories from the past, and another to anchor what her husband does. Then as I talked about her husband's behavior, I shifted to the tone that anchored the positive memory, to give her a new response to her husband.

Along with that, I was making a content reframe: I was changing the meaning of her husband's behavior. Now seeing or hearing her husband do those things will simply be an indication that he is the unique person who is special to her.

I included another pattern that we haven't talked about yet, and several that we won't teach you consciously. The pattern I'm thinking of is a fairly complex one, and makes use of a kind of metaphor that we haven't taught very often. You see, there are two kinds of metaphor. One kind is based on isomorphism. That is, if a woman comes in who has two daughters that argue, I might tell her a story about a gardener who had two rosebushes which were snarled together in his garden. If you use isomorphic metaphor to produce change, you tell a story that has a one-to-one relationship to what is occurring, and then either build in a specific solution, or provide a very ambiguous, open-ended solution. You can read about that kind of metaphor in David Gordon's book, *Therapeutic Metaphors.*

There's another kind of metaphor that elicits a response which is really a command to do something or to avoid something. This kind of a story elicits a response without necessarily being parallel to anything in the person's life. I might tell a story about a person I know who was completely convinced that he was right about a particular way of doing something. He and I and several others were all involved in designing a computer, and we all had our own ideas about how to do it. He wanted to do something with the transformer that none of the rest of us thought could be done. When we disagreed he yelled at us and told us that he wasn't even going to waste his time talking to us about it. He said that we didn't know, and we didn't understand, and he was smarter than us. So he just went in and took the transformer, hooked it up, flipped the switch, and it electrocuted him and killed him.

That kind of metaphor is very different from an isomorphic metaphor. It elicits a response of avoiding something. It's an exaggerated example of what I just did when I told Linda about the mothers who had forgotten about what they'd had children for.

I used other examples of this kind of metaphor. I told a story about myself, and how my tastes changed naturally as I grew up. That story isn't parallel to anything I know about Linda; it's simply a story that elicits a response—the response of things changing spontaneously. That's a response that can be very useful when doing hypnosis.

This kind of metaphor is particularly effective if you use stories that are universal in order to elicit responses. By universal I mean stories that everyone can relate to and will respond to in the same way. Almost everyone has experienced liking some food and later disliking it, or vice-versa, so I know that if I describe such an experience, almost everyone will respond to it in the same way: by accessing an experience which indicates that spontaneous change is possible.

Milton Erickson used to use this pattern very effectively. He put people into a trance, and then talked about going to school for the first time and being faced with the alphabet. "At first it seemed like an overwhelming task. But now each letter has formed a permanent image in your brain and has become the basis for reading and writing."

That's a universal example, for people in this culture, of something difficult becoming easy. Even if it didn't happen quite that way, as an adult looking back, it seems as if it would have happened that way. That means it's an experience that you can use with anyone to elicit the response of something difficult becoming easy. When people ask for help in making a change, you can be sure that the change will seem difficult to them. So it can be really useful to elicit the response of something difficult becoming easy.

Often Milton would talk to his clients about what it was like to be a small child. He would say "And when you were a very young child, and you first learned to crawl, you saw toes and table legs, and the world looked a certain way. And when you first stood up, you had a whole new set of perceptions about the world. The whole world looked different to you. When you bent over and looked between your legs, the world looked different again. You can gain new perceptions for yourself as you change your abilities. And as you change your perceptions you have the possibility of acquiring new abilities." This kind of description is really an instruction to do something—to change your perceptions. He describes an experience we have all undeniably had of doing so, easily. "And you may be able to remember being a child, or think about what it would be like to only notice the carpet, and the little mysterious things in the fiber . . . to only notice the relationship of the underside of tables . . . and then one day you learned to stand. Perhaps you held onto someone's fingers or the side of the couch, and you looked at the world. Rather than looking up or looking down, now you could look straight ahead. And what you saw looked very different. It changed the things that you were interested in, it changed how you saw things, and it would change what you could do."

When you tell that kind of story, it doesn't matter if things actually occurred exactly that way. All that matters is that if adults look back at what it must have been like to be a child, it *seems* as if that would have occurred. That means that adults will universally respond to that kind of story in the same way.

If you get someone to recall that experience, and the next things you talk about are experiences that could serve as the perceptual base for changing a particular problem, that sequence is a command. It's not just a story. The command is to change your perceptions using this particular data.

We aren't going to go into detail about this kind of metaphor during this seminar. However, you can make what you do more powerful and have more punch by using this in a simple way. You can think about what kind of responses you can elicit that will make your change work easier. Then you can think of universal experiences that include those responses, and describe those experiences to your clients after you put them in a trance.

One response that's very useful to elicit when doing hypnosis is the experience that one's unconscious is wise and can be trusted. What are universal experiences in which people respond appropriately without thinking about it consciously? . . . You can talk about how when you run, your body knows just when to make your heart beat faster, and your breathing faster, and when to slow them down again. Consciously, you have no idea just how fast your heart should beat in order to get the appropriate amount of oxygen to your cells, and there's no need to, because your unconscious has a wisdom about how and when such things should occur.

V

Reframing in Trance

Introduction

This afternoon, I want to spend some time teaching you reframing: an approach that you can use with hypnosis to deal with almost any difficulty. I also want to teach you how to arrange explicit "yes" and "no" signals, because if you know how to do that, you can go through any procedure in a trance and get accurate feedback as you do it. But first I want to give you some background.

How many of you have ever had a client with hysterical paralysis or something like that? Many people think it's uncommon, but it's not. It's an interesting problem. When I first encountered hysterical paralysis, I was fascinated by it. I had read that Milton Erickson had taken hysterical paralysis and moved it from one part of the body to another, and I had always wanted to do that.

When I finally got a client with hysterical paralysis, I decided to try something similar to what Erickson had done. I hypnotized her and moved her paralysis from one arm to the other. She walked out being able to use her left arm, which she hadn't been able to move for three years. However, her good right arm was now completely paralyzed. I was delighted, and had her come back the next day.

She was somewhat perturbed at me, because changing her paralysis made it obvious to her that her paralysis had a hysterical quality to it. Before that—no matter what the doctors had told her—she knew that the paralysis wasn't really in her mind. The doctors kept saying "It's in your mind" and she knew it was in her arm. But when it changed to the

137

138

other arm, it was hard to believe that it was *only* in her arm.

The next day I moved the paralysis from her arm to her leg. She had to limp out, but both of her arms worked perfectly. She began to get even more perturbed at me. Moving her paralysis around accomplished something very important. She had a belief, and I gave her counterexamples. She believed that her difficulty was not in her mind. But when you go into the office of somebody who is working with your mind and not your arm, and you walk out one day with your paralysis in the other arm, and the next day not in an arm but in a leg, that has a tendency to make you question whether or not you have a physiological problem. Not only did this serve as a counterexample to her old belief, but it began to teach her that the paralysis itself could be moved.

I assumed that the paralysis had some function in her life, so rather than take it away entirely, I moved it again. She ended up walking out with paralyzed fingernails, which she complained about bitterly! How would you feel if your fingernails were paralyzed? What if you started out with just a paralyzed arm, and ended up with the fingernails on *every single finger of your hands* paralyzed!

When Erickson wrote about the case in which he moved someone's hysterical paralysis, he alluded to the main criticism of hypnosis as a treatment procedure: that hypnosis only treats the symptom and not the "basic need," so a hypnotic "cure" will only result in some other symptom appearing.

This notion of needs evolved out of the work of Freud. He believed that people had certain needs. In those days they accepted "needs" as a well-formed description of something that happened inside someone's mind. Once someone had a need, there was nothing that could be done about it. It was only a question of how the need would express itself.

Let's say you had a need to get attention. If that need wasn't being fulfilled, you might break out in hives or something like that to get attention. The attention would be the "secondary gain" that you would get from having hives. If you had a need for people to be more supportive of you and take care of you, you might get a paralyzed arm.

Back in Freud's day there was another guy named Mesmer, and Mesmer used to do things that intrigued Freud. Mesmer would take somebody with hysterical paralysis and make the paralysis go away, but later on the person would end up having some other kind of problem.

Freud got the idea that if you cured someone's paralyzed arm, the symptom would *of necessity* express itself in another way. Her paralyzed arm might go away, but her face would break out in hives. He even gave this a name: "conversion." It's also called "symptom substitution."

Hypnosis has often been accused of only resulting in symptom substitution. Critics have claimed that while hypnosis may remove one symptom, the client will *of necessity* get another symptom in its place. When I entered the field of psychology, I was interested in testing this criticism of hypnosis.

I became very curious about hypnosis because just about everyone in the field of psychology told me "Don't learn about hypnosis. It only treats the symptom." I learned a long time ago that anything in life that is avoided strenuously is probably worthwhile, so this aroused my interest. While there are exceptions, I've noticed that people tend to avoid things that are very powerful.

People said "Don't learn hypnosis, because it only treats the symptom" and my first response was "Well, I'd like to be able to treat the symptom. If I can't do anything else, that might be worthwhile." They said "No, no. If you only treat the symptom and you cure it, it will pop out somewhere else."

Since I am a mathematician, the idea of getting something to pop out somewhere else was so much like an equation that it was attractive. I thought "Oh, I'd like to be able to do that!" So I started learning about hypnosis, and experimenting to find out what happened when you took away symptoms. I tried taking a few volunteers who had some problems, hypnotizing them, and removing symptoms *carte blanche,* without doing anything else. I wanted to find out where the symptom came out, to find out if there was some systematic pattern in how the conversion took place. Any good mathematician is going to ask the question "How does the symptom know where to come out next?" Nothing is random. If atomic particles aren't random, it takes a lot of audacity to think that symptoms can violate the laws of physics.

I began to notice that there were certain patterns to how symptoms came out. The new symptoms seemed to accomplish the same *purpose* that the old ones had accomplished. When I removed someone's symptom with hypnosis, she got another symptom that resulted in getting the same goodies.

The other thing that I noticed—which I hate to inform the world of psychology of—is that the symptom *didn't* always come back. In fact, people were better off when it *did* come back. If the *only* way someone could get attention was with her paralyzed arm, and I hypnotized her and took that symptom away, then she simply did not get attention. That seems to me less useful than having a conversion.

When I watched therapists work, I started noticing that very often they succeeded in "fixing" someone by making the person more *limited*! That may be a difficult idea to understand at first. However, if somebody is not in touch with her feelings—for example, if she is closed off to the world as a way of protecting herself against a lot of the hurt and suffering that one can feel in life—and you take that away from her, she ends up getting slaughtered emotionally. That doesn't strike me as being a useful outcome.

I know a man who had that happen. The clinician who worked with him thought his ideology was more important than his client's experience. The therapist believed it was good for people to feel everything intensely, so he set about teaching his client to respond intensely without asking the question "When he does feel things intensely, how is he going to deal with that?" That clinician didn't consider that the mechanisms which have protected his client from feeling things intensely must be there for a purpose.

The difference between conscious reasoning and unconscious response is that responses seem to have purpose and not meaning. It's very hard for people to understand the difference between those two, because they usually try to figure it out consciously. And, of course, consciously you are trying to discern the meaning of the difference between meaning and purpose. That is a really good way to confuse yourself. And as some of you begin to engage in that process, I want to speak to the rest of you.

Purpose is simply a function. If something has a function, it accomplishes something. What it accomplishes is not necessarily worthwhile. However, it is habitual. It accomplishes something that *at some time* in the history of that organism had a worthwhile meaning to it. Most of you who are clinicians have noticed that people engage in behaviors which would be useful and appropriate for someone who is five years old, but not for an adult. However, once the program for the behavior was set up, they continued to use it.

For example, there are some adults who cry and whine to get their way. They don't realize whining isn't going to help them any more. When you whined as a child, if you had the right parent, you got things you wanted. But when you go out into the world as an adult, it only works with a few people. So you whine about the fact that it doesn't work, and get even less of what you want.

When I learned about hypnosis, I decided I'd find out if you could just make something go away without ramifications. I hypnotized eight smokers, and just took away their smoking habit. There were no detectable ramifications at all with four of them. If ramifications aren't detectable, that's satisfactory to me. If there is some underlying "pressing need" that never surfaces, that's all right with me. If the Freudian analyst says it will hang on forever, that's OK, too. If it works, I don't care if it leaves some "pressing need" as long as it never has an impact on the person's life.

However, with the other four people whom I worked with, conversions did take place. I checked up on all of them periodically, because I wanted to find out if anything had occurred that was unusual, strange, inordinately pleasurable, or an interference in their lives. I also had them come in and sit around in my office, because I wanted to observe whether there were any radical changes in their behavior that they didn't report.

Another man who had been a smoker had a very interesting and unusual response. When this man called me to report, he said the following: "Everything is going beautifully. I haven't even wanted a cigarette. Everything has been really cool. I haven't had any other problems whatsoever. By the way, do you do any marriage counseling?"

Now, I noticed a certain incongruity in his communication, so I told him to get his wife and come over to my office immediately. When they arrived, I seated them in the waiting room and left the room. At that time my wating room had a videotape unit set up in it so that I could watch people. I discovered that I could learn much more about people in the waiting room in five minutes than I could in my office in an hour. So I used to spy on people a lot. I had it set up so that no matter where a person moved in that room, I could hear and see them.

This couple sat in there and waited and waited, and I waited and waited. I kept watching them until I noticed something interesting. They were both engaging in such meaningful activities as reading magazines and staring out the window. There wasn't a lot to do. He was pacing around, and she kept looking at him and trying to talk to him. At one point he sat down next to her, and she opened her purse and pulled out a cigarette. She lit the cigarette and then stopped and stared at him. She took a drag off of the cigarette and looked at him again. He glanced at her smoking, got up, and moved away from her. She continually tried to engage him in conversation, but he would just give her short answers and go back to his magazine.

At that point I went out into the waiting room, lit a cigarette, handed it to the man, told him to smoke it, and left the room. He took the cigarette, and although he didn't want to smoke it, he kept it in his hand. He didn't smoke the cigarette, but he began to talk to his wife.

It had occurred to me that there was a strong possibility that over the years they had developed a signal system using cigarettes. I later used a little hypnotic investigation and verified that my hunch was correct. In their day-to-day routine they both engaged in lots of activities until one of them paused and lit a cigarette. Then the other would do the same thing, and they would pay attention to each other. They hadn't done that in the last two weeks, since I took away his smoking. They had ignored each other completely because that signal system was gone. That's a good example of something which is not meaningful in itself, but which has a purpose.

Another man came to see me because of ringing and pain in his ear. It had started with a small earache some time earlier; then he went deaf in that ear and also had chronic pain in the ear. He'd had five operations, and now there were no nerves left in that ear. Doctors had taken everything out, yet his ear still rang, and he still had the same pain he'd had before the operations. The doctors knew there was nothing left in his ear to hurt or make noise, so they decided that it must be psychological. Their timing was not something I would be proud of, but at least they didn't keep operating. They have to be complimented for that. At least they didn't say "Well, maybe it's the other ear!" Or "Let's go for the left cerebral hemisphere!"

When this man came to me, he said "I've got to get the pain to stop. All I want to do is learn self-hypnosis to control the pain, because now I have to take so many drugs to control the pain that I can't function. I can't do anything at home. I can't work. And if I don't take the drugs, the pain is so tremendous I can't do anything. I'm trapped. I'm going broke. I'm going to lose my home. It's just terrible."

He wanted me to use hypnosis, and in a way I did. I used a particular model inside of hypnosis—a model we call "reframing" which is designed to do deliberate symptom substitution. Reframing takes one symptom and turns it into another one. It sounded to me as if this ear problem gave him a ticket out of having to work and do other unpleasant things. It wasn't a very pleasant ticket, but he didn't like his work, either. He was an architect and he didn't really enjoy it, and ended up doing most of the bookkeeping and other unpleasant jobs. So I switched the symptom from being pain and ringing in his ear—although I left the ringing initially—to hysterical paralysis. I instructed his unconscious mind that both his arms would become paralyzed *only* when it was appropriate for this symptom to be available, because I wanted to know how accurate my guess was.

He really became quite functional. Then his wife would say things like "I want you to take out the garbage and mow the lawn, because there are so many things that we're behind on" and suddenly his arms would become paralyzed. He would go "Oh, damn! I can't do it now." His business partners would ask him to engage in the most unpleasant of activities in their business—doing bookkeeping and things like that—and the paralysis would mysteriously emerge.

Once while I was trying to learn about symptom substitution, a lady who had numb feet came to me. Her feet were numb all the time. They were so numb that she couldn't balance herself, and she even had to have people help her walk. She had been in therapy for some time. Before she first went to therapy, her feet only got numb sometimes, and after being in therapy, they kept getting worse and worse. She thought that they had been getting worse all the time, and that the therapy hadn't helped, but my guess is that the therapy had made her have numb feet constantly.

I always think of symptoms as being people's friends, not their problems, because I think of symptoms as communication channels. However, as with most communications between people, the purpose and the outcome is often forgotten. Symptoms, like people, don't always realize the difference between what they *intend* to communicate and what they *do* communicate.

This woman was brought into my office by a very conservative counselor from a place in California where you have to be rich to qualify to live. The counselor explained to me how she had done family therapy with this woman, and the woman now had a perfectly happy family. The counselor had thought that the woman's numb feet had something to do with family interactions. But since she had worked through all the family difficulties, and the symptom was still there, something else must be going on. So they thought, as a last straw, they would try hypnosis.

The poor client was sitting there dressed in a sweatshirt and pedal-pushers. She wasn't an unattractive person, but she appeared to have worked very diligently to make herself look unattractive. There she

was, sitting next to a very well-dressed forty-year-old woman therapist, who was saying things to me like "Her family problems are
solved." Every time the counselor said that, the client didn't say anything, but her nonverbal response was dramatic. Her face would go
asymmetrical and her breathing would become shallow and rapid. I
thought "Hm . . . something is going on here."

So I looked at her, and said "You've come to me with numb feet
. . . and your therapist says . . . this has nothing to do with your
family problems. . . . Your therapist believes . . . your problems
have been solved . . . and your symptom persists. . . . Your doctor
tells you . . . this is not neurological. . . . He says the problem is not a
physical one . . . but it is in your head. . . . Now I know . . . and you
know . . . that the problem is not in your head. . . . It's in your feet
. . . because you can't stand on them. . . . If you stood on your
feet. . . without numbness . . . you wouldn't need . . . this therapist
. . . or that doctor . . . because that's the reason you've come
here. . . . Now I don't want to talk to *you* . . . because you've failed
utterly to cope with this problem. . . . You haven't learned to stand on
those feet . . . by yourself . . . without numbness. . . . I want to speak
to your feet directly."

If you take somebody from Middle-class America and say something like that to them, they get *weird.* The difference between hypnotic
communication and ordinary verbal communication is that when you
use hypnotic communication, you don't care about the content. You
only pay attention to the responses. I keep saying "Don't pay attention
to the content, pay attention to the *response.*" If you do that, you can
say *anything,* and communicate with people in a way that no one else
can.

Then I shifted my eyes and looked down at her feet and said "Numb
feet, I know you have something important to tell us." That therapist
looked down at the woman's feet, and the woman bent over and stared
at her feet, too.

I said "Now, I know . . . that biologically . . . the right foot is the
'yes' foot . . . and the left foot is the 'no' foot. . . . Is there something
that you want to say to me?" The "yes" foot moved, and the woman and
the therapist both gasped. I said "All right. Is there something that
you've been trying to tell this woman for years, and she hasn't understood?" The "yes" foot moved again. I said "Would you be willing to
tell her is a new way?" The "no" foot moved. I said "Have you noticed
that this way doesn't work as well as you would like it to, and that the

price is too high?" The "no" foot moved again. Her feet thought that what they were doing worked just fine.

Then I said "Would you be willing to try another approach anyway, if it worked better?" and the "yes" foot moved. So I said "All right, feet. If you like this idea, what I want you to do is to remove every ounce of numbness. Restore complete and solid and firm balance. And *only* at the moments that you need to communicate, I want you to become numb. But I want you to do a more thorough job. I want you to become numb from the tip of the toes to at least a foot above the knees. And then when you no longer need to communicate, go back to full balance. Because the way you communicate now, she doesn't know when you are communicating and when you are not, so she can't understand what you are saying. Even though she obeys, she obeys when she doesn't need to. And she could obey more fully, could she not?" And the "yes" foot moved. Then I said "Begin now."

The woman said "My feet aren't numb!" She picked her foot up and she looked at it, and she moved her toes. She stood up and she could balance. The therapist said "Now, I don't want you to get too optimistic, because sometimes these things don't last" and the woman got numb all the way up to her knees, and she fell over. She lifted herself up into the chair and said to her therapist "Don't tell me that!" and the numbness went away.

Now, her symptom became a teacher for her. When she left my office and went home, she was delighted. She cleaned the house and did things she hadn't done in a long time. When her husband came home, she told him the good news, and said "Why don't you take me out to dinner to celebrate?" He said "I'm too tired. Why don't you just cook me something." She responded "Well, OK" and the numbness began to creep up her legs. She said "No, I think we'd better go out" and the numbness went down.

Her numbness became her best friend for quite some time. It became a teacher. When a symptom becomes a teacher for you, it becomes an ally, because there is nothing in the world that can't be made useful in some way.

If you think of psychotherapy, hypnosis, and medical science in general as making war on symptoms, you will be very limited in what you will be able to do. Fighting with her own unconscious mind is something the client doesn't do very well, and your conscious mind won't be able to do it much better.

A long time ago, before I became an official hypnotist, I had a relative who had a tremendous problem with her weight. She was a member of Weight Watchers Anonymous and she did all kinds of things like putting signs on her refrigerator. What impressed me about her was that she always bought food so she could resist eating it. There was always food in the house to not eat.

I remember that one time when I was just a kid and didn't know much about things, I went to the supermarket with her. As we were walking through the supermarket, I was kind of bouncing along behind her. She was putting lots of things in the cart that she wouldn't eat. One of the things she was getting was a half-gallon of ice cream. I asked her why she was getting the ice cream, when the day before she'd gone to so much trouble to not eat it. She said she was getting it for me. I told her I didn't like ice cream, and that she didn't need to get it for me. She took the ice cream out of the cart and tried to put it back in the bin, but she couldn't do it. She said "Well, maybe your mother would like some." I said "No, my mother doesn't like ice cream, either." So she started to put it back again, and then she said "Well, you're going to have some friends over tomorrow." I said "No, I've changed my mind." She almost set the ice cream down, and then stopped again. She searched her mind, trying to put the ice cream back. I reached over, took the half-gallon of ice cream, and put it back down in the bin. Then I looked at her and asked "What's the matter?" She said "I don't know. I think I'm leaving somebody out."

I remember being struck by how confusing that comment was. It didn't make any sense to me until years later. She *had* left out somebody in her life—herself. She was a professional housewife who had a house that never got dirty, because nobody ever dirtied it. Her husband worked seventeen hours a day, seldom came home, and refused to talk business with her because he thought that was impolite. However, there was nothing left to talk about. They had no children. She didn't have a car, because her husband didn't think that she should learn to drive; it wasn't safe in California. So she had an empty house with nothing in it, and no one to talk to. One might say she was empty.

I wish I had known then what I know now—that there is an unconscious purpose behind behavior. The purpose does not need to be meaningful in the sense that Freud thought it did. When I was first interested in psychology, fool that I was, I took a couple of courses at the University. One of those courses was called "Interpretation of Interpersonal Documents." We were going to learn to interpret things the "real" way. In that course, I discovered that people attach much more meaning to behavior than there actually is. Behavior doesn't have that much meaning, but it has a tremendous amount of purpose, and I want to demonstrate this to you.

Reframing

How many of you in here know how to do reframing already? What I would like to do, both for those of you who do not know what reframing means and for those of you who think you know how to do it, is to give you a way of doing reframing with the unconscious mind. The way we usually teach reframing in seminars, it is a way for your conscious mind to communicate with the rest of you about something you want to change, and to generate new and more satisfactory behaviors to choose from. Today I want to teach you how to use reframing as a way of communicating directly with someone's unconscious *without* using her conscious mind as an intermediary.

The way we're going to do reframing today will be a little bit unusual, because you are never going to know what you are working on. The person that you work with is not going to tell you what she wants to change. She is not even going to allude to it, and in fact she herself may not know what it is. We are going to do this by setting up an unconscious signal system. Rather than talking to people's feet, you are going to talk to something else.

1) *Setting up Unconscious yes/no Signals with the Unconscious.* Before you can do the reframing part, you need to be able to set up a yes/no signal system, so that you have a way of getting feedback. There are many ways of going about this. One way is to use what are called "ideomotor responses." Whenever a person moves some part of her body without consciously doing it, that's an ideomotor response. Traditional hypnotists use what are called finger signals. They have one finger lift for "yes" and another one lift for "no." Erickson had a tendency to use arms—to have a whole arm move up relatively involuntarily. But you can use head nods, skin color changes—any signal that is nonverbal in nature and is something that you can observe.

Remember that unconscious movements are slow and relatively jerky. If you are using finger signals and your partner lifts her finger up quickly, the way she would if you just asked her to lift her finger, you say "That's the *wrong* mind. I am not interested in *that* mind."

The conscious reframing model that is in the book *Frogs into Princes* is designed to use the client's conscious mind as a messenger.

She notices responses internally and reports what they are to you.

Rather than using the client's conscious mind in that way, this afternoon I would like you to go through a procedure of learning to set up ideomotor responses so that you can see the "yes" or "no" responses. The way you are going to do that requires that you first substantially alter somebody's state of consciousness. You can alter her state in one of the ways that you have already learned. You figure out what would be a sequence of experiences that would lead your partner to be in a very altered state.

When you are working with the person, you might tell her to sit there and as she sits there, remember a time that she took a long trip in a car. She was driving down the highway—perhaps it was nighttime, perhaps it was daytime. Perhaps it started in daytime and worked its way towards evening. And as the dusk began to fall and she moved down that road, she began to notice the vibration in the steering wheel, the hum of the engine, the repetitive movement of visual objects rushing past her. The din of experience . . . as you moved on . . . and on . . . through the evening. And as you did so . . . you became more and more relaxed . . . and you told yourself you had to stay awake . . . this was very important. . . . But you felt very tired . . . and you might look at a clock . . . once . . . and look at it later . . . and feel as if an hour should have passed . . . but only minutes had gone by. . . . Sometimes you would appear to daydream for a second . . . and twenty or twenty-five minutes would have gone by. . . .

All of these descriptions . . . that you can use . . . will lead your partner more and more into an altered state. . . . And as she goes into that altered state . . . and begins to relax . . . and become even more comfortable . . . then I want you to begin . . . to suggest to her . . . that she can use her unconscious mind . . . as a resource . . . a resource that she can learn from . . . and communicate with . . . and really have an experience . . . which is one that will be satisfactory to her. . . . And that the only thing which is necessary . . . to build good rapport with her unconscious . . . is to have a channel of communication. . . .

Sometimes the unconscious communicates with the conscious mind by movement . . . . It might be movement . . . of relaxation. . . . It might be that your head nods . . . up and down . . . slightly . . . to communicate "yes," and back and forth . . . slightly . . . to communicate "no." . . . It might be that a left arm . . . very slowly . . . begins to lift up . . . as a way of communicating "yes" and a right arm

. . . lifts up slowly to communicate "no." . . . It might be that your right foot twitches . . . involuntarily . . . to indicate "yes" . . . and a left foot twitches . . . involuntarily . . . to communicate "no." . . . It might be that you look to the left . . . to communicate "no" . . . and you look to the right to communicate "yes." . . . Only your unconscious mind knows which it will be. . . . And if it should be that one of your hands is going to lift up . . . or one of your feet is going to move . . . it doesn't matter which it is at all. . . . It only matters that the choice that you make . . . is appropriate . . . to you . . . because your unconscious mind knows more about you . . . than anyone else. . . .

Now, you can then ask the person to unconsciously choose . . . what she would like to use as a "yes" signal . . . and watch what happens. . . . If you don't see anything . . . take your time . . . deepen her trance . . . and suggest other alternatives . . . until you find one. . . . Because some people choose to say "no" by moving an index finger . . . and "yes" by lifting a whole arm. . . . And I know that someone who does that . . . can allow their unconscious mind . . . to lift a right arm . . . off their thigh slowly . . . perhaps all the way up to their face . . . so that the person who is working with them . . . could never miss that signal. . . .

Now, it requires that you be astute when you do this . . . because very, very often . . . the signals will appear to be incorporated . . . into a conscious movement . . . and when that occurs . . . you don't want to miss it . . . do you? It's so easy for people . . . to miss signals. . . .

Now, you may get a signal . . . that you see once . . . but it doesn't appear . . . to come a second or a third time. . . . Just because you ask a question . . . doesn't mean that someone has a way of answering it unconsciously. . . . Because sometimes questions can't be answered "yes" or "no." . . . So try to ask questions initially that you can be sure . . . there is a "yes" or a "no" response to.

I want you to pair up and try this. First induce an altered state, and then lead the person into answering questions with an ideomotor response. If the person literally does not give you any signal and has trouble doing ideomotor responses, you might want to help her. Remember, never define anything as a success or failure. Leave it ambiguous as to when you are asking her to use one channel as opposed to another, and leave it ambiguous as to which channels you are paying attention to, so that it's hard for her to tell where you are getting the signals from. If you set up something that is limited and she fails at it, it may convince her that she can't do it, when in fact she probably already has succeeded. But she didn't notice that success; she only noticed when you defined something as failure.

I would like to instruct every unconscious mind in here that if you get the idea from the person who is working with you that you are failing, you are wrong. It's the *other* person who is failing. The fact that you got that idea is an indication that she didn't give you enough choices so that you could respond easily and appropriately.

Sometimes it's very difficult for people to do ideomotor responses because it's a new thing for them. If they are sitting there and you are not seeing any responses, very often you can tell them (He turns to a woman in the audience.) "Sally, I'm reaching over and I'm lifting up your left arm. And I'm not going to tell you to put it down any faster than you really relax comfortably and completely and learn to allow your other hand to float up involuntarily. So that hand will go down slowly while you think pleasant thoughts . . . and allow all the weight to drain out of the other hand . . . so that one hand goes down . . . only as fast as the other one begins and continues to lift up . . . and no faster. That's much too fast—slow down. Only as fast as the other hand learns to move involuntarily. . . . That's right . . . . Take your time. . , . Let the other mind do it. . . . Slow down. . . . There it goes. . . . You are learning now . . . really learning. . . . Enjoy it. . . . That's right. . . . All the way up, let it . . . all the way up. . . . Learn to allow your unconscious mind to make the movements and the changes . . . and allow that to continue, one moving one way . . . and the other moving the other way. . . . And you can continue that until you've learned to do this perfectly."

Hypnosis is a learning process. There's no way to fail unless the hypnotist allows someone to define something as failure. If you define the situation so that failure is not possible, it won't be a problem. If you continually give people the experiences and the internal responses that can serve as the foundation to build learnings so that they can have choices, you will do them the most service. That's true of any learning.

You can allow that hand to go down, now, Sally, and congratulate yourself on a job well done.

Now, I know that each and every one of you in here can learn to go into a trance, and you can learn to get anything you want from trance states. But if trance states are typically a time when you fail at things, that won't be the case. Traditional hypnotists have always done themselves a disservice in that they've asked people to do things that they weren't already doing. I don't do that, because I think it is unfair to them and it would make my work harder. I always allow people to do what they are already doing by giving them a lot of choices. I allow them to respond in ways that are most natural for them, and then slowly use that to teach them to do something else in an altered state. You can begin with simple things like movement, and extend that all the way to making pervasive personal changes.

OK. Find a partner, induce an altered state, and set up a nonverbal yes/no signal system. The signals can be responses other than just movements. You might have her blush for a "yes" signal and pale for "no." Or she could relax for "yes" and tighten up for "no." If you try a range of possibilities and don't notice a response, say "I would request of your unconscious mind that it provide me with an obviously recognizable signal that I can use validly as a "yes" response. Would you provide that for me?" And then you sit back and observe. If you see it, fine. If you don't, you say "Please make it more obvious for me. Because I desire to be instructed by your unconscious mind and to be fully respectful of your needs, I need a signal system that is unequivocal and unambiguous." Your partner will generally come up with some responses that you can see. Take about twenty minutes to do just that much with each other. Then come back, and I'll give you more instruction.

* * * * *

Many of you have told me that it was a lot easier than you thought it was going to be. Many of you, as I walked around the room, were succeeding brilliantly without noticing it. One of the problems with doing anything that deals with unconscious activity, is that very often things are really obvious. I noticed someone staring at his partner's fingers and asking questions, and the partner was nodding her head "yes" and "no." He was focusing on her fingers, and he kept squinting harder, as if somehow or other that was going to make the fingers lift higher. You have to understand that very often unconscious responses, since they are not meaningful, have a tendency to be very blatant. But if you look only in one place, you may miss them.

2) *Identifying the Pattern of Behavior to be Changed.* Now that you've established yes/no signals, I want you to put your partner in an altered state again and have her identify some pattern of behavior that she engages in but doesn't like. Now, consciously she may think "Ah, smoking" but unconsciously she may identify something else. It doesn't matter what she thinks she has identified, because I want you to *tell her unconscious to scan through all the things in her life that cause her problems and pick one that is of utmost and vital importance to her well-being.*

When her unconscious mind has selected one, *have it give you a 'yes" signal.* You will be guaranteed by these instructions that if she consciously picks something trivial like smoking, her unconscious can pick something more useful. Habit control is the most trite application of a learning tool. It's important, but it is not nearly as important to your well-being as other things. There are many patterns that occur in your life which prevent you from having intimacy with people, spontaneity when you are moving through the world, or the ability to learn from other people and enjoy them. There are patterns like that which are pervasive—throughout everything you do. A byproduct of that pattern may be that you can't control your smoking or that you wake up at four o'clock in the morning and have to eat pecans.

Once I worked with a man who did that. He woke up at four a.m., and if he couldn't get pecans, he couldn't get back to sleep. It didn't matter where he was; it didn't even matter if he changed time zones. It changed time zones too. It was a very sophisticated thing. This person, by the way, was a clinician.

The problem was that he would travel to places where you couldn't get pecans. he would take pecans along when he went to foreign countries, but sometimes he wasn't allowed to bring them in. And that meant he would wake up at four o'clock in the morning. Being clever, he learned to go to bed at nine o'clock at night and get up at four o'clock in the morning. However, his wife didn't like that much. It made life dull.

Now, I knew that the behavior he told me he wanted to change was only an example of a much more important and pervasive pattern. However, I know that working with an example is one way to work with the pattern, so I just went ahead with reframing.

So in the next piece, I want you to first put your partner back into trance, reestablish a yes/no signal with the person's unconscious, and then ask her to identify, both consciously and unconsciously, a significant pattern of behavior she wants to change. You can label this pattern X or Y or something arbitrary like that.

3) *Separating Positive Function from Behavior.*

a) Now you can go right through the standard reframing model. First you say something like *"I want you, Joyce's unconscious mind, to turn the finger signals over to the part of her that makes her do X. And when that part has full control over the finger signals, both fingers will lift up so that I know."* You always use the ideomotor signals as a feedback mechanism.

b) The next question is very important. You ask *"Are you willing to allow her conscious mind to know what it is of value that occurs when she does X?"* This is a yes/no question. If you get a "yes" say "go ahead and let her know, and when you've done that, then allow that "yes" finger to rise, that "yes" blush to occur—or whatever the signal is—so that I know you've informed her." You are always monitoring things. Use the yes/no signals not only as answers, but as monitors.

By the way, it doesn't matter if you get a "yes" or a "no" response to the question "Will you let her conscious mind know the useful purpose?" It doesn't matter because you already have what you wanted to accomplish: communication on the subject. If you go in and ask "Are you willing to communicate about this?" it might say "No." And if it says that, then you are stuck. Then you have to come up with some other scam.

If you ask a father in family therapy "Are you willing to change your behavior in relationship to your son?" he might say "No." But if you say to him "Do you love your son?" he'll say "Yes." If you ask "Do you *really* love him?" he'll say "Yes" again. If you then ask "Do you love him *enough* that you would be willing to make changes in your behavior so that he could have a happy life?" you won't find many fathers who will say "No" to that.

The reframing procedure I'm teaching you is very similar to that. You make it very easy for the person to respond in the way that you want her to by presupposing everything that's important.

So I presuppose communication. If his unconscious says "No, I'm not willing to tell the conscious mind" it's already communicated with me. I say "Then are you willing to figure out for yourself exactly what you consider to be the most useful aspect of this behavior?" You see, all

I want is the communication. It doesn't matter whether the response is "yes" or "no." Who cares if her conscious mind knows? Even if her conscious mind knew, it wouldn't help. Sometimes knowing gives an illusion of security, but informing the conscious mind is not profoundly useful in and of itself. What I want is communication.

Equally important, I want to make a distinction between the behavior that he doesn't like and its useful purpose. This separation is also presupposed by my question. I don't ask if there *is* a useful purpose, I ask if his unconscious part is willing to communicate what the useful purpose is. If the unconscious part is not willing to communicate its positive function, I say "Fine" and just go ahead. The important distinction between the behavior and some useful purpose has been made. This gives me lots of flexibility in making changes. She doesn't like the behavior, so I find some positive purpose which it serves. This opens the door to creating new choices.

4) *Creating New Alternatives.*

a) As soon as the conscious mind knows the useful purpose, or the part identifies for itself what it is, the next step is to generate alternative ways to accomplish the useful purpose. You can simply *ask that part if it would be willing to go into the creative resources where people dream and manufacture ideas*—you can describe anything which has to do with the manifestation of new choices, rearranging things, or creativity—*and get some new ways to accomplish this positive function* other than the one it is using now. Totally reassure the part that it does not have to accept any of these choices, and that it does not have to give up the old behavior. It can simply go in and get a whole plethora of other ways of accomplishing the same positive intention.

b) When you get a "yes" tell it to go ahead, and to give you a "yes" signal again when it has gotten ten new choices. If the conscious mind knows what the pattern of behavior is and the function it serves, then you can allow the conscious mind to know about the new choices. But there is no need for the conscious mind to know about the choices.

I want you to do just that much, even though it may not make much sense to you. You first ask her to pick a behavior that she most wants to have more choices about. Then you essentially say "Separate the behavior that you are using from what it is supposed to accomplish—what its purpose is." Then you say "OK, now that you have separated those and you know the difference, I want you to go into all of your creativity and come up with ten new ways to accomplish this purpose.

You don't have to use them. There's no commitment here to change anything. Just come up with ten ways that you would be able to accomplish the same purpose."

When the person signals you that she in fact has the ten choices, or that she only got eight, then stop. Bring her back to the waking state. OK, try that much.

* * * * *

In the piece that you just did, the basic thing that you are trying to accomplish is to get somebody to learn unconsciously to separate behaviors from what those behaviors accomplish. If a behavior is a way of accomplishing a particular outcome, once you've made that distinction you can easily get the person to begin to generate other possibilities—three, ten, fifty ways of accomplishing the purpose other than the problem behavior. You want her to end up with ways which are *as immediate, as effective, and as available* as the way she is using now. If you do this, typically it is not that difficult to begin to induce very pervasive change.

If you think only in terms of changing a behavior, like smoking, you don't have much room to move. You can either smoke or not smoke, and it's *very* difficult to get people to *not* do things. If you back up and work in terms of the positive function of smoking—for instance relaxation—this gives you a lot more flexibility. There are many ways a person can relax.

People sometimes try deliberate symptom substitution, but they usually get into difficulty. For example, take a person who unconsciously wants to feel satisfaction, and the way she achieves that satisfaction is by eating a piece of chocolate cake. Replacing eating with painting a picture is not going to work very well, because it is a lot easier to get a piece of chocolate cake than it is to paint a picture.

It's a lot easier to smoke a cigarette to relax than it is to go to Mexico. Smoking may not relax you as well, but it is much more immediately available. Unconsciously you don't really make the kind of qualitative distinctions that you might make philosophically. You might consciously decide that it isn't nearly as satisfying to eat chocolate cake, because then you have to regret it afterwards, and it detracts from the rest of your life. You might decide that if you took up a hobby or you found something else to do, that would satisfy you more. However, if what you try to substitute to give you that feeling of satisfaction is not as immediate and as available as the chocolate cake, you'll either go back to the same pattern of behavior or you will find something else that is easily available.

Now, sometimes when you find something else that is as immediate, you find something that is worth having. But often people quit overeating and begin to smoke. Or they quit smoking and spontaneously gain weight. Or they give up some habit that gets in their way, and they end up doing something even more destructive to them. So it's important that you have a way of evaluating the choices that you select.

5) *Evaluating New Alternatives.*

a) I'm going to ask you to pair up again with the same person and continue with the next step. Put her back into the altered state, reestablish whatever signal system you were using, and then *ask her to go through each of the choices, and to evaluate each one in terms of whether unconsciously she believes it is at least as immediate and effective and available as the way she is now using to accomplish the positive function.* Whatever the intention behind the behavior is, will these alternative choices work just as effectively to accomplish it? *Each time she identifies one that will, allow the "yes" signal to occur,* so that you can count the number of choices she unconsciously selects. You want to know how many choices she unconsciously believes meet that criterion. If you get ten, you are in good shape.

b) If you get less than three acceptable choices, have her go back to step four and generate more until she has at least three. If you only have one choice about how to do something well, that's not much of a choice. That's where most of you are now with whatever you are dealing with. If the *only* way you can get immediate gratification to satisfy yourself is by overeating or yelling at your children or whatever it happens to be, you don't really have a choice. If you develop only one more possibility, you still don't really have a choice. All you have is a dilemma.

If you have three possibilities, in addition to the one you don't like, then you are into the Land of Selection and that's really what choice is all about. So I want you to have her generate at least three possibilities that unconsciously she will accept as being as immediate, as available, and as effective, at accomplishing that particular purpose.

6) *Selecting One Alternative.*

a) Now, once you get a signal from her that tells you she has three, then have her unconsciously select which of those new ones to try out. You don't want her to select the old one, so the best way is to bypass that possibility by presupposition. You ask her to *select which of the new ways strikes her as being the most effective and the most available in satisfying whatever purpose she has, and to give you a "yes" signal when she has made the choice.*

b) Then *ask that unconscious part of her if it would be responsible for using the new choice instead of the old one for three weeks to evaluate its effectiveness.* If she discovers it will not work, then she can try out the other two, or go back to the old pattern. Going back to the old pattern of behavior doesn't constitute failure, but is simply a signal to generate more possibilities, perhaps at night while she dreams and sleeps, perhaps in a daydream.

One of the things I've discovered in my work with people is that when they go through usual therapeutic, hypnotic, or medical procedures in order to change, they often begin to change *less* spontaneously than a person normally would. When people fail to get the outcome they want, they begin to build the generalization that change is difficult and they can't do it, rather than simply taking no change as an indication that the choices they developed were not adequate, and that it's time to find even better ones.

When you get that part to take responsibility for trying a new choice, ask it to give some signal if it discovers the new choice is not good enough. Then have the part use that as a signal to generate a new choice that's even better. It could do this in the process of dreams, or fantasies, or just totally at the unconscious level. *An inadequate new choice becomes a signal to build new learnings rather than an indication of failure.* Does that make sense? It's a really important principle, even if you don't do hypnosis. When you change people, always define anything that might be considered a failure as an indication that it's time to expand. That's a much better overall learning than any specific change you could give someone in psychotherapy. If somebody comes in with numb feet, and you build in that learning and help her make the numbness go away, you teach her that if the numbness comes back, it's time to do something. It doesn't mean that therapy didn't work, or that she failed.

Sometimes a therapist tells me she used a procedure with somebody and that person changed for six months, but then the same old problem came back, and the therapist doesn't know what she did *wrong*. It strikes me that the therapist must have done something really *right* to get it to last that long. Even if the change only lasted a week, she must have done something which was very appropriate. What she missed was taking what she did that was appropriate, and using it as the basis for knowing what to do next. A symptom is like a barometer; it tells you when the choices you have are inadequate for your being able to cope and respond in a way that is appropriate for you.

Stress can also be considered a barometer for when you are not handling your behavior appropriately. Once I worked with people who were in what was called "The Stress Clinic." I thought this was an interesting name for the place—kind of a metaphor. They were attempting to help other people reduce the amount of stress in their lives by learning relaxation techniques. But what they failed to do in that clinic with their clients and with themselves was to define stress as something useful. They defined it as a disease that had to be cured, instead of as a useful way of monitoring when your way of dealing with problems isn't working well. Stress can be an indication that it is time to sit back and use the relaxation techniques *and* that now is an opportunity to begin to think of more creative ways to cope.

I would like you to get back with your partner and have her unconscious select the choices that will really work, and then select one of those new choices to test for a limited period of time. If the choice doesn't work, it tries another choice or begins some behavior that will generate more choices. If it does work, she keeps it, and that alleviates the need for the unwanted pattern of behavior.

7) *Future-Pacing.* If you get total verification at the unconscious level that your partner is willing to accept the new response and use it, then without even knowing what the problem is, tell her to *go into a fantasy of being in the situation where she would be most apt to respond with the pattern of behavior that she doesn't like, and surprise herself delightfully by trying out the new behavior.* Have her unconscious mind notify you either "yes" it's working or "no" it isn't. *If there is any way in which the new choice doesn't work or has harmful side effects, have her unconscious give you a "no" signal, and then have her go back to generate more choices.* I'd like you to spend about twenty minutes doing this, so that you can take what you did previously and bring it to a conclusion.

*   *   *   *   *

Reframing Outline

(1) *Set up yes/no signals with the unconscious.*

(2) *Identify a pattern of behavior to be changed.* Ask her unconscious to select some behavior, X, that *it* doesn't like. Ask it to pick something that it thinks is of utmost and vital importance to her well-being. Have it give you a "yes" signal when it has identified one.

(3) *Separate positive function from behavior.*

    (a) Ask her unconscious mind to turn the yes/no signals over to the part of her that makes her do X. Either ask that part to give you a "yes" signal, or a "yes" and a "no" signal simultaneously, when that has occurred.

    (b) Ask "Are you willing to allow her conscious mind to know what it is of value that occurs when she does X?" If "yes," say "Go ahead and let her know, and when you've done that, give me a 'yes' signal." If "no," proceed.

(4) *Create new alternatives.*

    (a) Ask that part if it would be willing to go into the person's creative resources and get new ways to accomplish this positive function other than X. (The part is under no obligation to accept or use these choices, only to find them.)

    (b) When you get a "yes," tell it to go ahead, and give you a "yes" signal when it has ten new choices.

(5) *Evaluate new alternatives.*

    (a) Ask that part to evaluate each new choice in terms of whether unconsciously it believes the choice is at least as immediate, effective and available as X. Each time the part identifies one that it believes *is*, have it give you a "yes" signal.

    (b) If you get less than three, recycle to step (4) and get more choices.

(6) *Select one alternative.*

    (a) Ask the part to select the new way it considers the most satisfying and available in achieving the positive function, and to give you a "yes" signal when it has selected.

    (b) Ask the unconscious part if it would be responsible for using this new choice for three weeks to evaluate its effectiveness.

(7) *Future-Pace.* Ask her unconscious go into a fantasy of trying out the new behaviors in the appropriate context. Have her unconscious notify you either "yes" it's working or "no" it isn't. If there is any way in which the new choice doesn't work or has harmful side effects, recycle to step (4) and create new choices.

160

Those of you who already know the reframing procedure in *Frogs into Princes* will notice that the procedure we're offering you today has slightly different steps and a slightly different order. The basic technique is the same, and you will accomplish the same things when you use it.

Discussion

The generalization that underlies the reframing technique is that when things aren't the way you want them to be, you can change them. Find out the purpose that you are trying to achieve, the outcome you are working towards, and then generate more choices. That is a worthwhile learning no matter what you're doing, and every inch you get closer to it will be in your best interest.

When therapists work with clients and the therapist notices that a procedure is not working, it simply is an indication for her to vary her behavior. As I walked around the room this afternoon, I noticed that some of you forgot to control the tempo of your voice, and you kept bringing people out of trance instead of putting them in. One man in the back of the room was doing beautifully until his voice began to rise. As his voice went up slowly in pitch, his partner kept coming out of trance and trying to force herself back in—the mark of an overly cooperative client. It has been my experience that all clients are really very cooperative if they are provided with the right stimulus.

Once I had a client who came in and sat down and said "Nothing ever works with me. There's nothing you can do that will ever work and I know this already." And I said "All right, I'm going to do something that will make you stay in that chair." I opened my desk drawer and took out a piece of paper. I wrote on it, and folded up the piece of paper. Then I looked at him and said "Now, you feel so heavy you feel compelled to stay in that chair, and everything you try to do will be in vain, because every motion you make will keep you in that chair." The guy immediately stood straight up. I opened the piece of paper and showed it to him. The paper said "You are standing now."

There was nothing profoundly important about what I did. However, it convinced him that I could make him do things. In his case, that was very useful. That's very rare. Most people don't need to be convinced of that. If you create a context in which whatever response you want from a client is appropriate, it will occur naturally.

A funny thing happened years ago. I had a student who failed at everything. He was a compulsive failer. I soon discovered that if I defined a particular success as the most likely failure, he could go in and succeed with people, and then come out and say "Well, it didn't work." His client would change, and the student would never notice it! I would tell him that the most likely way to fail with this person was to have X happen. I made sure X was a change that would be very useful to the client. He would work with the client and "fail" every time with precision. He succeeded consistently at failing in exactly the way that I specified.

Any rigidity in behavior allows you to do things like that. The ones I'm describing are outlandish rigidities. But if you think about your clients, most of their rigidities are fairly outlandish, too. It is only a question of establishing a context in which their natural responses are the ones that will lead them where they want to go.

There's an old gestalt technique to use when the client says "There's no way in the world that I can think of anything that would be helpful." You look at her and say "You're right. You could never do it. You are an absolute failure; you could never think of anything that would be helpful, not even the smallest thing." Typically she will then respond "Well, there is this one little thing." That's part of the natural polarity response of many people.

Some people, however, will respond in the opposite way. I once saw a gestalt therapist work with a client who said "I don't know what to do." The gestalt therapist said "Well, guess." The person said "I don't know. I'm a lousy guesser." And the therapist said "You can never guess anything that's appropriate." The client's face began to droop and she looked pathetic. If you use that gestalt technique with someone who responds congruently, you will only convince her that she is a failure. If you notice her response, you can utilize it to lead her where she wants to go. So you need to notice what kind of response you are getting, and vary your behavior in order to get the response you want.

When you do reframing using nonverbal yes/no signals, you don't need to worry what response you get, because it doesn't matter whether you get a "yes" or a "no" response. Whatever response you get on any step of reframing simply tells you what to do next. If you tell her to get new choices, and she gets them but the choices are not good enough, that only means she needs to go back and get more.

If she keeps doing it and she can't get ones that will work, then have her redefine the context. If you had her go to her creative part that manifests dreams and dream up new ways, and those ways aren't good enough, then have her go to "the brain center that creates all devious behavior." You can make up anything. Act as if it is real, and it will be.

There are thousands of people in this country today who have a "parent," a "child," and an "adult" in their behavior. They weren't always that way, but they are now. The only clients I ever saw with those behaviors were ones who had been in Transactional Analysis. That is not a criticism of TA. It's a compliment about the flexibility of humanity to create anything, as long as someone else acts as if it's real.

The TA therapists who have come to me for private help always had difficulty with their parts. They couldn't do adult things and have childlike fun doing them, because those are separated in their psychotheology. That's a byproduct of their belief system and their psychotherapy.

It seems to me that rather than having a gestalt topdog and underdog that fight, a psychoanalytic unconscious that tortures you wantonly, or a TA parent and child that don't mix very well, or any other aspect of your personality that leads to limitations, you should make up a psychotherapy for each client in which all the parts flexibly generate choices for coping. I want you to have choices. The parts that I make up for you are creative parts that can do anything. I make up an unconscious that is concerned and caring and willing to work on your behalf, because I don't want parts of you that have limitations. You are too good at doing that already.

If any of you want to know more about how to do reframing in a different way, read *Frogs into Princes*. In the last chapter of that book we do reframing with someone as a demonstration and answer a lot of questions. We also have a book *Reframing: The Transformation of Meaning* that presents several models of reframing in great detail.

You don't need to put someone into a formal trance in order to do reframing. However, it can be fun as a variation. The basic steps of reframing can also be done in the context of a normal conversation. The only difference is that you need to be more observant to notice the responses you are getting. In a normal conversation you can get the same unconscious responses, but they usually go by more quickly and that makes them harder to notice.

Let me tell you a funny little story that's an example of how you can reframe someone in a normal conversation. Last year I was visiting a friend in Southern California. I was in a liquor store buying a couple of bottles of champagne for a party we were going to have at his house.

In the liquor store I noticed a little old alcoholic woman. It's quite easy for me to pick out an alcoholic by muscle tonus, skin tone, posture, and breathing, even when she's not loaded. I'm sure all of you who have spent time noticing the difference between alcoholics and non-alcoholics also find it easy to make that distinction. She was short, and although she looked ancient, my guess is she was actually about 65. I nodded to her and smiled and went about my business. I knew the woman behind the cash register, and we made a couple of joking remarks to each other and laughed. This little old lady also laughed and made some comment which was actually pretty funny, and I laughed too.

The old lady turned to me as I was leaving and said "You don't happen to be going up the hill by the Post Office, do you?" I said "I'd be delighted to give you a lift home. I'll wait outside in my car."

She came out, got in the car, and we started driving. As she sat on the seat next to me, she was wringing her hands and looking over at me furtively. It was obvious to me that somehow I'd tapped something inside of her. Finally she said "Why do you drink?"

I did my best to keep from laughing, because she was obviously wondering why *she* drank but making a referential index shift. I said "Well, personally, *I* drink for taste. I drink very fine wines, and I drink champagnes. I don't particularly like the taste of whiskey, so I don't drink whiskey, and I drink beer when I'm at the beach and it's hot." And then I said "But that's not *really* the question you want to ask me. The question you want to ask me is 'Why do *you* drink?' " That was such a good match for her experience that she burst into tears.

Crying wasn't useful for me, and it wasn't useful for her, either. I looked outside and saw a dog walking along. I pointed at it and exclaimed "LOOK! IS THAT YOUR DOG?" just as a way to get her to stop crying. Because of the urgency in my voice, she responded congruently to my question. She looked out, then looked back at me confused, and said "I don't even have a dog." But she had stopped crying entirely, which was the point of the maneuver.

Then I told her a story. "Well, you know, that dog reminds me of this little dog that I knew—a very small dog—that lived in San Francisco. This dog believed that nobody in the world understood it. That's what the dog told me, and the dog was *almost* right. Because it was true that *almost* nobody in the world really understood her. And the dog didn't realize that there is a big difference between *no one* understanding it and *almost* no one understanding her." She burst into tears again.

We continued driving, and soon she said "You're right, the question is 'Why do I drink?' "

"And even that is the wrong question" I said. "Your whole life you've been asked that question, and you've been asking yourself the question 'Why do I drink?' Everybody's been saying 'Why do you drink?' but you've been made a fool of. Not only did you ask me the wrong question, but you've been asking yourself the wrong question for the last 30 years. Everybody around you has been asking you the wrong question, and they've made a fool out of you by focusing your attention on that question, because it's not the right question."

I pulled into her driveway. She looked over at me, and first she said "Who are you *really*?" I just smiled. Then she said "Well, are you going to tell me what the right question is?"

"Well, I'll tell you under one condition. The condition is this: after I finish telling you, I'll reach over and touch you on the shoulder. When you feel my touch on your shoulder, you'll get up, walk out, go into your house, and begin to find answers to the question I give you. As soon as you know what the answer is, you'll call me." And I gave her my friend's phone number.

She said "OK. I agree." So I said "Well, the question is not 'Why do you drink?' the question is (slowly) *'What would you do if you didn't drink?'* "

Immediately her whole demeanor changed. Different expressions began tumbling past one another on her face. She went through breathing, skin-color, and posture changes. That was precisely what I'd wanted. She'd never considered what else she'd do if she didn't drink. She went into a fairly deep trance, and I let her sit there for two or three minutes, and then I reached over and touched her on the shoulder. She roused a little bit, got out of the car, and went into her house.

Five minutes after I got to my friend's house the telephone rang, and sure enough it was this woman. She said "Is that really you? . . . I just wanted to tell you that you saved a life this afternoon. I was going home to commit suicide. But I decided I just didn't know how to answer that question, and I want to tell you that. I don't know what it meant to you, but that is the single most beautiful question in the world."

I said "I don't care whether you like the question or whether you believe it's the most beautiful question in the world. That's not my interest. My interest is in the *answer* to that question. And you call me tomorrow with several answers to that question."

At one point in the conversation she used a perfect idiom. She said

"Well, I just felt like I was going down the drain." And I said to her "*People* don't go down the drain. *Other* things *do!*" And sure enough, when she called me the next day, she'd dumped all the booze in the house down the drain. I was there for two weeks, and I know she didn't drink again during that period of time.

I consider that a really interesting example of conversational reframing. There wasn't a wasted move in the conversation on either my part or her part. And what made it work, of course, was my ability to notice the sensory-grounded responses I was eliciting, and her ability to do that as well. She was quite sensitive to minimal cues and so forth. I suppose a person who is about to commit suicide would be, since this is their last time around.

In this example I skipped most of the steps I asked you to go through in reframing. However, the essence of what I did was the same kind of symptom subsititution—"What would you do if you didn't drink?"

One of the big advantages of hypnosis is that people's responses are amplified and slowed down. There's nothing you can do with a person *in* trance that you can't do with a person *out* of trance, as far as I know. I'm able to induce every deep trance phenomenon in the waking state. However, hypnosis slows the person down enough so that you can keep track of what's happening, and stabilize states long enough to be able to do something systematically. To do it in the waking state requires sensitivity, speed, and flexibility. With hypnosis, you stabilize a person in a particular altered state, so that she will stay there long enough for you to be able to do something.

Woman: In general, when do you use hypnosis—with what kinds of problems?

When I feel like it. Seriously, that is the only distinction I can figure out that makes hypnosis more relevant than something else. I started doing hypnosis for only one reason: I got sick of listening to my clients talk. I was so tired of it that I was becoming ineffective as a therapist, because I was not paying attention and responding to them in a way that was useful. I was responding to them out of boredom.

So I began just zapping them into a trance and finding out how little information I could work from and still give them what they wanted. Then the whole process of therapy became interesting again. Now I use it intermixed with everything else as a way of coloring what I do, mostly to keep me interested. I know I could get the personal changes more quickly and methodically, but for me, to sit down and do formal reframing is a boring task. Even though it's fast, it's laborious, because

I have done it too many times. If I do something too many times, I don't want to do it anymore.

Hypnosis is a way of doing things in a bizarre and unusual way. Now I mainly create alternative realities with hypnosis. I create realities other than the ones that a person lives in—for instance, one in which she is a unicorn, because unicorns can do what she wants to be able to do but thinks she can't. I regress people to a younger age than when they first had to wear glasses and have them keep child-like eyes and grow up, as a way of working with myopia. It depends upon what people want. I just go for it in whatever way I think would be interesting.

Man: I'm becoming more and more interested in giving up my glasses and having normal vision. Could I do that using hypnosis?

Do you have any astigmatism?

Man: Yes. My left eye's really bad.

Well, that makes a difference. So far I haven't been able to do much with astigmatism. That doesn't mean it can't be done; I just haven't figured out a way to do it yet.

Myopia isn't too hard to deal with, because nearsighted people are just squeezing their eyeballs too hard. When they try to see something, they squint and strain, and that results in improper focus and blurred vision. All they have to do is learn the meaning of the word "focus." That's not really very difficult. William H. Bates developed a way of doing that years ago, and wrote *Better Eyesight Without Glasses*. It's just that people don't use it.

Do you know that optics is the only field that has ever claimed to be closed? If you read the literature from the 'forties and 'fifties, opticians thought there was nothing more to discover. Now it's opened again. Recently there have been some whackos who blew the field apart completely with light fibers and lasers and holograms. However, earlier introductory texts actually stated that the field of optics was a completely closed science! They claimed proudly that they knew everything that could be known, and that theirs was the only closed science.

The behavior of most modern eye doctors is still based on the idea that optics is a closed field. Most eye doctors have a very strong and very limited belief system about what is possible. Corrective lenses were originally designed to correct your eyeballs. Originally they gave you one set of glasses to wear for about three days, and then a weaker set for another three days, and so on, until your eyes got better. Then you gave all of the glasses back to the doctor. They don't do that anymore. Now they sell you one, and you keep it until your eyes go one way or another, and then they sell you another pair.

Man: So how about myopia? You say your cure for myopia is teaching people how to focus. How do you do that?

The way I go about that is to regress them to a time before they first wore glasses. Then I test their eyes, to make sure that they did not have myopia at that age. When I bring them back to their present age, I leave them with "child eyes" and grow up everything else from the eyeball out. I don't know what that means, but I've done it with a lot of people and it has worked.

I discovered this method when I did age-regression with someone who wore glasses. We used to do weird hypnosis groups where we just went around and zoned everybody out. I had age-regressed a man who was wearing glasses, and as he got younger, he couldn't see anymore. He was regressed to five years old, and he said "Hi there. I can't see anything. Why do I have to have this thing on my face?" and he reached up and took his glasses off.

I became curious, so I gave him a fairly standard eye test with his glasses off. I didn't have an eye chart, but there were letters on a poster on the wall, and I asked him to tell me what the letters were. He didn't know the names of the letters, so I had him draw them for me. He drew whatever he saw with squiggly lines. His writing was just like a child's. Then I brought him back up to be an adult and gave him the same test. Without his glasses he could no longer tell what the letters were. I regressed him to five years old, and he could see again. That was spontaneous. I gave no suggestions for that to occur. When I brought him out the last time, I gave him these instructions: "Now your eyes are going to stay five years old, and the rest of you is going to grow up." That's all it took for him to be able to see.

Woman: Did you do that all at one time?

Yes, during one evening. The results lasted for about two months, and then slowly his eyes started to get bad again. That's when I started using reframing to find out what his purpose was for having blurry eyes. It turned out that over the years he had learned to do lots of things by having blurry eyes. Ordinarily he had what we call "see-feel circuits." When he looked at something, he instantly had feelings about it. Having blurry vision stopped the see-feel circuit. During a time of stress, if he couldn't see something unpleasant, he wouldn't have the unpleasant feelings. I had to give him other ways of interrupting see-feel circuits, to take care of the secondary gain that came from having blurred vision.

Man: That's difficult with contacts. I wear contacts and I can't just take contacts off in times of stress like I could glasses. So I've learned how to defocus with my contacts still on.

You have an interesting presupposition, which is that you have to blur things somehow. You're assuming that in times of stress you don't want to be able to see what's going on until you can cope. It seems to me that times of stress are times when it's particularly useful to be able to see clearly. As soon as you have effective ways of coping, you won't need to blur your vision.

As I said before, years ago Bates came up with eye exercises to improve vision. For the most part his program was very successful, although it took time and was a lot of work. The main drawback was that the Bates program didn't deal with secondary gain. So if you were diligent and exercised, you could wipe out the only way you had to do something useful. That part of you would have to come up with a new way. It's a lot easier to change if you don't have to overcome your own internal parts.

Woman: Could you use reframing for weight problems?

That's definitely a heavy subject. Ambiguity is very important in hypnosis, you know. Obesity is no different than most anything else. You can do it with reframing.

Woman: Well, I haven't had much success. I've done reframing and clients have lost weight, but then they haven't been able to maintain their new weight.

Well, think about it. There is something which makes it more advantageous for them to be fat than to be thin. One possibility is that none of their responses will work as a thin person. The choices that they have available as a human being work as a fat person, but not as a thin person. If you grew up your whole life being heavy, you were never the fastest runner. You were never the first one chosen to be on your track team. You weren't the first one chosen to be a square dancer. There are lots of experiences that you didn't have, which constitute the basis for knowing how to respond as a thin person.

If this is the case for your clients, you could create an alternative childhood for them   one that contains experiences which serve as a basis for responding in new ways as an adult. I do that with most people in whom I make radical changes.

In what I just said, I'm making assumptions about what the secondary gain is. I would use reframing to find out which part gets her to get fat again. I would find out what it does for her, and then I would know what experiences to provide.

One very nice thing about hypnosis is it gives you the ability to create alternative history. Erickson's story about the "February Man" is a good example. Erickson had a woman come in who didn't know how to bring up children and be kind to them and be a good parent, because she hadn't had one. She had been raised by governesses. Erickson went back into her personal history and appeared every so often as the "February Man" and gave her the experiences she was missing. Those experiences then provided her with the basis upon which to relate to her own children.

Hypnosis is just a tool. You can do just about anything with it. It's a tool to create any context or any response. But you have to know what response you want in order to be systematically effective.

Woman: I have a question about dealing with smoking. Could you regress somebody to a time just before they smoked and then reframe her to go the other way? She decided to smoke at some point, so could you reframe her to make some other choice?

Yes, and then she'll end up having total amnesia for ever having been a smoker. That's a slick move; however, you have to be very careful when you do things like that. I've done that with people. I've hypnotized them and removed their knowledge of ever having been smokers. I have regressed them to before they smoked and then given them an entirely different set of experiences. The problem is that other people in their lives began to think they were nuts.

If you do this with someone who has just moved to a new city, it doesn't matter. I did this with a client who was married, and when she got home, her husband offered her a cigarette. She said "I don't want one of those." "All right" he said, "You quit, huh?" She looked at him and said "I never smoked." He said "Don't give me that. You've smoked for twenty years." "I *never* smoked in my life!"

Woman: You could give the person amnesia for those conversations, too.

You could, but if you do it that way, you have to keep building on the change. You have to have her go into an amnesic state every time somebody says "Oh, you used to smoke." She will eventually begin to become confused and disoriented, because so much of her experience is in the amnesic state. She has yellow stains on her teeth, and she doesn't know where those stains came from. She asks her dentist, and the dentist says "Smoking stains." She says "But I've never smoked." The dentist says "You're kidding!" Your client says congruently "No, I've never smoked." The dentist then writes a journal article about this new phenomenon.

You have to be somewhat graceful about how you do these things. I did it one time to try it. It worked very well, but the ripples that resulted from that change were a bit disastrous.

Man: Couldn't you include in the instructions that other people will assume that she has been a smoker? You would instruct her not to be too disturbed by that, just to ignore it.

Yeah, I did that with the woman I told you about, but it became disturbing for her anyway. I said "People will act bizarre and unusual about you, but you'll take it with a grain of salt and figure that they are just confused." But she began to become upset about how *many* of them were doing it. She thought the whole world was going crazy.

Woman: So what do you do now instead?

The simplest way is to just use reframing. You don't even need to put people in a trance; you can just use standard reframing. It works perfectly. Then you put them in a trance to remove the physical addition.

Woman: How do you remove the physical addiction in a trance?

Direct suggestion.

Woman: Do you say "You are no longer addicted?"

No. That isn't direct suggestion. That's dumb. I'm serious. If you say "You will no longer have the physical addiction" you haven't said *how*. Some of your clients will be flexible enough to find a way, but most won't. You need to build up a context in which they can respond that way easily. If you do it too directly, you won't get the response very often. If you say "You will no longer want cigarettes" you're less apt to get it than if you say "Cigarettes taste unpleasant." You're even more apt to get it if you have the *thought* of smoking a cigarette be unpleasant. Better than that, you have them be totally proud every time they refuse a cigarette, even though they really do want one. You can create contexts in which the response is a natural one.

Usually I remove the addiction in this way: I go in and verify— either through finger signals or verbalization or head nods—that the unconscious knows what feeling accompanies the physical addiction. Then I ask the unconscious to spontaneously connect that feeling with another set of sensations, like pleasure or delight or curiosity, each time the feeling occurs. That way they'll end up doing something other than smoking.

You can use reframing with smoking and other drug addictions, obesity, and most other problems people want you to cure with hypnosis. You can reframe them first to solve the problem, and then hypnotize them in order to satisfy their request for hypnosis. You can make reframing a prerequisite to doing hypnosis. Rather than challenge what they came in for, hypnosis, tell them that you're a very special hypnotist. Explain that you're very thorough and don't want to use hypnosis to do anything detrimental, so you need to make lots of careful checks first. Then you go through the standard reframing. "Before I can put you into a trance, there are certain things I have to know. Go inside and ask if the part that is responsible for this pattern of behavior. . . . " If you act as if reframing is just the preamble, they'll hurry through the reframing so that they can get to the "real stuff."

After they are completely changed, you say "Now we can begin the trance. Close your eyes. . . . " Then you go through any hypnotic routine you want to. Afterwards they'll tell everyone "Hypnosis worked!"

Reframing is the simplest way you can get change in many symptoms. However, I'm not always for doing things simply; I'm for doing them artfully. Once you've done five smokers with straight reframing and you know you can get results that way, then begin to do it more creatively. Do yourself and your client a favor by doing it in a different and bizarre way. Do reframing in trance and take her to the Goddess of Cigarettes. Have her burn a package of Marlboros at her altar or something. Sometimes all you have to do for smoking is put the person in a trance and say "What I want your unconscious to do is find the most creative way for you to stop smoking without even knowing that you've done it." And sometimes you have to do a lot *more*!

People keep wanting to learn to do hypnosis so they can stop people from smoking and do weight control. When people ask "What do you do with smokers?" sometimes I say "Hand them a book of matches." Hypnosis is much too elegant a set of tools to think about as something that you use just for weight control or for smoking. That's like buying a Ferrari to go to the grocery store. There is something repulsive to me about using a really elegant set of tools in a trite way. Smoking and weight control are important, but the way you use hypnosis to deal with a smoker is idiosyncratic to the person. What's much more important to me is to learn hypnosis as a set of skills, so you can use it idiosyncratically for anything.

Man: I did reframing in trance with a man on smoking, and got a lot of resistance. First he burst out of trance, and then he became a little kid. He started wiggling his feet and—

In NLP we have a principle that says "There is no resistance; there are only incompetent therapists." I mean that literally. I do not believe that there is resistance; there are only unskilled therapists. That shouldn't be taken critically. That should be taken as follows: every time you begin to encounter "resistance," you are presented with an unprecedented opportunity to delight yourself. If you say "Aha! I have done something which is incompetent, so now I am going to surprise and delight myself by doing something else" you will continually improve. If you think "He's not ready yet" *he* may change, but *you* will be stuck.

There's no resistance if you utilize every response. If somebody spontaneously goes into any state, utilize it. If he becomes a little kid, tell him to enjoy himself. If he comes out of trance, you can say "And what can I do for you now?" To be an effective communicator, all you have to do is respond appropriately to whatever spontaneously happens. If a person comes out of trance and you ask yourself "What did I do wrong?" that isn't an appropriate response. No formula works perfectly every time. People aren't willing to do anything rigidly. All kinds of strange things happen.

Once I put a man into trance, planning to do standard reframing. I said "Lift your right index finger for "yes" and your left index finger for "no"—and the guy went *"Pur-ple!"* At that moment, if you don't have patterns for utilization, you are stuck. I said "That's right, *pur-ple!*" I just fed it back to him in the same tonality and tempo. Then he said *"Au-ra!"* So I said *"Pur-ple! Au-ra!"* I continued "Now we'll take this meaningful message . . . " and I gave him some bizarre set of instructions for utilization. I had no idea what he was doing.

When he came out of trance, he reported to me that as I told him to lift up his "no" finger, he became engulfed in a big purple aura. The more he was in the aura, the more he knew that he was making some change. The aura was somehow or other saturating him and changing him. Who knows what that was about. Some purple cloud came down and changed him before I could get around to it.

If I had interrupted the purple cloud, I would have really gotten stuck. Instead I just went along with it, and it did my work for me.

I've had people who go way down into trance while I am doing unconscious work, and they are doing fine. Suddenly there's a pause, and they come all the way out of trance. They look at me, and I just sit there and look back at them blankly and wait. They look around and then all of a sudden they go back in. I don't even say anything; I just wait. When people come out spontaneously, I'm fairly patient and let them give me something to respond to. A lot of people are floaters. They go in and out of trance. So when they come out, I just wait, and then they will go back in, and I can continue. Then later they may float back up again. If you ask people to maintain an altered state, you are asking them to do something artificial. You have to be fluid in responding to their varying states.

Man: Could you use reframing for psychosomatic symptoms like headaches?

Reframing is great with psychosomatic problems. You have the option of using the symptom itself for a yes/no signal. If the symptom is a migraine, for instance, you can have it hurt more for "yes" and less for "no."

Man: A lot of physicians' wives come to see me with psychosomatic symptoms. The symptoms don't do anything for the wives—the physicians just sneer at them and don't give them any attention or do things for them. It's hard to find a secondary gain.

You've already made an assumption about what the secondary gain is: that is has to do with getting attention. In the cases like that that I've done reframing with, the secondary gain has *never* been to get attention from the husband. It's usually a way of making a fool out of the husband. It's a way to keep the husband from being too pompous about being a doctor, by presenting him with an illness he can't treat.

They must give doctors courses in being pompous at medical schools. I meet lots of different kinds of therapists. I meet programmers from computer firms, and they are really different from each other. But most doctors have a really standard set of pompous analogues. Not all of them are pompous, of course; there are always exceptions to everything. But as a class, I don't know what they do to those poor people.

Man: If you spend two years interning, following other doctors around, it will make you pompous. It's modeling and mirroring.

Susan: I've got a cold. Can you use hypnosis to take away a cold?

A man came to me with a cold that he'd had for six months, and I made it go away. But his unconscious specified exactly how long it would take to go away. He'd had it for six months, and his unconscious wanted two days to make it go away.

174

Susan: I've only had mine for three days.

Well, I'm not going to take the time to do it now, if that's what you are asking. But I'll certainly give somebody else a set of procedures to do it with you. Is that acceptable?

Susan: Yes.

Who wants an interesting task?

Woman: I'll do it.

OK. Do the following sequence. Put her in a deep trance and send her conscious mind away. There are several ways you can do that. You can send her conscious mind back to some pleasant memory. You can have it walk down a long tunnel and come out at the end in a place with gardens and fountains where she can swim, and then close the door so she doesn't eavesdrop unhelpfully. Set up a feedback mechanism so that you know when her conscious mind is there, and when it's not. You could have one of her fingers be up when her unconscious mind is there alone, and have it go down when her conscious mind returns. Use something like that so that you have feedback.

Then I want you to ask her unconscious if it would be willing to remove the cold, *carte blanche.* Get a "yes" or a "no." If you get a "yes" ask it if it will be willing to do so right now. If there is any hesitation whatsoever, whether you are using verbal or nonverbal signals, then go into the reframing format and find out if the cold serves any function whatsoever. If it does, come up with new ways of accomplishing that function. Get the unconscious to specify exactly how long it will take to make the cold go away. You do this with yes/no questions too. You ask questions like "Would you be willing to take it away in one hour?"

In addition to that, as you bring her out of trance, overlap her into situations that will take care of all the physiological parameters of the cold. Overlap her into an environment where her cold symptoms would disappear spontaneously. If she has body aches, overlap into a hot tub or a whirlpool. If she has a drippy nose, take her into the desert where everything gets dried out. Find out what symptoms she has before putting her into a trance, so that you'll know where to overlap her to when you bring her out.

Woman: Where would you overlap her to in order to take care of a sore throat?

That's a good question. Where does a sore throat go away? What do you do to get rid of a sore throat?

Woman: You gargle with salt water.

What are the odds of having a sore throat when you get out of the ocean after swimming in warm, tropical, salt water? About zero. If you actually went swimming there with a really bad sore throat, you might make your cold worse eventually. But if you go swimming in the ocean, especially if you go where there are some good-sized waves, chances are that all the salt water around will dry out all your membranes.

If you ever get a runny nose, and you can't get to the nose sprayer, or you don't want to get addicted to nose sprays, you can do something very simple instead. Nowadays there are some very addictive nose sprays on the market. They are more addictive than cigarettes. You can watch people in drugstores furtively going up to the counter and buying boxes of nose spray. It's really bizarre. All you need to do for a simple, non-addictive alternative to nose spray is to buy one of the nose-spray bottles and pour out all the nose spray. Then you make a salt water solution, put the cap back on, and spray the salt solution in your nose. That will work as well as anything else to dry out your nose.

Woman: Could you use the procedure you just outlined for a stomachache or any ordinary psychosomatic problem?

Yes. Put the person in a trance and do reframing first, to make sure that you give her alternatives if the problem is functional. Then do overlap for each symptom that the person has, as you bring them out of trance.

Susan: My cold is better—not entirely better—but while you were talking, it already started going away.

One time I got somebody's poison oak to go away on the spot as a demonstration. I put him in a deep trance and explained to him that poison oak is a mistake. "It's a mistake" I said. "Allow me to tell you the story of antigens and antibodies. Poison oak rash is a response to a plant to protect you from the danger of it, when the plant isn't dangerous. And then you get all this stuff over your skin, but it is your body responding. And it's just a mistake; and when you make mistakes, the best policy is always to go back and *clear them up*." Within two hours that person didn't have a trace of poison oak, except for little red marks on his skin in the places where there had been open pus wounds.

It is amazing what you can get away with if you are congruent. People frequently send us their "impossibles" to work with. We got one client who had neurological damage that impaired his ability to walk. We referred this man to one of our students, David Gordon, since we don't have a private practice anymore. The man brought lots of X-rays and records to his first session that "proved" that he was unable to walk normally. He hobbled in with a walker, sat down, and showed David all of his records. David did a few things, and sent him out.

The next time this client came in, David remembered something he had seen me do effectively with somebody, and tried it out. He told that man the story of the plasticity of the human brain. You should read neurology journals; they have the best metaphors of all. All of science is a metaphor. Plasticity means that one part of the brain is able to take over the function of another part. They've documented that this actually occurs. If a child learns a language, and then at the age of four gets his language hemisphere cut off, he will learn language again in the other hemisphere, even though that hemisphere wasn't supposed to be the one to learn language. If the part of your brain that moves your index finger gets destroyed, you can learn to move your index finger with another part of your brain. That's what plasticity is all about.

David put this man in a trance and explained how you could grow new pathways, and also use different pathways to recreate a function that has been blocked by injury. He told about studies which indicate that about 90% of the brain is not used. These are total lies, as far as I can tell, but he told them well. And since science documents that these lies are actually true, David referred to various journal articles while this guy was sitting there in a trance.

Besides direct explanations of central nervous system plasticity, he told more general metaphors about finding new streets to drive on when you're driving across a city and you come across an area where the streets are all torn up for construction. Then he gave this man's unconscious rather direct instructions to rewire: "Discover exactly where the damage has occurred, and check adjacent nerve pathways which are either uncommitted to other functions, or which may be recommitted safely without interfering with other functions, until you have restored the functions of the damaged area."

Whether that man actually grew new pathways or not, I don't know. But he got up and walked out normally after the session. Given the scientific argument David had presented, the logical response of that human being was to make whatever changes were necessary to be able to walk normally. Whatever that scientific metaphor was a metaphor for, the appropriate response was to get up and walk out. That's the way I think about designing everything that I do. We've also been successful in using this method with other clients who have standard medical evidence of neurological insult and trauma.

Man: Is that what faith healing is all about?

I don't know. Is that what neurology is all about? You are asking me a question about verification of reality. It's probably *all* wrong. I don't know. Faith healers present a context in which the logical response is to change, and they do a much better job of it than most therapists do! They do a much better job than most of our students, because they have convinced themselves, so they are more congruent.

I did a faith healing one time. I walked into a religious meeting and looked holy. All the people stared at me; finally I communicated to them that I had this thing with God. I told them I'd had a moving experience where God had made me a healer with these hands. I convinced the people in this group, and healed some of them. I don't know how they actually healed themselves. All I did was provide a context in which they could respond appropriately, and since I didn't point at them afterwards and laugh at them, they stayed healed and their lives were changed.

These stories are designed to show you that *there is some mechanism within people that is capable of doing these things, but it needs to be convinced, it needs to be motivated, it needs to be communicated with, and provided with a context in which to respond.*

Otherwise it won't respond, because *it* doesn't care. Whatever that part is, it doesn't limp, it doesn't itch with poison oak. If it did, it would go ahead and take care of the limping or the itching. But if you provide a context in which it can respond appropriately, it will.

This is what we accomplish with all our NLP tools. Reframing is just a context for people to respond to by changing themselves. That's all anything is, as far as I know.

VI

Specific Utilization Techniques

New Behavior Generator

Today we want to teach you other specific ways to utilize trance states. First we want to give you a very useful procedure that you can use for a wide variety of behaviors: the new behavior generator. You can use this for any situation in which the person makes some response they're dissatisfied with. That description could fit the major complaint of most of your clients. I'm going to assume that you've already put the person in a trance and established some kind of ideomotor yes/no signal system, either overtly or covertly.

The first thing you do is have him select some behavior that he is dissatisfied with. Then you have him watch and listen to himself behave in that situation. You want him to *see himself* doing it *out in front of himself* as if he were watching a movie. This is an instruction for dissociation; this makes it possible for him to watch and listen with comfort to something that could be unpleasant if he were actually in the situation. You say "Give me that 'yes' signal as soon as you have completed watching and listening, with comfort and security, to this piece of behavior that you want to change."

When you get the "yes" response, you ask "Do you know what new behavior or response you would prefer to make in this situation?" It's important to phrase everything in terms of yes/no questions so that you always have clear feedback from the person.

If the answer to that question is "yes" the person does know what response he would prefer to make, you say "Good. Now watch and

178

179

listen to yourself as you make that new response in the situation that used to be a problem for you. Give me a 'yes' response when you're done."

Then you ask "Having observed yourself making a new response to that situation, was that completely satisfactory to you?" If you get a "no" response, you have him go back and select a more appropriate behavior.

If you get a "yes" response, you go ahead to install the new behavior by asking him to re-associate with the dissociated experience. "This time I want you to run the same movie, but from the point of view of being yourself doing the behavior. Put yourself *inside* the movie and experience what it is like to actually carry out those behaviors in the situation."

When he has done that, ask "Was that still satisfactory?" and be sure that you get a congruent "yes" response. Sometimes a behavior looks great from the outside, but doesn't feel good once you get inside. If you get a "no" to this question, you need to back up and make modifications in the behavior until he is satisfied when he experiences it from the inside.

Now that you've got the change in his behavior, you need to do something to be absolutely sure that the change transfers automatically to the appropriate situations in his life. We call this future-pacing, or bridging. You can ask "Will you, his unconscious mind, take responsibility for having this new behavior actually occur in the context where the old behavior used to occur?" If you want, you can be even more explicit. You can add "Now raise your 'yes' finger as soon as you, his unconscious mind, have discovered what specifically you'll see, hear, or feel, that will indicate that this is a context where you are going to make this new behavior occur." You are finding a contextual cue that will automatically trigger the new behavior. Automaticity is one of the characteristics of changes made by a refined hypnotist. When you make this kind of change, the conscious mind doesn't have to remember to do anything. If the conscious mind has to remember the new behavior, you haven't wired it in appropriately. Why tax the conscious mind? It's the most limited and undependable part of the person.

With some people, explicit future-pacing isn't necessary. They have a good future-pacing strategy and they will do it themselves. Other people will not be able to do that bridging on their own, and you need to do it explicitly if you want to be thorough and systematic in your work.

If the person doesn't know what new response he would like to have in the problem situation, then you begin a step-by-step selection process. First you say "Go back in your personal history. Have you made a response in some other situation that you think would be an excellent response to make in this situation?" If the answer is "yes" then have him relive that situation and incorporate that response, going through all the steps that I just outlined.

If the answer is still "no" then you have him continue the search for a model, using what we call "referential index shift." You say "Do you know anyone who responds to that kind of situation in a way that you think is quite appropriate, elegant, and effective, and a way in which you would like to respond?" You can say "I know by the fact that you are dissatisfied with your present behavior, that you have some standard for what kind of response you would like to have. Pick some human being—someone whom you respect and admire—who has what you consider to be a much more integrated and appropriate response to this kind of situation." The model they select can be "real" or "fictional." A fictional character from a movie or a book is as real an internal representation of a possible response as are actual people in your life experience, and can serve as excellent models.

Once he has selected a model, you have him go through a three-step sequence to incorporate that model's behavior into his own repertoire. First you have him see and hear the model responding to the situation that he wants to have a new choice about. You can ask him to raise his "yes" finger to indicate when he has completed this. Then you reach over, push the "yes" finger down gently, and say "Good. Having watched and listened to this other person do this, do you now believe that this is the kind of response you would like to be able to make?" If you get a "no," you have to back up and ask him to find another model, or see the same model respond differently. If you get a "yes," you go on to the next step.

In this second step you say "Now substitute your own image and your voice into this film strip and sound track. Watch and listen to it again, and raise your "yes" finger when you are done. Here he watches and listens to *himself* doing the behavior, but he is still dissociated kinesthetically.

When he finishes this step, you ask him "After seeing and hearing yourself do this, do you still want this as a piece of behavior? Do you still think that this is appropriate for you?" If you get a "no" you back up and modify the behavior until it is appropriate—either by making small changes, or by going back to selecting a new model.

If you get a "yes," you ask him to step into the image and have the experience a third time, from the perspective of being there and having the feelings that go along with that particular response. When he has done this, you ask "Was that still satisfactory?" If the answer is "no," you back up and modify the behavior. If the answer is a congruent "yes," that means that the new behavior has been tried out in that situation and found to be satisfactory.

This is a really respectful and graceful way of approaching change, because you keep the change dissociated from him until he has decided that it would be useful. Then you wire it in.

Next you do a future-pace in the same way I described earlier. You can ask his unconscious mind to give you a "yes" signal as soon as it has discovered what external cue it will use as an automatic trigger for the new behavior.

At the end, you can give him some general suggestions for amnesia. "It is important to remember to forget the things that you don't need to remember" is one way to say it. Your outcome is behavioral change. You don't care whether he has any consciousness of it or not. You might suggest that he will remember only as much as his unconscious mind believes is useful for his conscious mind to know about. If his unconscious decides to give him nothing, ask minimally that he has a warm tingling sensation as he comes out of trance as an indication that something useful has happened, and that he can look forward to being delightfully surprised by some new behavior when he gets into the context.

Man: What do you do if you get a "no" response when you ask the question "Does your unconscious know what the cue is?"

You could say "Then I would like you to recall to your unconscious mind the particular situations that you watched and listened to in which you want your behavior to be different. I would like you to create exactly that context again with those same people, those same surroundings, and watch and listen to what it is that happens right at the *beginning* of that experience, which could be used as a cue to trigger that new behavior."

I think it's time to act. Go through this in pairs so that you get some experience now with the basic outline. Let me reassure you that it is

182

quite appropriate for you to stumble a bit with this material. I'm asking you to employ an entire strategy for generative change, with a brief amount of instruction. If you were already able to do these things gracefully and smoothly, you would have wasted your time and money coming here. So I'm delighted that you are courageous enough to feel free to limit yourself to the choices I offer here. I remind you that these are simply more choices to be added to your general repertoire as an effective communicator. With some practice these choices will become as smooth and graceful as any other techniques you have learned to use.

New Behavior Generator Outline
(1)   Select situation in which new behavior is desired.
(2)   Pick a model.
(3)   Watch and listen to the model behaving in the situation.
(4)   Substitute your image and voice for the model's.
(5)   Step into the movie to experience the kinesthetic feelings.
(6)   Future-pace: What cue will trigger off the new behavior?

*   *   *   *   *

The strategy you all just used is designed for straight behavioral change. The only difficulty I noticed people running into was in dealing with "secondary gain." Let me use the problem that Nora worked on as an example.

Nora was interested in learning to have choices about smoking. Smoking is a habitual problem that has a profound set of secondary gains for most people. In other words, there are certain things that smoking does for Nora and other smokers that serve a positive purpose. It's actually better that she smoke, and get access to those experiences and those resources, than it would be for her to quit smoking. She wants to give up something that she knows is physiologically damaging. The difficulty is that if she were to give it up without anything else happening, she would lose access to certain resources and states of consciousness that are important to her.

I'm confident that if we were to get Nora to stop smoking without doing anything else, her unconscious mind is flexible enough that she would begin smoking again within a few months. If we were to make an overall judgement about her functioning, it is probably better that she smoke—even with the damaging physical consequences—and retain access to certain resources, than that she stop smoking and lose access to those resources. Any difficulties that involve secondary gain can be dealt with easily by using reframing. The new behavior generator is primarily for simple behavioral change. If there is secondary gain, use reframing.

The new behavior generator can also be combined with reframing in a useful way. If on the "generating new choices" step your partner doesn't create new alternatives quickly enough to satisfy you, you can say something like this:

"And as you continue to work, developing and considering various alternatives . . . I'd like to remind you of . . . some additional resources . . . sources of models that you might consider. . . . There may be other times and places in your life . . . when you had alternative behaviors which are more successful . . . at protecting you and getting you what you want and need . . . than X. . . . If there are, you might consider those alternatives. . . . In addition . . . you might quickly go on . . . a thorough search visually . . . and auditorily . . . for people whom you really respect and admire . . . who seem to have alternative choices . . . which are more effective than X . . . and still allow them the kinds of experiences that you desire for yourself . . . . Evaluate each one of those . . . allowing the part of you that runs X . . . to determine for you which, if any, of those are more effective than X. . . . Of course once your unconscious has determined . . . that it has these three methods of proceeding to do what X was supposed to do . . . more effectively than X . . . it will give you that 'yes' signal, and cause you to arouse . . . taking all the time you need."

The procedures we are teaching you do not have to be used in isolation. As you practice them and become more effective in using them, you can begin to combine them and vary them in ways that make your learning more interesting for you.

Man: Have you ever gotten a congruent "yes" signal, and then not gotten the new behavior?

No. If I get a congruent response that says it will happen, it will. Sometimes the person has the new behavior for three or four months, and is just delighted, and then he goes back to the old behavior. To me that's a statement that I'm an elegant master of the art of change, that the person who was my client is quite responsive and easily able to make profound changes, *and* that some context in his life—his job, his family relationships, or something else—has changed so that the old behavior has become more appropriate than the new behavior we found. It's now my job to create new alternatives more appropriate for the new context.

Larry: I've heard that you could just take a person into the future and ask him what he would like to be like.

You're talking about pseudo-orientation in time. When you do that you put the person in trance, orient him into the future, and presuppose that he has already solved the problem he had when he first came to see you. Then you ask him to recount in detail just how he solved that problem, and what you did with him that was particularly useful. We've actually used this method as a way to develop new techniques that we then use with other clients.

There are lots of ways to do pseudo-orientation in time. It's one of my favorite approaches, but it's a little more advanced. If you can do the steps I just gave you, you've got the essential steps for making useful changes. This is the bare skeleton of how to proceed effectively. Variations such as pseudo-orientation in time require some artistry. I'm giving you what I consider the essential ingredients. The particular flavoring of the cuisine that you cook up in your office is going to be your artistry. I recommend that you feel free to restrict yourself to this bare outline until it is an automated part of your repertoire, and then get artistic. The bottom line is to be effective. After you can do that, you can get artistic.

I like the work that you all did very much. Are there any other questions or comments about your experience that I might respond to now?

Beth: Kitty did this exercise with me, and I was dealing with something I've worked on for six or seven years in all different kinds of psychotherapy, from Reichian to gestalt to everything else around. This was something that happened way back in childhood which I alienated myself from, and couldn't get closure on. Anyway, using this new behavior generator with the help of Kitty, who was doing it for the very first time, the whole thing just fell into place. I don't know just what words to use. It just happened. There was unification, acceptance, and forgiveness, that I had never been able to experience before. And I have spent a long time trying to get at this with many different approaches. Thank you.

That was a testimonial, not a question. But I also asked for comments, so it was perfectly appropriate. Thank you.

Deep Trance Identification

Using exquisite models for the new behavior generator is based on what we call a "referential index shift"—"becoming" another person. If you do a really complete referential index shift, it's called "deep trance identification," one of the hardest hypnotic phenomena of all. Deep trance identification is a state of consciousness in which you assume the identity of someone else. You do it so completely that for that period of time you don't know you are doing it. Of course, there are varying degrees of this. It's possible to adopt the nonverbal and verbal behavior of another person so completely that you automatically acquire many skills that he has, even though you have no conscious representation of those skills. It's essentially what we did with people like Milton Erickson in order to learn quickly to be able to get the results they got.

There are certain necessary elements to assisting someone in doing deep trance identification. First, you have to remove the identity of the person with whom you are working. That presupposes a lot of amnesia: he is going to have amnesia for who he is. Secondly, it presupposes that he is going to have the ability to generate his behavior based on what he has observed about somebody else. In other words, if he is going to do deep trance identification with Melvin Schwartz, it means that all of his behavior has to be generated from Melvin Schwartz' verbal and nonverbal behavior. You need to give instructions to his unconscious to sort through his experience of the model's behavior: This includes voice tonality, facial expressions, posture, movement style, and typical ways of responding.

There are many ways to go after deep trance identification. Let me give you one way. The first thing I would do is work for a total age-regression to get rid of the identity of the person that I am working with. By the way, doing this will tell you how much work you are going to have to do to get deep trance identification.

Now, how could you get age-regression? What kinds of experiences would lead to age-regression? Think of universals for a moment. What universal experiences do people use to age-regress themselves?

Woman: The first time you learned to walk.

Man: Childhood memories.

No. Let me rephrase the question. You are mentioning things that are out of people's childhood, but not things that you've *used* to age-regress yourself. Let me give you an example. One of the things that people use to regress themselves is their college yearbook. People pull out their yearbooks specifically to regress themselves. College reunions are another classic example of an age-regression technique. What else?

Woman: Photograph albums.

Man: Boxes of memorabilia.

Yes. Exactly.

Man: Odors.

Odors is one way it happens spontaneously, but not a way that people deliberately use.

Woman: Old music.

Now there's a zinger.

Man: Souvenirs.

What else do people do? People return to their home town and go back to the old neighborhood. The things we're talking about now are things that people characteristically do. If I'm going to go for a hyp-notic phenomenon, I want to design an experience in which the spon-taneous reaction is the response I want—in this case regression—so I'm going to use these kinds of universal experiences.

One of the ways of doing age-regression is to induce a trance and have somebody see before himself the book of time. "And in that book there will be photographs from your entire life, and the page you are open to now is your present age totally and completely. But as you turn the page back one year, suddenly and completely, you are back there again . . . feeling what you felt then . . . and knowing only what you knew then and nothing more . . . honestly and completely . . . such that you can turn back one page . . . of time . . . at a time . . . going back fully and completely in each year . . . until you go all the way back to age six . . . such that when you are back there fully and completely . . . at age six . . . honestly knowing what you knew then and *only* then . . . will you be ready to continue . . . spontaneous-ly . . . one of your hands will begin to float up, *only* as an indication to me . . . that you are honestly six years old."

That's how I design a technique to accomplish any phenomenon. There is no trance phenomenon that people don't already do anyway. Age-regression is not something that only hypnotists do. It's some-thing that people do to themselves. They open a box of memorabilia; they pick up each object and they return to the age they were when they had the object. They discover that the box is really a time machine. "So you can cut a small hole in the side, and pick up something from your childhood and make it very small and you *see* the door . . . the open-ing in the box before you . . . and slowly you begin to walk into the box of time . . . and as you step through that door you have strange and confusing feelings. As you step through you look around and there are big objects lying all around you and each object has a door . . . . And you *know,* although you are slightly frightened, that if you walk through any of those doors . . . you will become the *age* . . . at which that object appeared in your life. . . ."

You see, it's utter nonsense that I'm saying. However, I'm designing a context in which it is possible and logical for people to experience an alternative reality. Of course, you always use feedback to notice if the person is responding or not. You use all the usual behavioral cues to let you know if the person is actually regressing.

Once you get age-regression, you can do something with it. You have a six-year-old sitting in front of you. What do six-year-olds do to become somebody else?

Man: They play dress-up.

Exactly. They go up to the attic and play dress-up; they play "pretend." So you have them put on a set of clothes, only they don't know whose clothes these are. "This is a funny set of clothes. It's not like mama's clothes. It's not daddy's clothes. It's not army clothes. I have no idea whose clothes these are. It doesn't make any sense . . . but suddenly, unconsciously . . . you begin to forget that you are the child . . . and you begin to become a person whom you don't know at six years old . . . but your unconscious knows who it is . . . and can *take that person's* tone of *voice* . . . that person's responses . . . *only* that person's movement . . . and *only* that person's behavior such that for the next ten minutes you will sit there . . . and develop unconsciously . . . a personality which is based on only what you know . . . about that particular human being . . . so that in ten minutes your eyes will spontaneously flutter open . . . and you will *be completely that particular human being.*"

Does that make sense to you as a way of doing it? You see, we could give you many specific strategies for using hypnosis to get different results. What we are trying to do now instead, is to give you an idea about how we conceive of using hypnosis to do *anything.* I build any particular hypnotic phenomenon by figuring out how I can get to it as naturally and easily as possible. If you can't get age-regression and identification this way, you can always use reframing to get it.

Man: Isn't there a lot of variation in how fast you can go when you do deep trance identification? And don't clients have to have some flexibility before they can do it?

Yes. Typically I don't attempt to do deep trance identification until I have somebody who is an exquisite subject, and who is trained to respond to me quickly. I would try to get many other trance phenomena before I would try deep trance identification. It seems foolish to me to attempt it with somebody who does not already know how to do amnesia and negative and positive hallucination, because those are minimum requirements. So I would do many other things first.

If I were a teacher in elementary school, deep trance identification would be one of the things I would teach. I would get videotapes of Albert Einstein and Irving Berlin and other great geniuses of our culture. I would have videotapes of them doing different things: talking and interacting with people—and especially talking about and doing whatever they are famous for. Then I would have the kids use those samples of behavior as the basis for becoming these people and accessing their abilities.

Man: It seems to me that this is what other cultures have called spirit possession.

Yes. What people experience as demonic possession, as far as I can tell, is nothing more than deep trance identification. I know a man who is famous for working with multiple personalities. He always has about twenty clients who are MP's. He's also a good Catholic, so of course a lot of his clients are possessed. He does exorcisms out on the helicopter pad behind a hospital. He gets national awards for being a straight psychiatrist, but I'm considered weird!

I went to see him because I was curious about his multiple personality clients. I met one of his clients in an altered state and met four or five of her personalities and the demon that possessed her. As far as I can tell, I can induce that in anybody. In fact, the way he went about introducing me to these personalities is exactly the way I would go about inducing them as a hypnotist.

The woman was sitting there in a chair, talking to us about how she has a lot of amnesia in her life. Nobody else does, right? Yet this psychiatrist's convincer for knowing that you are a multiple personality is if there is any period of your life that you can't remember! He makes up a name for whatever period you have amnesia for. According to this psychiatrist, the period that you don't remember wasn't you; that was another personality. He would give it some name like "Fred." Then he ignores your ongoing behavior, hits you on the head unexpectedly and calls this name "Fred! Fred! Come out! Come out!" If you say "What do you mean 'Fred, come out?' " he ignores you until suddenly some other personality emerges. That's a great way to make multiple personalities. I'm convinced that MP's are manufactured by parents and well-meaning therapists; they are not spontaneously derived.

Man: When you do deep trance identification, you don't want to have the person become someone else at six years of age. How do you get him to grow up again?

You just tell him to be someone else. Children don't pretend to be somebody else who is only six years of age. They pretend to be someone else at whatever age they know the person at. You can tell children anything, and as long as you do so meaningfully, they'll obey you. Once you have age-regressed the person, you say "Now, while you continue to play and have a good time, your unconscious mind is going to learn about. . . . " Then you just give him direct suggestions: "Sort through everything you know unconsciously about so-and-so—the way he looks, the way he sounds, the way he moves, the way he responds—and make that a single unit so that you will emerge spontaneously in fifteen minutes being totally that adult."

Let me caution you again. Deep trance identification is fairly complicated and difficult. It's useful as a learning strategy, but there are much easier ways to accomplish most of the things you want to do. For most changes, the new behavior generator or some other technique will work equally well and be a *lot* easier to do.

Pain Control

Pain is a fascinating thing in that it's very useful up to a point, and then it's no longer useful. This is true for a lot of other things as well. A little adrenalin in an emergency can be useful, but too much can be incapacitating, depending on the task. For something really simple and strenuous, like lifting a car off someone, the more adrenalin the better. But for any task that requires fine coordination, like fixing a watch or putting a key into a keyhole, too much adrenalin is *disastrous.*

One thing I do to deal with pain is provide a context in which the natural response is to *miss* pain. *This is an overall strategy for hypnosis: to create a context in which the natural response is the one I want.*

In the classic Erickson story on pain control, they brought in a woman who was dying of cancer. They brought her to Erickson in an ambulance, put her on a gurney, and rolled her into the office. The woman looked at Erickson and said "This is the dumbest thing I've ever done in my life. My doctor sent me here so that you could do

190

something about the pain. Drugs don't help my pain. Surgery doesn't help my pain. How are you going to be able to help my pain with just words?"

Erickson, sitting in a wheelchair, swayed back and forth and looked at her, and paced all her beliefs by saying "You came here because your doctor told you to come here, and you don't understand how just *words* could control your pain. *Drugs* don't even control your pain. *Surgery* doesn't even control your pain. And you think this is the dumbest thing you've ever heard of. Well, let me ask you a question. If that door were to burst open right now . . . and you looked over and saw a great big tiger . . . licking its chops hungrily . . . staring at *only you* . . . how much pain do you think you'd feel?"

The point is, he presented a context in which nobody is going to be aware of pain. Pain simply doesn't exist when you're about to be eaten by a tiger. An experience where there is no pain is something that can be anchored and continued as a particular altered state. Erickson said "Later the doctors didn't understand her when she said she had a tiger under her bed and she just listened to its purr."

There are lots and lots of ways of approaching pain control. You have to think of what it would take, if you had physiological pain, to get you to not notice it. Going to the dentist and having him drill through your tooth hurts. When he hits a nerve, physiologically the signals go through your nerves and your brain goes "Uggh!" That happens. Yet there are people who go to the dentist, get no novocaine, and feel nothing. They don't do hypnosis, either. Dentists will tell you about them. The dentist drills right into their nerves, and they don't respond. The last dentist I went to said "I can never understand this. It hurts *me,* but *they* don't feel a thing!"

Who are the people who can do that? They are people with no consciousness of kinesthetics. They are people who haven't got *any* feelings, so they can't feel pain. The only thing that will get through is putting their hand on a hot plate. By the time it burns up to the elbow, they may notice. These are people who typically get hurt a lot. They have a tendency to get skinned knees and bump into things, because they have no consciousness of their kinesthetics and haven't learned to be cautious. As a strategy to work with pain, you can *make* somebody into someone like that.

The questions you always need to ask yourself are "What is it that you want?" and "Where would that happen naturally?" There are contexts in which you can move around and feel things but not feel pain. Have you ever hurt your hand? Have you ever cut your finger so that it really hurt? Or have you smacked it with a hammer so it really throbbed with pain? And during the period of time when it was throbbing, did you ever forget about it for some reason? In what context would that occur?

Man: In an emergency.

Sure. An emergency is one classic example. For most people it doesn't even take an emergency. All they have to do is be distracted by anything else. Humans have such a limited amount of conscious attention. The rule is that 7 ± 2 chunks of information is all people can attend to. So give them nine chunks if you want to distract them. Give them something else to do—anything else.

Once I worked with a man who had severe pain. He had been in an accident that had resulted in a back injury. I don't know the medical details, but there was some physical reason why he ought to have pain. He came in and said he wanted hypnosis. I said I didn't know if I could help him with his pain. I had a procedure that worked very well, but only on people who are mature and intelligent, and frankly, I didn't know if he was mature enough.

I told him "Look, the most mature and intelligent people are the ones who are able to see things from different perceptual points of view." By the way, according to Jean Piaget, this is actually true. So I explained Piaget's theory and test of intelligence to this man.

According to Piaget, being intelligent means being able to tell what things would look like from different perspectives. If I wanted to test a child, I could use a block of wood and a thimble. I'd bring the child over, show him the thimble, and place the block of wood in front of the thimble to block the child's view of the thimble. Then I'd ask "Is there anything behind the block?" If the child says "No" he's not very "mature." The "mature" child can visualize the thimble when it's hidden, and he can also see what the thimble, the block of wood, and they themselves would look like from the other side of the table. The testers literally ask "What would it look like if you were over there on the other side of the table?" The better you can see things from different points of view, the more "mature" and intelligent you are. One consequence of that kind of visualization is that you become dissociated from your feelings. This is what some modern methods teach kids to be able to do. They teach kids to grow up and be dissociated from their feelings, because that's what it means to be "mature."

I told this man that there was something I wanted him to go home

192

and practice, because I was going to test him extensively on it the next week to find out how mature and intelligent he was. What he needed to do was to find out what he would look like lying in his bed, first from the perceptual viewpoint of one corner of the room, then from the viewpoint of the opposite corner, and then from *every* point in between. I told him that next week I would pick one viewpoint at random, and have him draw it in detail. I would measure it and find out exactly what the angle was, and by looking at his drawing I would be able to compute his intelligence.

He went home, and when he came back a week later he had done this task. He had worked on it methodically. He was highly motivated; he wanted me to treat him and thought I could help him. And when he came back, he said "You know, the strangest thing is, I haven't had much pain at all this week." Giving someone an appropriate task is another way of going after the same outcome.

There are other bizarre ways to deal with pain. You can do anything in trance as long as you presuppose it. Once I told a man who came to see me "I want to speak to the Brain. As soon as the Brain is ready to talk to me, and no conscious parts know anything about what is going on, then the mouth will open and say 'Now.' " He sat there for twenty minutes and then he said "Nowwww." I said "All right, Brain, you fouled up. Pain is a very valuable thing. It allows you to know when something needs to be attended to. This injury is already being attended to as well as it can be. Unless you can come up with anything else that needs to be done, it's time to shut off the pain." It said "Yessss!" I said "Shut it off now, and turn it back on only when it's needed; not before." Now, I have no idea what all that means, but it sounds so logical, and presupposes that the brain can do what I ask. After that he had no pain whatsoever.

Amnesia

I want to comment on something from one of the exercises. One man did something that can be used to get amnesia. He did the exercise, and as the woman he had induced into a trance returned, he looked at her and said "Notice how quiet it is in the room." When a person returns and opens his eyes, if you look at him and immediately comment on anything other than the experience he just came out of, you will abruptly direct his attention elsewhere, and you will tend to get really profound amnesia. This is true whether he is coming out of a deep trance, or whether you are in the middle of an ordinary conversation with him. For example, you could be talking about hypnosis and suddenly you turn and begin to talk about the necessity for checking your brakes before you go down mountain roads, and very congruently go into extreme detail about it. If you then ask "What was I just talking about?" he probably won't remember. Since there's no continuity, the probability that what happened just before the interruption will be consciously remembered is really small. So you get amnesia.

Try this with your clients when you aren't doing official altered states work. Deliver the set of instructions you want them to carry out for homework, and then immediately change the subject. They will have amnesia for the instructions; however, they will typically carry them out. There won't be any interference from the conscious mind when you do it that way. They won't remember the assignment, so they won't be able to have any "conscious resistance" to carrying it out.

Man: I've had clients apologize for not remembering the homework assignment I had given them, and then describe exactly how they fulfilled it.

Excellent. That's really good feedback to know that you've gotten the message across.

When you are doing official trance work, as soon as the person arouses from trance, you can begin in the middle of a sentence to comment about something that is completely unrelated to what occurred before or during the trance. That's an unconscious cue to him that you would prefer not to talk about what just occurred, and that it need not be available to his consciousness, either. Amnesia is as easy to get as most other "deep trance" phenomena, and this is one way to get it.

Man: I used to have trouble eliciting amnesia with my clients. Then I started doing just one thing differently: I waited about fifteen minutes before bringing up anything that happened in the trance. That's the only thing I changed, and amnesia started to occur.

Man: I've found that if I say to somebody "Then you will make a decision on this by next Tuesday," change the subject abruptly, and—

Well, I wouldn't be that direct. I would presuppose the decision. I would say "And when we get together to continue the discussion next Tuesday, I would like you to go ahead and indicate what your decision is in some way that is particularly interesting for me" and change the subject. If you do that, the behavior will occur and there won't be any consciousness about what's going on. That's an advantage if there is any conscious resistance to what you propose.

By the way, amnesia is a way to convince a "non-believer" that he's been in a trance. When he arouses from a trance, immediately engage his attention on something else and then later demand that he describe all the events that occurred, to prove to you that he wasn't in a trance.

Milton Erickson's office was the Land of Clutter. There were four hundred thousand objects in his office, so he had lots of choices about what he talked about and what he directed your attention to. He always arranged the clocks so that he could see them and you couldn't. He loved to bring people out of a trance, change the subject, and then say "Now, before you look at your watch, I would like you to make a guess about how much time has transpired." Of course you never knew what time it was, because Erickson did time distortion really well.

That is usually a convincer for people. If they can't account for the last two hours, they become convinced they were in a trance.

Another way to get amnesia is by producing dissociation. For example, if a person is highly specialized visually, I may do an overlap induction with him and lead him into a kinesthetic state of consciousness. When he comes back to his normal state of consciousness, he will automatically be amnesic for his trance experience. He will have no way to access the information because his consciousness is visual, and the altered state experiences were kinesthetically grounded. "He"—the visual part of him—won't know about that.

Any time you radically alter someone's state of consciousness, and then bring him back to his normal state abruptly without building bridges between those states, he will tend to have amnesia for what occurred when his consciousness was altered. He has no way to get to that information in his normal state; the information is linked to another state of consciousness.

Research on learning has been done on mild forms of this phenomenon. It's been discovered that if you memorize information while listening to music, you'll be much more apt to remember the information later if you listen to music again. What you learn when you're drinking coffee or altering your consciousness in some other way, you'll be more apt to recover if you drink coffee again or alter your consciousness in the same way.

You can use this same information to get amnesia. What you *do* want to insure is that you've transferred the behavioral changes to the person's normal state of consciousness. It's very important to build bridges that make such a transfer automatic. That's the purpose of having you do explicit future-pacing. It insures that the change you have made will transfer to the context in which it is needed.

Lynn, what did I just say? (He raises his arm directing her to a visual access. See Appendix I on eye accessing cues.)

Lynn: I don't know.

I don't care if you understand what I said. Just tell me what words I used.

Lynn: I don't know; I don't remember. It's erased.

Did you all notice that when I asked her that question requesting auditory information, I waved my arm directing her gaze up and to her left. She followed, so she was looking in a direction that allowed her to access visual information, but not auditory. That's another way to get dissociation. So it's no surprise that she reported being amnesic for what I said.

Do you remember what I said this time? (He waves his arm down and to her left.)

Lynn: You said I was amnesic, since you directed me to access visual information and not auditory.

Right. She can recover what I said when I direct her to the appropriate channel. If I want amnesia, I direct her into an inappropriate channel. Since I asked her to recall what I said, it's appropriate to direct her to look down and to her left, if I want her to be able to recall it. If I want her to be able to recall the movements of my arms, I would direct her gaze up and to her left. So if I deliberately direct her into a channel other than the one where the information is stored, she will be amnesic.

Amnesia is traditionally thought of as one of the most difficult deep trance phenomena to get. If you understand accessing cues and states of consciousness in the way that we have been describing them here, all you have to do is misdirect a person and you get amnesia.

Man: What about getting the amnesia to last later on?

It doesn't matter later. A good time to go for amnesia is right after you've made some change or given some instruction. If a person doesn't consciously remember, it can be easier for the new behavior to emerge without conscious interference. If he remembers later on, that's OK.

Sometimes I verbally suggest a dissociation between the person's conscious and unconscious processes in order to get amnesia. For example, I might say: "And as you sit there . . . I'm going to speak to you . . . and the more you listen to me . . . the less you will understand with your conscious mind . . . the more you will understand with your unconscious mind . . . because it's your ears that I am speaking to."

What could it mean to tell someone you aren't speaking to him, but to his ears? The result is generally dissociation. Another variation is to say "I'm not speaking to *you* now; I'm talking to *him*."

Earlier I offered you another way to suggest amnesia verbally. Before you bring someone out of a trance, you can give him instructions like "And your unconscious mind can sort through everything that has occurred here so that it can let you know only those portions of what has occurred that it believes would be useful for you to know . . . because it can be so delightful to find yourself using new choices . . . and you don't know where they came from." Or "And you can remember to forget to remember any material best left at the unconscious level."

Recovering Personal History

Organizations known roughly as "the law," and also organizations that exist to protect people from too much justice, frequently hire experts in hypnosis to aid them in recovering information about past events. One of the things that people do exquisitely in altered states is relive experiences. In fact, most of the psychotherapies that have people relive past experiences use hypnotic technology to get them to do so. Some psychotherapists use these hypnotic techniques much more effectively than many professional hypnotists.

The easiest way to get someone to relive an experience is to do the same thing you did when you practiced the induction method of accessing a previous trance. All you do is begin with the first thing that you know led up to the event, have the person recall that in detail, and then proceed from there. If you do this, the person will have the same responses he had the first time.

Once I worked with a businessman who told me that he went into a meditative state when he got on airplanes. He said "The way I experience it, one moment we're taking off and the next thing I know, the plane is landing." I was curious about what happened, so I had him reaccess that experience. First I had him walk up the ramp onto the airplane, sit down and put on his seat belt, and then have the usual conversation with the stewardess about his coat and whether he wanted a drink. Then as the plane was taking off, I had him listen to the captain announcing how high they would be flying.

As soon as I went through all that, his head dropped forward, and he ceased to respond to me. Then he started snoring. He didn't go into a meditative state on airplanes; he went to sleep. Each time I led him through the same progression, he fell asleep, and I had to shout "Hey, you! Wake up!" Later on I discovered that if I just made the sound "Urp Urp" and jiggled his chair a little bit, he'd arouse and ask "Are we there yet?" If you want to know what happened in the past, you'll find out if you have the person relive the experience fully enough.

A man who is fairly skilled at using these techniques came up to me in a workshop and told me about two young female clients of his. They had been abducted and raped when they were out somewhere together. One of them remembered the event vividly, and had given the police all the necessary information. The other one had complete amnesia for the event and didn't quite believe the story that the first one had told. The one who remembered the rape vividly was a psychological mess as a result of it, while the other one had no response to it. She was fine.

In a situation like this, you need to consider carefully whether there is any point to her knowing what happened. If there isn't, recovering the memory may only give her pain.

This well-intentioned therapist was working diligently to get the woman who didn't remember anything to remember the event in detail, so that she could feel all of the pain. He decided that she had repressed all that unpleasantness, and he was right! However, repressing unpleasantness is an excellent choice in some situations. He placed a value judgement upon "truth" and assumed that since it was repressed, it would come out and be harmful to her later on, so she might as well have the pain now and get it over with.

If you use hypnosis to lead people into awareness of unpleasant experiences, I think you should first make a choice about whether that is worthwhile. Many of us were taught that reliving unpleasant experiences makes them less harmful, and *that absolutely, categorically, is not so.* If there is one thing that academic psychology has learned, it's that that assumption is false. Academic psychology has learned that if a certain set of experiences teaches you to have a generalization, going through the same experiences again will only reinforce whatever you learned from them. If what you learned from an event causes you limitations, reliving that event over and over again in the same way will only reinforce your generalization and the limitations that result from that generalization.

Therapists like Virginia Satir and Milton Erickson all have people go back and relive events, but they have people do it *differently* than the event occurred the first time. Satir describes this as "going back and seeing with new eyes," whatever that means. Erickson had people go back into the past, and then he changed things totally. He reorganized history so that it had no alternative but to be different.

Once Milton did a fascinating thing with somebody. A client came in who had made a mistake as a very young child; he had committed a crime. Something about the course of events convinced him that from that point on he would engage in criminal activities. He became convinced that he would always make the same mistake, and so he did.

Erickson took him back into his personal history and gave him an experience in which he became convinced that he would no longer engage in crime, because he wasn't good at it. That event never actually occurred. However, if you ask that man today about that event, he will recall it for you with a great deal of detail, and it will be as real to him as anything that actually occurred.

Sometimes there is some meaningful purpose in taking a person back through unpleasant memories. It might provide you with information so that you can catch a criminal and prevent him from committing a crime against someone else. Possibly information from that event may be needed for some other purpose.

A friend of mine worked with a couple who had been assaulted, and they both had complete amnesia for having been assaulted. In fact, the only way they knew they had been assaulted was that they were both covered with bruises and lacerations. They were told that the lacerations were inflicted by some weapon, and that their money and their property were gone. The police kept insisting that they had been beaten and robbed. The man and the woman both said "We don't know. We don't remember anything."

I did some hypnotic investigation and discovered that this couple had not been attacked; they had gotten into a car accident. After the crash, somebody pulled them out of their car and stole the car and their belongings. When I went through the experience with them to find out what had occurred, I chose to do it with only one of them, and took the other one out of the room; there was no need for both of them to suffer. Being the sexist I am, I decided it was best that the man suffer. However, I had him go through the experience in a different way to minimize any unpleasantness for him. Instead of going through the experience in the way he had before, I had him *watch himself* go through it.

I took this precaution both because I wanted him to be able to do it comfortably, *and* because he had been knocked unconscious. If someone got knocked out the first time through an experience, if I have them relive it in the same way, they will get knocked out again.

A student of mine had been in an accident and wanted to relive the experience. A lot of people had tried to work with him to get him to do this. They would have him start out with the feeling of the steering wheel and the sound of the engine, and then the visual experience of the trees, and then a horn honking, and then he would pass out. They would have to do all kinds of things to wake him up, and then they'd try again.

They could have anticipated that he'd pass out, because in the accident he hit a tree and got knocked out. If you relive something and do it in exactly the same way, you will go through the same experience in the way that you did the first time. If you got knocked out the first time, you'll get knocked out when reliving it.

If somebody has been attacked or raped or been in a car wreck, reexperiencing the feelings they had then is not going to be useful. If someone is telling you about his heart attack, you don't want him to relive it in exactly the same way. "Oh, you had a heart attack last week. What happened?" That is the craziest thing you can ask somebody. If you do it well enough, you are going to give him another heart attack.

Many women who have been raped or attacked, subsequently have trouble with men. I'm not talking about having trouble with the man who attacked them, but with their husbands and their loved ones. Sometimes they can't even live in the house that they lived in, or walk down a street without absolute terror. Those women are reliving their unpleasant experiences over and over again. No one should have to suffer that way. If somebody was unfairly attacked, that is enough unfair pain. Having any more than that seems very unjust to me.

There is a procedure that allows you to separate out part of an experience, so that it's possible to relive it in a new way. You have them begin the experience, and then step outside of it so that they *see themselves* going through it. They hear what was going on at the time, but they watch themselves go through the event as if they were watching a movie. When they do it in this way, they don't have to have the feelings that they had when they were there. They can have feelings *about* the experience. This procedure is described in detail in Chapter II of *Frogs into Princes*, so I won't explain it here. We call it the phobia technique or the visual-kinesthetic dissociation.

When you have people relive unpleasant experiences, keep these ideas in mind. As a precaution against them reexperiencing the feelings, have them *see themselves* going through the experience. If you want to be really safe, have them *watch themselves watching themselves* go through the experience, as if they were in the projection box at a movie theatre, watching themselves watch the movie. If you have them go through an event this way, when they remember it later on, they won't experience the terror. That is a real gift to give someone who has been beaten or brutalized somehow. If they go back through that event from the position of watching themselves watching themselves, it will diffuse the intensity of the feelings and prevent them from building any generalization that would make them have to feel those unpleasant feelings again.

VII

Calibration

Next we'd like to spend some time teaching you what we call calibration exercises. Calibration refers to the process by which you tune yourselves to the nonverbal signals that indicate a particular state in a particular person. Throughout this workshop you have all been calibrating yourselves to recognize the signs of altered states in another person. Some of those signs will be fairly universal, while others will only be useful with a particular person.

In a way everything we're teaching you in this seminar can be summed up in three statements. To be an effective communicator you need to: 1) know what outcome you want, 2) have the behavioral flexibility to vary what you are doing to get the outcome, and 3) have the sensory experience to know when you've got the response that you want.

Most of what we've taught you so far is designed to give you specific ways to vary your behavior in order to get the results you want. We suggest that you think of it in this way: *The meaning of your communication is the response you get.* If you use this as a guiding principle, you will know that when the response you get is not the one you want and expect, it's time to vary your behavior until you get it. We teach many specific ways to do this, and when those don't work, we suggest you try something else. If what you are doing is not working, then *any* other behavior has a better chance of getting the response you want.

If you don't have enough sensory experience to notice the response that you're getting, you won't have a way of knowing when you've

201

202

succeeded or failed. You see, sometimes people ask me if I ever work with the deaf and the blind. I tell them "Yes, always."

We use calibration exercises to increase your sensory acuity. Your ability to notice minimal nonverbal responses will dramatically increase your ability to be an effective hypnotist in particular, and an effective communicator in general.

When Frank, a friend of mine, was about eighteen or nineteen years old, he was a very good Golden Gloves boxer. He was also supporting his family by working as a janitor at a state mental hospital. As he walked around on the wards, he would shadow box just to stay in shape for boxing.

On one ward there was a catatonic who had been in the same position for two or three years. Every day the personnel stood him up at the end of his bed and locked him onto it. He had catheter tubes and feeding tubes and everything. Nobody had been able to make contact with this man. Once as Frank walked by on an errand, shadow boxing as usual, he noticed that this guy responded to his boxing with little flinches in his head and neck. This was a major response for this guy. So Frank ran down to the nurses' station and pulled out the guy's file. Sure enough, he had been a professional prize fighter before he became catatonic.

How would you make contact with a prizefighter? Any professional has to make certain motor programs automatic, just as most of you have automated driving a car until it functions as an unconscious program. In the boxing ring there are so many things you have to do that you need to make most of what you do unconscious. Your conscious attention can then be used to notice what's going on in the situation. My friend went back and started shadow boxing with this guy, and he quickly came out of the catatonic altered state that he'd been in for some years.

Woman: Did he start boxing when Frank started shadow boxing?

Yes, of course. He didn't have a choice, because those were programs that he had practiced for years and years.

The main point of this is that my friend was able to notice the responses that he was getting. That made it possible for him to use his behavior to amplify them. If you don't notice the responses you are getting, everything else we're teaching you will be worthless.

Exercise 8
We want to start with a fairly easy calibration exercise to increase

your ability to make sensory discriminations. Pair up and ask your partner to think of someone he likes. As he does this, watch for small changes in his breathing, posture, muscle tonus, skin color, etc. Then ask your partner to think of someone he dislikes, again watching what changes occur. Have him go back and forth between thinking of the person he likes and the one he dislikes until you can clearly see the differences between his expressions.

Next, ask a series of comparative questions in order to test your calibration. Ask "Which one is taller?" I don't want him to tell you the answer. Your job is to watch his response and then tell *him* which one it is.

Any comparative question will work for this: "Which one have you seen most recently?" "Which one has darker hair?" "Which one is heavier?" "Which one lives nearer to you?" "Which one makes more money?"

When you ask a question, your partner will go inside to process the question and get an answer. He may first consider the person he likes, then consider the person he doesn't like, and finally think of the person who is the answer to the question. So you may initially see some back and forth responses, and then you will see the response that answers the question. The answer will be the response you see just before he comes back out and looks at you or nods his head to indicate that he has determined the answer internally.

When you've guessed correctly four times in a row, switch roles with your partner. Take about five minutes each.

*   *   *   *   *

As I went around the room, I noticed that most of you were doing very well. In fact, for some of you this was *too* easy. This will vary considerably from person to person, because some people are much more expressive than others. If you found your task too easy, there are several things you can do to make this something you can learn from.

One thing you can do is to artificially limit the information that you are receiving. If it's easy for you to discriminate differences on the basis of facial changes, use a notebook or something else to cover your partner's face. See if you can make the same discrimination by watching changes in his chest or his hands, or some other part of his body.

Another thing you can do is to ask about more neutral subjects.

204

"Think about a chair that you have in your home." "Now think about a chair that you have in your office." This will also make the task a challenge again. Another way is to find someone who is generally less expressive. His responses will be less obvious.

On the other hand, if you *didn't* notice any differences in your partner when thinking about the two people, you can do something to make the task easier. Ask him to think of the most obnoxious, disgusting person he has ever met in his life. It helps if you do this with a congruent tone of voice. Then ask him to think of the person whom he loves most dearly in the whole world. This will exaggerate the differences between his responses, and make it easier for you to detect them. You could also find someone who is more expressive.

The point of this is to do whatever is necessary in order to make the task difficult enough so that it's just beyond what your capabilities were in the past. If you do that, you will learn the most, and increase your sensitivity most quickly.

Exercise 9

Next we want you to do another calibration exercise to determine the nonverbal signals that go with agreement and disagreement. Pair up again and ask mundane questions conversationally. "Your name is Bob?" "Were you born in California?" "Are you married?" "Do you have a car?" Ask uncontroversial yes/no questions and pay attention to his nonverbal responses as he gives you a verbal "yes" or "no." You learn what constitutes a "yes" response nonverbally by noticing what distinguishes the nonverbal responses that accompany "yes" from the ones that accompany "no."

Some people will spontaneously and unconsciously tense their jaw muscles for "no" and relax them for "yes." Some people will turn whiter for "no," and redder for "yes." Others will tilt their head forward when they say "yes" and back when they say "no." There are lots of idiosyncratic responses that you can notice which are already paired with agreement or disagreement.

When you can distinguish "yes" from "no" nonverbally, ask your partner not to answer your questions. After each question, observe the nonverbal response and tell your partner whether the answer is "yes" or "no." When you have guessed correctly four times in a row, switch roles with your partner.

*   *   *   *   *

Some of you may recognize what you just did as a conversational way to do what you did earlier in this workshop when you set up yes/no signals in trance. Being able to do it conversationally allows you to use this information at board meetings, and in many other contexts where it's inappropriate to induce a formal trance, but you want feedback from other people.

If you are a salesperson and have calibrated for "yes" and "no," you can know immediately when the potential buyer agrees or disagrees with what you say, even if the person says nothing. This means you know what selling points to emphasize and build on. You also know what points to drop, or what objections you may need to satisfy before you can make a sale.

If you are making a proposal to a board of directors, calibrating to "yes" and "no" can let you know exactly when to have the proposal voted on. You say to the group "Now I don't know if this proposal already makes sense as a beneficial plan for this organization." Then you pause, and watch to find out if most of the members give you a "yes" response. If you get yeses, you bring the proposal to an immediate vote. If you get noes, you continue to discuss the proposal until you find ways to get the agreement of the entire group.

Exercise 10

I would like to give you another calibration exercise to do this evening. Carry on a normal conversation with someone who is not in this seminar. As you are talking, say something about him that you know is not true, and notice what his response is. A little later, say something about him that you know has to be true. It doesn't matter how mundane your comment is, just notice how he responds, and if this response is different from the first one. Go back and forth three or four times, until you can discern the difference between the way he responds to statements about himself that are true, and statements that are inaccurate.

I recommend that what you say about him not be derogatory. Say something complimentary that you know he doesn't think is true. That way he won't get mad at you, and you won't have to justify what you say. You can still provide yourself with the experience of making this calibration. You don't ever need to tell him what you're doing, and you don't ever have to do anything with this information. Just notice if there is a difference.

The more you do to increase your sensory experience, the more often

206

you will *notice* the nonverbal input you are getting from other people that can make a big difference in your communication.

Crystal Ball Gazing Exercise

Now I want half of you to go out of this room and have a coffee break or something. Stay fairly close by, because in a few minutes the people who stay here are going to get you and do something with you . . . .

For those of you remaining, I'm going to have you learn to become "psychic." I'm going to have you all do some crystal ball gazing, or if you prefer, palm-reading. The point of this exercise is that it's an excellent way to further develop your ability to perceive minimal nonverbal cues. Being able to do this makes *all* the difference when you're doing hypnosis, and you need systematic ways to develop such perceptual skills.

In a few moments you are going to find one of the people who is now taking a break, and do either crystal ball gazing or palm-reading. You will actually be using the kind of subtle visual or tactile feedback from the other person that you have been using in the last several calibration exercises. Using your newfound "psychic" abilities, you are going to tell him something about his own personal history that you have no way of knowing. You will surprise yourself as well as him.

Choose someone you don't know for a partner, so you won't be able to draw upon stories and unconscious information that you have about that person from the past. I want you to demonstrate to your own satisfaction that you can do this without prior knowledge. Your unconscious mind knows you can, but your conscious mind needs to be convinced of it.

When you first pair up with this person that you don't know, conversationally ask a few mundane questions to get acquainted. Use this time to calibrate to yes and no: agreement and disagreement.

As soon as you've done that, you can begin crystal ball gazing. If you can simply begin congruently, great. If that seems awkward to you, you can say "I think this is a ridiculous exercise, but John and Richard are asking me to do it. I've usually gained from following their instructions, so I'm going to try it. Would you be willing to cooperate?"

Then you say "OK, I'm going to read this crystal ball, and tell you something significant about your past experience." As you say this, you cup your hands in front of you and stare at your hands as if they contain something. Your partner will probably look at your hands too.

As with any exercise, the first thing you need to do is to get rapport.

An excellent way to get rapport is to move the crystal ball that's not there up and down slightly as your partner breathes in and out. At this point you've already done two things with the crystal ball. You've established rapport by pacing the breathing, and you've riveted your partner's conscious attention on something that's not there. That's always a good indication that someone is in an altered state.

Now you begin doing something like the following: "As I look into this crystal ball . . . I see the mists swirling . . . and as they swirl, it looks like a figure is emerging . . . a very important figure . . . from your past." Then you pause until you've got your partner's attention focused on the crystal ball, and he has had time to identify "someone important from the past." So far what you're doing is like a process instruction: you are giving no specifics.

Then you say "It looks like a man. . . ." Now you wait until you can see some indication from your partner that he agrees or disagrees. If you get some minimal cues that indicate "no"—that your partner consciously or unconsciously had already selected a woman—then you say "No, it's a woman! The mists are clearing now!"

Many people will actually shake their heads slightly and indicate very obviously to you whether or not you're following their experience. All you need to do is give your partner time to select a person or experience from his past, and then make statements about that person and watch the response to find out if you're correct or not. If you're not, you very congruently shift what you "report" as if that's what you actually see in the crystal ball.

If I play a game with you, and I place a pea under one of two shells and ask you to guess which one it's under, how many questions do you have to ask to know the answer?

Woman: One question.

Sure. You say "Is it this one?" If the answer is "yes," you know. If the answer is "no," you know it's under the other one.

If I have four shells and one pea, now how many questions do you have to ask to know the answer?

Man: Two.

Right. You only need two, because you can chunk the problem you are going to solve. "Is it under these two?" When you get the answer to that question, your second question is "Which shell out of the remaining two is it under?" If you have eight shells, you need three questions, and so on.

This kind of guessing strategy is very effective for what you are going

208

to do. You can always divide the world into exclusive binary classes. "It's a man./It's a woman." "He's inside./He's outside." "He's older than you./He's younger than you." "He's close to you./He's not very close to you." "He wants to be close to you./He doesn't want to be close to you." Language allows you to make these absolutely artificial distinctions that divide the world up into binary choices: it's either this or that.

Woman: Do you feed the person both options?

You start by feeding one possiblity. "It looks like a man." You then wait for the response, to find out if your partner accepts or rejects what you say. He might have already selected a man, in which case what you said is congruent with his experience. Alternatively, he may not have made a choice yet, either consciously or unconsciously. When you proposed a man, he may have considered it and accepted it. Or, he could have chosen a woman, but when you waited, he made a substitution and found it acceptable.

The other class of responses your partner might have is to find what you say not acceptable, in which case you simply change. "Oh no, the mists have cleared away now, and I can see that it's a woman."

The whole point of this exercise is for you to give yourself an opportunity to notice that you can use a person's unconscious nonverbal signals to guide you to a description of an experience in that person's life history that you don't know anything about. In *his* perception of the process, you will have somehow gotten information that you couldn't have gotten in normal ways, and it will seem "psychic."

As soon as you have calibrated to your partner, you can begin with the general category of "an important person." Everybody has an important person somewhere in their life, so that's a good way to get started. Then you can use binary categories. What are some additional binary categories you can use?

Woman: Short/tall.

Man: Happy/unhappy.

Sure. These are all pseudo-categories, but they are categories everybody operates with all the time. "Concerned about you./Not concerned about you." "It's night./It's daytime." I want you each to have a list of at least six binary choices such as these before you begin.

At the end of using these binary categories, you can practice using Ericksonian patterns by doing a process instruction. You *could* do the whole thing with just Ericksonian patterns. There are plenty of "psychics" who actually do just that. You could say "And that event from your past contains *some* information, *some* learning, that you hadn't realized was there. . . . Because the meaning which that event has for you now may be different than the meaning you drew from it . . . at the time. . . . So that as your unconscious mind makes sense out of your past . . . in a new way . . . it doesn't matter if it allows your conscious mind to appreciate that understanding . . . a lot . . . or a little. . . . Your unconscious mind can apply that new understanding . . . in a meaningful . . . and surprisingly delightful way . . . to some experience . . . that will occur within the next forty-eight hours."

Or, once you've described the important person, you can say "And I don't know if you've realized that there is an important message which that person had never verbalized to you, but always wanted to relate . . . that could be useful to you now. . . . And as you watch and listen to them now . . . you can begin to hear what that message is. . . ."

When you use Ericksonian patterns, you can use this same yes/no feedback system to guide what you say. Make sure that you stay out of content.

After going through an experience like this with you, it will take a relatively sophisticated communicator to know what you actually said. His internal experience projected into the crystal ball will be so rich and detailed that he may mistakenly think that you specified the entire experience that he actually created internally. You mentioned some appropriate variable, and he filled in the specifics. Typically at the end of this, unless you've got someone really sophisticated, he will say "How did you know those things?" And of course the answer is, you didn't.

Woman: You are not getting verbal feedback from them at any time?

No. The point of this exercise is for you to learn to trust your ability to see nonverbal signals and to use those to guide what you say. Using the binary category approach, you will get more specific by following the yes/no signals down the binary tree. When using the Ericksonian approach, you will stay completely general, but still use the nonverbal feedback to know if and when the person is following you. If you notice particularly powerful involuntary responses as you go along, then you know to emphasize nominalizations in that general area. You still have no idea what his experience is, but as long as you have rapport, the person will be perfectly capable of filling in rich detail for himself and making it a very meaningful experience.

Crystal ball gazing is designed to refine your ability to make visual

210

discriminations. If you would prefer to develop your tactile abilities, do palm-reading instead. When you do palm-reading, you hold the other person's hand, and learn to *feel* the difference between your partner's "yes" and "no" responses when you are calibrating.

Ann: I do psychic readings for people and get information outside of the sensory channels. Are you saying that being psychic is really doing this?

I have no objections to notions of ESP and other psychic phenomena. At the moment the word "psychic" in the psychological realm has about the same meaning that the word "viable" has in the medical world. It's a term for things that are powerful somehow but we don't yet understand what they are or how they work. Some psychics certainly do their readings in the way I've described this exercise.

My hope is that there are hundreds of information-passing channels between human beings which lie outside of our recognized five senses and which I don't yet know anything about. I don't know. I do know that I now see and hear and tactilely feel things that I would have considered in the realm of psychic phenomena a few years ago.

I would be delighted if I could discover extra channels. One of my programs for discovering whether there are other such channels is first to refine my sensory channels as much as I can, and then model people who can do "psychic" phenomena. If I am getting the maximum amount of information I believe I can get out of the normally recognized channels, and I am getting other information as well, then I've got some evidence that there might be other channels.

Go find someone outside to try this exercise with, and find out how accurate you can be using just nonverbal feedback. Take about ten minutes.

*   *   *   *   *

How did you do?

Woman: I made a mistake at the beginning. My partner got right into it. His head was starting to go down toward the crystal ball. I said the person was a woman, and his head jerked back up and he said "I see a man."

How did you respond to that?

Woman: I said "Oh, yes. I see now it *is* a man out there."

OK, good. Calling something a "mistake" instead of an "outcome" or a "response" is an unnecessary judgement on the part of your conscious mind. If it's useful for you to set your own high criteria for how good you want to be in doing these kinds of things in order to motivate yourself to become increasingly more adept, I respect that. Do recognize, however, that what may seem like a "mistake" to you, may be totally unrecognizeable as such to the other person. *You* know what steps you are planning to go through. If for some reason you don't carry out that plan, that may or may not be apparent to other people. I recommend confidently utilizing whatever extra pieces of information they give you as you go along. "Of course you see a man, and examine carefully the expression on his face."

Woman: Your partner may be testing you to find out "Is this person going to be flexible and allow me to do what I want to do?" So it could be an opportunity to establish rapport.

Exactly. Erickson talks a lot about idiosyncratic needs that particular people have when going into altered states. It's possible that no matter what you propose, they have a polarity response to the first thing you say. Whatever their response is, you utilize it to go where you want to go.

Ann: I found it difficult to do this. When I started thinking about it and first took off, I started to go into the state that I go into to get psychic information.

Right. I thought that might happen.

Ann: Telling the other person I'm going to do crystal ball gazing immediately puts me into that state. When I do psychic readings, I close my eyes and get images on the inside, so I kept my eyes open to make this different. Even with my eyes open, it was difficult to stay out of the state where I receive that information, and just stay with the binary choices.

Right. Let me say several things in response to that. You have the ability to go to a special state in which you either have access to channels of communication I don't know about yet, or you have a really fine sensitivity to minimal cues so that you don't have to use the binary method. Whichever it is, is not important for me at this moment. You already have a well-developed strategy which you can use in order to get the same kinds of information that you can get using this step-by-step model of binary choices.

The question is "Is it worthwhile for you to *add* to your repertoire *another* way of doing it, independently of the special state you've learned to use effectively for yourself?" *If* you are interested in that, then before you engage in activities like crystal ball gazing, palmistry, or anything else we do that's associated with the special skill you've already developed, you can reframe internally to make sure that your special state and all the skills connected with it are kept specially protected, separated from your learning a whole new way of getting information. If you do this, then you won't have the interference of constantly sliding into that special state.

It may turn out that the programs for reading a person may be the same in both states. I don't know. The point is, in order to protect the special skill you've already developed *and* to add a new way of approaching the same subject matter to your repertoire, I think it would be useful for you to dissociate one from the other initially. Spend some time and energy, if you are interested, in developing *another* way of doing something you already do well. You will then have two ways to proceed and you can exercise more choice.

VIII

Self-Hypnosis

This afternoon we'd like to give you two methods of self-induction, and then a very elegant method of utilizing self-hypnosis. These methods can be useful to you personally, as well as in your work with clients. If you instruct your clients in self-hypnosis, you can then have them put themselves in altered states in your office. All you will need to do is utilize those trances. You can have your clients practice entering altered states at home, and when they come back in, have them access those trance states by asking them to recount in detail what they did. You say "Now, tell me in detail, which of the ways that you tried secured the deepest trance?" They'll say "Well, this one's pretty good," and they will begin to go back into a trance as they describe what happened. You will essentially be accessing a previous trance.

The first self-induction method I want to describe is Betty Erickson's technique. Betty is Milton's wife, and she is extremely sophisticated in putting herself into various altered states. She can jump in and out of many different states very quickly. The technique that she developed presupposes representational systems. Erickson, by the way, is the only person other than us who had an explicit understanding of representational systems; he knew that there are three major ones, and that there are predicates which identify them.

Betty uses representational systems in this induction. She seats herself in a comfortable place and finds something that's easy to look at. I would probably choose some place where the light is reflecting, such as some of the cut glass that is hanging from that chandelier. I fix

213

my gaze on that, and then I say three sentences to myself about my visual experience. "I see the light glittering on the various pieces of cut glass; I see the movement of somebody's bare arm; I see that somebody just looked up at the chandelier."

Now I switch to auditory, and make three statements about that portion of my experience. "I hear the sound of the ventilation system; I hear the sound of paper being rustled as people are making notes; I hear the sound of somebody clearing her throat."

Then I make three statements about my kinesthetic experience. "I can feel where the soles of my feet are making solid contact with the platform I'm standing on; I can feel the weight of my jacket as it lies across my shoulders; I can feel the warmth where my fingers are interlaced as I stand here." I've made three statements about my ongoing visual experience, three about my auditory, and three about my kinesthetic.

Then, maintaining the same position and the same direction of gaze, I recycle through each sensory channel, making *two* statements for each. I pick out two additional visual, auditory, and kinesthetic parts of my experience. Then I recycle through the three channels again, picking out *one* of each. Typically, even for beginners, about the time you get half way through the cycle of two sentences for each system, your eyes start to get drowsy, and you get tunnel vision. If your eyes get drowsy, you just allow them to close and substitute internal visualization for external. You can still use external experience for auditory and kinesthetic statements.

Man: Do you say the statements out loud when you are doing it for yourself?

It doesn't matter. Use whichever is easiest for you. Many of you will find that after you've done this half a dozen or so times, all you have to do is say "Well, I think I'll do that induction" and you're there! All I have to do is look over there at the cut glass and I get tunnel vision, which is one of the indicators that I'm going into an appropriate trance.

Woman: Do you have to do it in that sequence: visual, auditory, then kinesthetic?

No. If you happen to know your own preferred sequence, use that to pace yourself. If you tend to go visual, kinesthetic, and then auditory, then use that sequence. That will make it more powerful for you, but it will also work the other way.

Woman: You don't use the same sentences each time you cycle through, do you?

Use different ones each time, consistent with whatever your experience is at the moment. Notice that you are setting up a biofeedback loop. That is, you are representing in words exactly the experiences you are having visually, auditorily, and kinesthetically. One of the essential characteristics of all good hypnotic or altered states work is that particular loop. This is very similar to the 5-4-3-2-1 exercise that we discussed earlier, and it is the first phase of the Betty Erickson technique.

In the next phase I first sense which hand and arm feels lighter. Then I give suggestions to myself by saying that the hand that feels lighter will continue to feel lighter, and will begin to float up with honest unconscious movements, feeling attracted toward my face, so that when it makes contact with my face, I will sink into a deep trance.

The second self-hypnosis method is similar to the first, but you use internal representation instead of external representation. You sit or lie down in a comfortable place and make an internal visual image of what you would look like if you were standing five feet in front of yourself, looking at yourself. If you have any trouble constructing such an image, you already know a pattern which will assist you in doing that—overlap. Begin with the kinesthetic sensation of your breathing, or the sound of your breathing, and overlap to seeing your chest rising and falling. Continue to develop and stabilize that image of yourself until you can see it in greater detail. Eventually you will be able to see the rise and fall of your chest, which will be correlated with the kinesthetic sensations of your chest rising and falling as you breathe.

Continuing to see that image of yourself, you then shift your awareness to the very top of your head and kinesthetically sense temperature, tension, moisture, pressure, etc.—any distinction you are able to make kinesthetically. You work your way slowly down through your body, sensing each part of your body. As you look at that visual image of yourself from the outside, you're sensing what's going on in your body kinesthetically.

Next you add on auditory representation. As you see the image and sense your body kinesthetically, you describe your experience to yourself internally. "I feel a tension in my right eyebrow, and as I sense it, it begins to go away." All three systems are representing the same information. You are seeing, feeling, and hearing what your actual experience is at that moment.

After you've gone all the way through your body in this way, then you can add the same piece on at the end that I gave you for the other method. As you sense which hand and arm feels lighter, you see that hand and arm in the image beginning to lift up, feeling attracted toward your face. Then you describe it auditorily "My left hand is beginning to lift with honest, unconscious movements." Even if you don't know what honest, unconscious movements are, your unconscious does. Leave that to her. "My hand will continue to feel lighter and be attracted to my face. When it touches my face, I'll sink into a nice deep trance." You can say these things to yourself either sub-vocally or out loud if that is more convenient. If you say this out loud, shut the door, or people will think you are very weird.

Man: I have found it easier to get my hand up if I see a long handle pulling it up.

Or you can use a helium balloon. There are lots of extra things you can add to this. Use whatever else you can incorporate into your images and feelings and words that will help you accomplish each step. I'm giving you the basics. There are lots of nice artistic ways of doing it.

Man: If I'm using the internal image of myself out there and I feel my left hand lighter than my right, do I see that as a mirror image or the other way?

Try it both ways and find out which is more effective for you.

Man: What's the purpose of having your hand touch your face?

The exact task that you pick to do is arbitrary. Most people report that their hand and arm did lift, and when it touched their face they felt a sudden, radical change, and that they had amnesia after that point.

Before you begin either one of these exercises, and any time in the future when you decide to do self-hypnosis or meditation, give your unconscious an instruction about how long to keep you there and when to arouse you. You might say to yourself before you begin either one of these exercises "I would like you, my unconscious, to arouse me in fifteen minutes, allowing me to feel refreshed and renewed by this experience." Your body is an exquisite time clock. If you measure the time it takes a person to come back out of trance, it's usually within a quarter minute of the time they had specified. The worst that would ever happen, even if you forgot that instruction, is that you might go into a nice deep physiological sleep and wake refreshed several hours later.

Try both methods until you discover which is most effective for you. For the first half-dozen times, don't attempt any specific change work other than just relaxing and refreshing and renewing yourself. Wait until you have full confidence about your ability to get in and out; in other words wait until you know that you can get yourself into a deep trance and that your unconscious will arouse you after the appropriate length of time.

As you practice these methods, you will develop confidence about being able to get in and out. You will also notice that the procedure is beginning to streamline. Instead of deliberately going through the whole sequence, when you sit down to do it, you will begin to go into a trance immediately. At that point self-hypnosis becomes available to you as a really nice tool for your own self-evolution.

To use self-hypnosis for your own development, give your unconscious an entire set of instructions before going into a trance. First, decide what dimension of your experience you would like to alter. Ask your unconscious to review with sounds, images, and feelings, those occasions when you did something particularly creatively and effectively. Ask that when your unconscious has finished making this review in all systems, it extract from the review those elements of your performance which are distinctive, and to have them naturally and spontaneously begin to occur more frequently in your everyday behavior in appropriate contexts.

Suppose you are about to make a sales presentation to a board of directors in a corporation, and you want to make the very best presentation you can. Before you drop into the trance, at the time you state how long you want to stay down, you might say "When I get into a deep trance this time, I would like you, my unconscious mind, to review with images and sounds and feelings the five times when I have been most dynamic, effective, and creative in making sales presentations.

If you want to be effective in family therapy, you ask to review the five times you were most creative, etc. in doing family therapy. If you want more general self-evolution, you can say "Review the five times in my life when I behaved most gracefully, or most assertively, or most creatively." You ask for a review of the best representations of whatever it is that you would like to be effective at. Then you drop into trance and allow that to occur. If you do this, you will discover yourself changing; you will indeed evolve yourself.

You can also ask for a conscious output of what you went through in trance, but I recommend that you don't. I recommend that you simply get in the habit of trusting your unconscious processes. You will discover new patterns in your behavior, or old patterns which are occurring more frequently in the appropriate context. When that happens, you can use your own behavior as examples from which you can then come to a conscious understanding of what changes you have made. It's more efficient to go from unconscious change to behavior and *then* to a conscious digitalization of it, than it is to begin with a conscious understanding which you attempt to apply to behavior. Do yourself a favor and do it the easy way.

Bob: What if you want to do something that you have never done before?

If you don't know that you've ever succeeded with a particular behavior, then use the New Behavior Generator that we taught you this morning. Think of someone else who does this behavior very well. Pick yourself a really elegant model—somebody whom you really respect and admire—who does this behavior particularly elegantly and effectively. Then use a variation of the same instructions. Ask your unconscious mind to review all the internal stored images, sounds, and feelings of this person doing that particular behavior. Do this in three phases. In the first review, you just see and hear what is going on. Watch and listen to that person do what you want to learn to do. In the second phase you ask your unconscious mind to substitute your image and your voice for the other person's. So the second time you run the movie, you will see yourself doing the things that you just observed and listened to the other person doing. In the third phase you step into the movie and experience it from the inside, feeling yourself do the behavior, as well as seeing and hearing from that new point of view.

For instance, I might use Milton Erickson. I have spent a lot of hours watching and listening to his behavior. I give myself the instruction before I go into trance "Pick out the times when he has responded to incongruency with clients when I have been present. What specifically does he do?" The first time around I would see and hear him do whatever he does. The second time around, I would put myself in his position and see and hear myself doing the same thing he did. In order to actually get that into my behavior—which is where I want it—I have to step into the movie myself and feel the muscle movements and feelings that I would have if I were actually doing it.

This third step is designed to get those feelings and muscle patterns into your body so that when the situation comes up, you will automatically begin to respond in that way. After you have finished this third step you ask your unconscious to have this behavior naturally and spontaneously begin to occur more frequently in your behavior in the appropriate contexts. This works very, very well as a self-programming device.

Woman: Are you doing that as instruction to your unconscious before you go into a trance?

Yes. It's too complicated to do for yourself inside the trance. And I suggest that you start with small behaviors. For example, "I want to learn to smile when I want to get a certain response." Then later take bigger and bigger chunks of behavior.

I've given you a step-by-step process for inducing and using altered states for yourself. If you find these instructions tedious, let me reassure you that after you've practiced them, they will streamline very quickly so it will take only a matter of sixty seconds or so to alter your consciousness. You will be able to do it between sessions or during short breaks.

Discussion

Harry: Would you talk about how to distort your perceptions of time? How would you use hypnosis to speed up or slow down your perceptions of events?

How I would do that would depend upon whether I was going to do it to myself or to someone else. With myself, I would instruct my unconscious to find lots of experiences that have one factor in common: changing the speed of my perceptions. For example, you know what happens when you are zooming down the freeway and then exit from an off ramp into regular city traffic and seem to be going zero miles an hour. Or when you're really enjoying something, time seems to fly by, and hours seem like moments.

Those are examples of changes in your perception of time, which are indications that such changes are possible. I would ask my unconscious to find every example that it can think of, and to put me in those experiences. The only common thread that goes through all of the experiences is having control over time and the speed of reality.

While my unconscious was doing this, I would ask it to create some sort of control knob for me, so that I could speed things up or slow them down. I would set it up so that after I went through twenty experiences my eyes would open, I would still be in a trance, and I would be able to turn the knob one way to speed things up and turn it the other way to slow them down.

That is how I would go about it. I know that time distortion exists in

220

my normal experience already, so that is where I would find it. Then I could make tennis an opportunity to use time distortion. I could make the time slow enough so that I could respond easily, and then adjust the speed in between serves. After each serve I'd go back and evaluate "Was it fast or slow that time?" and adjust the knob accordingly.

Harry: Is there a way that I could speed up learning things, like hypnosis?

My guess is that you should be able to tell me the answer to that question. I can give you an example of how to do it, but I'm more interested in your knowing how to do it yourself. You know what it is that you want. So what are the parameters you are working with? If you want to speed up your perceptions, find some examples of having done it, and then give yourself some control over the process. You know that you've learned things. You know that you can integrate them. You know you have a standard speed. So how can you speed that up?

Harry: By going to the contexts in which I would do that normally.

Sure. But the factor that is really going to allow you to learn more quickly is the presence of *more time*. All you have to do is create two months. Is that enough? In other words, do what's called "pseudo-orientation in time." Put yourself into a trance and project yourself into the future. Tell yourself that instead of being tomorrow, it's two months from now. Then, in trance, relive fully all the time between now and then; create all the necessary history for it to be two months from now. You can make up all the clients you worked with and all the things you did; you can make up everything that happened between then and now. Create in detail all the history that you need in order to have already learned lots about NLP and hypnosis.

Whenever you want anything, all you have to do is think of where it would happen anyway, and then make that up. Hypnosis is a way of making a reality. If you know that something you want will happen in a specific reality, then use that reality to create what you want. If it doesn't happen in any reality that you know of, then create a reality in which it would happen.

Woman: Is it possible to create an overload of other realities?

Yes. It's called psychosis. When you use alternative realities, you must do so as a lawyer would. You must make sure that when you build realities, you build ones that are thorough and complete. You must make sure that they will accomplish what you want, and you must make sure that there's a doorway out of them. If you create sloppy realities and live in them, then you will respond in a sloppy way, and that will make you a junky person.

There's a book written by a well-known hypnotist that gives people inductions to read aloud to each other. There are programs in those inductions that make people really junky. People who read them will install strategies in each other which will not be beneficial for their overall functioning. To me that's foolish, and it's a kind of foolishness that I call indulgence. It's important not to be indulgent about using hypnosis. *When you build a reality, build one that will work, and build it completely and thoroughly so that you get exactly what you need.* You don't want to just build a crazy reality and go live in it, because you have no idea how you will respond to it. You may respond to it with emphysema! You want to make sure that you build one that is going to work well for you.

Most of the hypnotic realities that people have built for themselves and live in most of the time—what they call the waking state—are not profoundly useful. I mean that literally. The majority of the people I meet in the world have built a hypnotic reality which, on the whole, weighing the good against the bad and the pleasure against the pain, isn't really beneficial for them. To me that's indulgent. You don't want to make matters worse, only more useful.

Erickson's criteria of usefulness were for all his clients to get married, get a job, have children, and send him presents. Those are not my criteria. People sent me presents but I never got anything I wanted, except once. I'm not going to change everybody so that they get married and so on. Erickson did, because he believed that you must do those things.

I do think that you've got to be thorough when you build alternative realities, or when you build your own reality. For instance, I think the reality that humanistic psychologists have built is incredibly indulgent and not useful. That kind of indulgence is dangerous. Sometimes I get invited to do a keynote address at some humanistic psychology conference, and I find being there more terrifying than being in a criminal institution. The ethic that criminals have is at least conducive to survival. Many of the programs and kinds of realities that people are installing in each other at humanistic conferences are not even conducive to their own survival. If anything, they are detrimental. Those realities have a tendency to put people in situations of danger where they might actually get hurt. It may never happen, but it could. People don't usually consider the premises of what they do, and it's not just humanistic psychologists who operate that way. Everybody does.

Woman: What kind of realities do psychologists create that are destructive?

For example "To be a good person is to meta-comment." So you come in and say "I'm really mad about your walking out on me last night" and I say "Well, I really feel good that you can express your anger towards me." That kind of response is built into the fabric of most humanistic psychologies. That is not a useful response in any way. It does not help either of the two human beings. If anything, someone who uses that particular kind of response will end up becoming more and more alienated, and having unpleasant feelings more and more often. That's a *logical* outcome of using that particular kind of response. Just look at the people who use that response a lot, and you can find out for yourself.

There was a guy at the college I taught at who was a humanistic organizational development consultant. He used to be a hero, but now he's only a counterculture hero. His whole world is built upon those kinds of responses. He meta-comments about everything. He is also lonely, depressed, miserable, and alienated. It's no surprise to me, because his responses are never responses *to* people; they are always responses *about* people. He doesn't respond to people, so he can't have any intimacy or any feeling of connection. That limitation is built right into the fabric of his reality: he believes that a meta-comment is a "genuine" response.

People often create realities or pick outcomes that aren't worth having. That is a limitation in self-hypnosis. One of our students had a client who had decided that it was crazy for one person to carry on a conversation with himself. He read in a book "It takes two people to have a conversation." Since conversations are for two people to talk to one another, he decided that talking to yourself is stupid. So he just stopped having internal dialogue. When he stopped, he lost the ability to do certain things that he had used internal dialogue for—little things like the ability to plan! All he could do was see pictures and have feelings. He couldn't ask himself questions like "What would I like to do today?" He hadn't considered the overall impact of that change before he made it.

Clients often come in asking for things that wouldn't make them happy. Sometimes I give it to them and let them suffer for a while. Then it's easier for me to go back and give them something more meaningful.

One client of mine came in saying he didn't want to be able to feel anything. He told me that everything he had felt for years had been terrible, that people had hurt him over and over again, and he didn't want to have to feel things anymore. So I hypnotized him and hypnotically removed his kinesthetic experience. Of course he lost his sense of balance and could no longer stand up. Then I brought him back out of trance, still without any feelings, and asked if he would like to come back next week. He said "Please! Do something!" I said "All right, now we'll do it my way."

When you do self-hypnosis, consider the outcomes you go for very carefully. Play the counter-example game and ask yourself if there is any way in which your outcome could be harmful, and then use that information to improve your outcome. In both the examples I just gave you the person was trying to improve his life by limiting himself. Giving yourself *more* limitations is rarely a way to solve limitations. A guiding principle is to always *add* to your abilities and *add* to your choices.

IX

Questions

Man: Would it be OK to give you a case description and get suggestions from you?

Well, it would be OK. I don't know if I'll be able to say anything about it. A lot of times people describe a client to me, but since I don't have the person in front of me, I don't know what to do. Most of our procedures are based on moment-to-moment sensory feedback, and that doesn't exist in a verbal description. But I'm certainly willing to take a shot at it.

Man: This is a nineteen-year-old young man whom I saw once last week, and I will see him again tomorrow.

He certainly elicits a response from *you*! The first step is for you to use the phobia cure on yourself! OK, what about *him*?

Man: He told me that he's worn a surgical mask for four years.

How is that a problem? Does it mess up his French kissing, or what?

Man: Several years ago he became very preoccupied with his nose and—

Do you have any idea how this occurred?

Man: Yes. He developed acne on both sides of his nose, so he started wearing a surgical mask to cover it up.

Does he still have acne on his nose?

Man: No. When he came to see me, it was the first time he'd left the house in four years.

He's a courageous young man.

Man: He was totally housebound, and is convinced that his nose is the most deformed nose in existence.

224

Well, I'll give you an amusing approach you can try. I can't guarantee you that this will work, but it's something I have done.

If you have a secretary, get her to type up a short article on the positive relationship between unusual noses and sexual attraction. Get her to use a selectric typewriter that has one of those type faces that looks like magazine print. Type up this article and make xerox copies of it and put the name of some prestigious journal or magazine on it. Then leave the article somewhere in the waiting room. When your client comes in and sits down, have your secretary watch him until he sees the article. The minute he sees it and picks it up, have her run up and take it away from him.

I had a guy who wore a splint on his nose when he went out. The tape went all the way around his face so it covered his cheeks and his nose, because he was very concerned about acne.

I typed up an article about the relationship between bandages and severe acne. The whole thing detailed how people would put on band-aids, and it would lead to severe acne and sexual impotence and homosexuality and just about everything. I left the article in my waiting room, and let him read just enough to start to get into it, and then I had my secretary take it away. When he came in to talk to me, he demanded to see the article, and I insisted there was no such thing. Finally I opened the door, went out, and asked my secretary if she had taken an article away from him. She handed me an article about breast-feeding babies! I gave it to him, and told him that it was just his anxiety. When I said that, I looked at him very suspiciously. Probably now he'll never wear one of those splints again, even if he breaks his nose!

You have to create a context in which the response you want will occur naturally. You also need to use hypnosis or metaphor to talk about the responses that you want him to have, because not only does he need to be able to go out in public, he needs to go out in public with a sense of purpose. One of the things you might have him do is to go out in public with his surgical mask on, and go into places where he will meet people whom he will never see again. Have him pick some woman whom he *knows* would be really repulsed by his nose, and find out if he can go over and flash the surgical mask at her and make her throw up. The odds are you won't be able to get him to actually *do* that, because it will be too frightening. But you *can* talk about it and get him to laugh about the idea. You anchor his response of humor, and then begin to talk about going out into public. You can use that anchor to begin to associate a sense of humor about the ridiculousness of his nose with going out in public. Rather than getting him to feel OK, get him to feel ridiculous about it. It's much easier to diffuse the existing response, rather than try for a meaningful one.

I'll tell you something else you can do. We did this one, too, but we did it with a twenty-two-year-old woman who wore very unusual clothes. She wore *very* baggy clothes. She wasn't fat at all, but she believed that if people saw her body, they would find her hideous. So she wore hideous clothes to cover up her body.

I hired a bunch of guys from downtown to help me carry this one out. I got guys who wear vests with no shirts on. You know the type. They had big muscles, and tattoos and everything. I had them come into my office right before her appointment and sit there reading magazines. When she walked in the door, they turned around and laughed at her, and said "Those are the weirdest clothes I've ever seen." And there *they* were, dressed in a totally bizarre way. When she came into my office she was totally freaked out. I said "What's wrong?" and she said "Oh, those guys laughed at my clothes." I said "Oh, don't pay any attention to them. What do they know?"

The next week when she came back, her dress was not quite so baggy, but it was still kind of weird. When she came in, a man was sitting there in a suit and tie, dressed very nicely. As she walked in the door, he looked at her, then looked away and started sputtering, trying not to laugh, and said "I'm sorry. Excuse me." That was all it took to get her to wear reasonable clothes.

I use whatever my clients are afraid of to pump them out of whatever they are doing that is absurd. You can do lots of things using other people to help you get results. I've set people up out in the world to do these kinds of things, too. Sometimes I can get parents to work cooperatively with me. I go to schools and recruit people to work with me in the best interest of my clients.

You never know what will happen with any particular individual. I don't know this guy well enough to know for sure that what I've suggested would work, but in lieu of something impressive in my sensory experience, that would be the tack I would take.

Man: I've had him evaluated by a plastic surgeon, and the plastic surgeon made an allusion that there is a relationship between the length and width of the nose, and the length and width of the penis, so he's already started thinking in that direction.

You can tell him "Well we can shorten your nose for you, but. . . ,"

Or you can get the plastic surgeon to say "Well, what we do is we take it and we go whack." (He makes a chopping gesture.) That might change his mind!

I'll tell you another story. A woman that I worked with had a daughter who was really uptight about her nose. She really thought she had an ugly nose, when it didn't actually look any different than anybody else's. She wanted to have surgery and had saved up her own money for it, but her family was fighting with her about it. They told her she had an attractive nose and shouldn't change it, but she didn't believe them. Finally one day I said to the family "What difference does it make, anyway? In fact, I suggest that you insist that she go in and get rid of her hideous nose. Just say 'We've been lying to you all these years. Actually your nose is totally—ugh!—it's so repulsive! So just go down there and get the damn thing chopped off, for God's sake.'" They did this, and she went in, had the surgery, and then everybody said "Wow! You look so much better!" She didn't look different at all, because the surgeon didn't do very much. He'd been bribed, so he took just a little skin off the end and that was all. But she was happy after that, so everything was wonderful.

Never underestimate the nature of absurdity. There are some people who dye their hair, and their personalities change. If you can do something to your appearance, and it really does change your personality, then it's worthwhile. How many of you have gone out and bought some new clothes, and when you put them on you felt totally different?

Let me remind you of the general principle that we have mentioned over and over again: *Create a context in which the person will naturally respond in the way you want them to.* We have talked mostly about how to create a context in internal experience by using hypnotic technology. You can also use your creativity to create an external context which will get the desired response without any overt hypnosis. Sometimes that's a lot easier, and sometimes it's a lot more fun.

For instance, traditionally psychiatrists and psychotherapists have thought that it's really difficult to make contact with catatonics. It's easy, if you are willing to do things which are not usually considered professional, like stomp on their feet. They'll usually come right out of their trances and tell you to stop. That may seem unkind, but it's a lot kinder than letting them rot inside for years.

If you don't want to stomp on their feet, you can just pace them. The thing you need to keep in mind is that catatonics are in a very altered state, and you'll need to pace them longer to get rapport. They don't have much behavior to pace, but they will be breathing, blinking their eyes, and in some kind of posture. I've sometimes had to pace a catatonic for up to forty minutes, which is quite a taxing chore. However, it works, and it is very graceful. If you are not worried about being graceful, just walk over and stomp hard on their feet.

I know one psychiatrist who was working with a man who had had a very traumatic experience: his whole family had burned to death before his eyes, and he was powerless to help them. The man went into catatonia when this happened some years ago. The psychiatrist had worked and worked year after year with this guy and finally had gotten him to come out.

When this major event occurred, there happened to be an attractive 18-year-old candystriper in the office. The psychiatrist wanted to go get a colleague to help him with the next stage of therapy, but he didn't want the man to go back to catatonia while he was out of the room. The psychiatrist turned to the candystriper and said urgently "Keep him out! I'll be right back!" and ran out of the office.

So here is this young woman who had no experience doing therapy or anything like it. She knew enough about what this man had looked like before and what he looked like now, to know when he was going back in. Sure enough, as soon as the doctor went running out to get his friend to help, the man started to go back into the catatonic state. Her intuitive response was magnificent: she reached over and grabbed this guy and gave him the biggest, juiciest French kiss you can imagine! That kept him out!

The catatonic is making a decision that the internal experiences he is having in catatonia are richer and more rewarding than the ones he is being offered on the outside. And if you have ever been in a mental institution for any length of time, you might agree with those people! What the candystriper did was put him in a situation in which he would naturally prefer staying out.

We once saw a little woman in her late sixties who had been a dancer. She was having marital difficulties with her husband, and her right leg was paralyzed from the waist down. Doctors couldn't find any neurological evidence for this paralysis.

We wanted to test her to see if her paralysis was psychological rather than physical. In the office we had at that time you had to go upstairs to get to the bathroom. So we took a long time gathering information, until she asked where the bathroom was. We put her off and started discussing some aspects of her life that really got her interest. She got so excited that she put off going to the bathroom, and when she asked, we'd put her off. Just when we thought she was about to give up on us and go to the bathroom without our permission, we opened up the subject of her husband and their sexual difficulties, which was one of her major concerns. Then we told her "Go ahead to the bathroom now, but *hurry up and get back!*"

She was so excited that she forgot to be paralyzed. She literally ran up the stairs and then ran back down. Then she realized what she'd done, said "Oh, oh!" and went back into her paralyzed posture.

That gave us a demonstration that her paralysis was behavioral, and it also gave us an anchor for the state of not being paralyzed. We used that anchor indirectly by making veiled allusions to "taking steps to overcome difficulties," "being happy to respond to the call of nature," and "running up and down different possibilities."

Jack: How else can you tell when something is a physical problem versus a psychological problem? For example, I get seasick. It would be nice not to get seasick. I'm not sure if this is really a physical problem or a mental problem.

OK. Your question is "How do you distinguish between physical and psychological problems?" and my answer is "I don't usually bother."

Jack: Would you apply these techniques to my seasickness?

Immediately.

Jack: Would you expect to be successful?

I wouldn't bother to apply them if I didn't. I do make a distinction between psychological and physical problems in some ways. Let's say someone arrives in my office after she's had a stroke. All her behavior indicates aphasia, and she hands me a set of X-rays that show a tremendous trauma in the left temporal lobe. That is important information in shaping my response to her.

If a client has difficulties indicating definite physical manifestations, my immediate response is to make sure she is in the care of someone I consider a competent physician. I have several physician friends whom I trust. They have philosophies that match mine: "If you medicate, do it only as a last resort, because if it is successful, it destroys access to the part of the person you need to get to in order to make a behavioral change." Medication isn't for cures; typically, it's for management. That's what medication is designed for.

I can work with a person on medication; it's just that her responses are contaminated. It's hard to know how much of her response is to me and how much is to the chemical. Also, medication creates a severely altered state of consciousness. If you use our procedures with someone who is on medication, when she comes off it be sure to use the same procedures again. You've got to build some kind of a bridge between changes made in a severely altered state of consciousness, and someone's normal state of consciousness.

So if I have a client who is on medication, my first step is to get her off it, so that I have access to the part of her that is causing difficulty in her life. Once I've done that, if the client is supposed to have brain damage, I tell her metaphors about the plasticity of the human brain. The human central nervous system is one of the most plastic things I know of. There is a mountain of evidence that people can recover functions that they have lost through organic insult by rerouting—by using alternative neurological pathways. I will often induce a rather profound trance and do this programming in an altered state. That's the difference between a psychological and a physical program for dealing with problems in my way of proceeding.

Man: Does your position on medication include all drugs or are you talking about just "psychoactive" drugs?

I'm talking about anything that changes a person's state of consciousness. Some of the non-psychoactive drugs also have profound effects on consciousness. Since I've never been trained as a pharmacologist, I check with my physician friends whom I trust. I ask them "Are there consciousness-altering side effects to these drugs?" If not, I have my clients continue with their medications.

If you have a person who is diabetic, or something like that, you can teach her how to regulate her internal chemistry so that she doesn't have to be a diabetic. Then you take her off of the medication only as rapidly as she gains control over altering her chemistry. You tie reducing the medication to being able to regulate her own body chemistry in those areas.

Most people don't believe that kind of change is possible. Many people have very strong beliefs about what can and can't be done about problems with known chemical or physical aspects. Rather than opposing those beliefs, you can often use them to help you to make the changes that you're going for.

Once I went to a rest home at the request of a friend and worked with a man who had had a stroke. He had something called Broca's aphasia, which impairs the ability to generate language, but doesn't impair the ability to understand it. Someone with Broca's aphasia can understand well enough to obey commands. Another aspect of Broca's aphasia is that there is usually some paralysis, in a right-handed person, of the right side of the body and parts of the face. One of the most common characteristics is that the right hand becomes paralyzed in a very tense position with the hand drawn in toward the arm.

This man was particularly tense on the right side of his body, and since he had not been responding to physical therapy, my friend asked me to use hypnosis to get the muscles on that side of the man's body to relax. He thought it was possible for this man to get back partial control of the right side of his body, but not until after he had gotten that part of his body to relax.

I knew, partly from reading case histories, that it was possible to use hypnosis to do this. So I went in and worked diligently for two and a half hours with this man in very deep hypnosis, and at the end of that time, his hand was as loose as it could be. I was really impressed, because I'd never done it before. I didn't even know for sure if I would be able to do it. I just went in thinking "Well, I'll pretend as if I do this every day, and it's matter of fact, and if faith healers can cure people of things, maybe that's all hypnosis is. I don't know." I went in and took a shot at it and it worked. I thought it was great.

I was still with the man when the doctor and the physical therapist came back in the room. Neither of them was the person who had brought me to work with this man. They told me it was time for his physical therapy, and that I would have to leave and come back later on another day. I was sitting there, gloating on the inside, thinking "Wait until they see this. This is going to blow their minds!" I was sitting there chuckling to myself about the change.

The doctor and physcial therapist went over and helped the man out of his chair and back on a bed, and neither one of them noticed the fact that while they were doing that his arm was hanging loosely at his side! That was astounding to me. But I thought, if you're not really thinking about it, and you've got other things on your mind, that's possible. Then the physical therapist reached over and took the man's arm and folded it neatly back in the position that it had been in when it was tense. She did this as if she were making a bed. She laid him there and put the arm back into position, while she and the doctor were talking to each other. She then began a series of exercises to help him open up his hand and relax it. That completely amazed me! His hand was so limp, it was ridiculous. She took his fingers and moved them all the way open, and then moved them back again. She was still talking to the doctor, half paying attention to what she was doing, when she shifted and started to work on his right leg. She still hadn't noticed!

Suddenly it occurred to me that I was faced with a really powerful choice. I could astound them by making them notice what had occurred, but I didn't know what results that would have. I was concerned that since hypnosis was not scientifically acceptable, they would *believe* that his arm and hand were going to go back to the way they had been, and then set about making sure that they did. So I interrupted them and said "I want to show you something." I walked over and picked up the man's arm, and it was just like butter. They both looked at it the way you would look at a ghost. I looked at them and said "I want to tell you that hypnosis is not a valid scientific treatment, and that this is only a way to aid physical therapy, and probably it will go back. In fact it usually will go back in 24 hours. But every once in a while for some strange reason, it doesn't. And when it doesn't, it's usually because the person has been treated by a really skilled physical therapist before he was treated by hypnosis."

What I did was to pace their beliefs in order to enlist their support and make the hospital system help me. I kept in mind the outcome I was really after—for the man to have the choice of tension or relaxation. Who gets credit for that is not that important. What's important is that he gets to move his arm. And if people don't like the way that he got his choice, unconsciously they'll engage in behaviors that are likely to undo the change. It's not that they're malicious, just that their conscious minds can't deal with what's happening in front of them.

It's always easier to make changes if you work within the belief structure of the system or individual you are working with. At one seminar a participant, Pam, asked if she could bring in a nine-year-old male client, Dave, who was in really bad shape. She told me that the kid hadn't been able to sleep more than half an hour at a time for the past four or five days, and was now exhausted and starting to get sick. Apparently every time he dropped off to sleep, 15 or 20 minutes later he would start having nightmares about monsters, break out with sweat, thrash around, and wake up screaming. Pam didn't know how to cope with this, and wanted some quick assistance.

So during a break in the afternoon, I went in another room with Dave, Dave's mother, and Pam. I didn't have much time, so I went straight for rapport. Since I'm the oldest of nine children, I have no problem getting rapport with kids. By the time we sat down I had gotten rapport by the way I walked into the room, touched, and so forth.

Rather than going through an extended information-gathering phase, I immediately asked "What color are the monsters?" I didn't ask him "Can you see the monsters?" "Are there monsters?" "Do you have dreams?" "Are you upset?" "What is the problem?" The question I asked jumped past all that. "What color are the monsters?" presupposed all of the things I just mentioned. It's a huge leap, but since the kid and I were in rapport, it wasn't a problem. Dave replied by listing several colors. I said "I take it they're really big and really scary-looking." He said "Yeah!"

I asked "Who, of all the people and creatures that you know, would be tough enough to deal with these monsters?" He responded "Oh, I don't know," so we began fishing around. "Would the six-million-dollar man be strong enough?" He said "Nah."

Then I happened to hit upon one. I asked "Have you seen Star Wars?" This was several years ago when every nine-year-old kid was going to see Star Wars. His face lit up at the mention of that movie. I said "I'll bet I know which of the characters you like the best." Of course he asked "Which one?" I said "The Wookie." "Yeah, that's the one."

I said "By the way, let me teach you something about your dreaming arm that will be useful, so that you can control your dreams. I reached over, lifted his left arm, and asked him to see an image of the Wookie in a particular movie scene. With his arm in the air, cataleptic, I said "Now this is your dreaming arm, and let it drift down only as quickly as you watch, and see once again, the part of the movie that you especially like where the Wookie was doing things."

I could see rapid eye movement as his arm started down with unconscious movements, so I knew he was visualizing. I said "Hold it there. Can you see the Wookie?" He said "Umhum."

"Ask him if he'll be on your side, and be your friend, and be there to help take care of you." I could see him move his mouth and lips as he asked the Wookie the question. When he came back, I asked "What did he say?" Dave said "I couldn't understand him; he just made a sound." If you saw Star Wars, you know that the Wookie's speech was unintelligible. So I said "OK, have him move his head up and down for 'yes' and sideways for 'no.' Ask him again." So Dave went back and asked, and the Wookie nodded his head "yes." I asked "Look, is the Wookie tough enough to handle these monsters?" He thought about it for a while and then said "I don't think so. They're even bigger and meaner than the Wookie is."

I said "But he's *faster* than the monsters, right?" Dave said "Yeah." I put my hand on Dave's shoulder and said "OK. The Wookie's going to be standing there, and you know he's going to be there for you because you'll feel the pressure on your shoulder as he stands next to you with his hand on your shoulder, knowing that if worse comes to worse, he'll sweep you up into his arms and run, because he can outrun the monsters. So you'll always be able to get away if you need to." He processed that and nodded.

"However, we haven't dealt with the monsters yet. Who else could do that?" We cast about for other possibilities, and he came up with the answer, as the client always does if the therapist is smart enough to arrange the context. He chose Godzilla.

I said "OK, go in and see Godzilla." Dave closed his eyes immediately and raised his arm. It was one-trial learning; he understood exactly. I again saw rapid eye movements as he went inside and watched. Then he stopped and said "I'm having trouble getting an answer." I said "Well, watch his head." Dave said "But he's facing the other direction." "Tell him to turn around!" I said. So Dave went "Turn around."

Now that in itself was a *very* important change. *He* was now controlling powerful creatures in the domain in which he had been terrified. I was operating entirely within his belief system, his own metaphor.

Godzilla turned around and nodded "yes." I said "Now there's only one problem left. You've got someone to defend you and take care of the monsters if you need it. But Godzilla is big and clumsy. He's strong, and he'll take care of you, but you don't want him tromping around in dreams when you don't need him."

Listen to the presupposition in that statement. That statement said to him "You will have dreams. Some will have monsters and some won't. Godzilla will be appropriate in some dreams and in some he won't be." I was beginning to convert dreaming back into a normal, even enjoyable activity, rather than the time to have nightmares.

At that point Dave told me that in the story about Godzilla, there's a kid who wears a special necklace. When this kid wants Godzilla to arrive because he's being threatened by other monsters, all the kid does is touch the necklace. That's the signal for Godzilla to arrive.

I asked Dave's mother "Would you be willing to spend an hour this afternoon taking Dave around to some jewelry stores to find a necklace that will work for him as a signalling device?" I needed to be careful about over-all ecology here. In his town a little boy running around wearing a necklace wouldn't go over very well. I told him that he was only to wear it on evenings when he knew he would need it. Again, this was a way of putting the whole thing under his control.

In this example I didn't challenge the child's belief system; I didn't challenge the way he labeled things. I did no interpretation, but rather had the flexibility to enter into the child's world of beliefs. I then used devices within that world that were appropriate for getting the choices that the child needed at the time.

Man: What if the nightmares were just a symptom of something else?

All you know about when you work with an individual or family are the symptoms. My guess is that the nightmares did represent something going on within the family system, though I have no idea what. I asked Pam to keep a watch on the family to find out if any other symptoms emerged. Six months later she reported that there were no other symptoms. If other symptoms had emerged, I would go to reframing.

By responding to Dave's nightmares the way I did, I changed their meaning. In essence, I reframed them. The fact that I did this in the mother's presence was also important, because that changed *her* response to the nightmares. I gave her an example of a different way of responding to the nightmares.

Woman: Why did you use the dreaming arm technique?

It's just a game, and I wanted to begin with a game. With children, framing things as games produces a much more useful response than framing them as problem-solving. The dreaming arm is particularly useful in dealing with nightmares because it places visualization under the control of the child.

Benediction

Man: You have about eight minutes for your benediction. I just thought you might like to know that.

You want us to put you into trance, huh? We decided not to do it this time. We were going to give you lots of post-hypnotic suggestions, but we decided we wanted to find out what would happen if we just left you hanging. We wanted to know if we could come back here next year and you'd all still be sitting here.

OK. During the course of the past three days you have gone through a whole variety of experiences and learnings. There, it feels much better already, doesn't it? Now take a few moments and think about the sequence of what has occurred here. Go back to the beginning—three days ago—and quickly run through and review internally the things you learned. What are the things you want to take with you when you go back to your office, your home, your family? . . . Because the learnings you had here in the Grand Ballroom could stay in the Grand Ballroom, but they won't if you notify yourself when and where you want them to go.

You see, learning can remain in one state of consciousness. State-conditioned learning is a fact. Once a group of medical students I worked with were given an examination in the same room in which they learned the material. Each one passed the exam beautifully. Five minutes after the exam, they were taken across the campus to the gymnasium and given the same examination. Seventy-five percent of them flunked it, because the learnings of their classroom were not always available in other contexts. And the learnings of the gymnasium weren't very useful in taking a medical exam.

This selective availability of information keeps your mind from being cluttered unnecessarily, but it can also prevent you from having learnings when and where you need them.

The best way to have a learning is to have it *only* when you need it. You see, if you constantly thought of your phone number all day long every day, you'd go crazy. If you can think of it whenever you want to, except when you are near a telephone, it doesn't work for you. If you try to understand *why* that's the case, you still won't be able to call home. But if you *only* think of it when you want to tell it to someone else, or to dial your home, it's a learning that serves you well.

So think of the things you want to take out of the Grand Ballroom . . and think about the places you want to take them. . . . You don't have to think about what you are going to do with the learnings when you get there. . . . Just think about the furniture in your living room . . . the bed that you sleep in at night . . . that favorite office chair . . . your secretary . . . the carpet in the place where you work . . . the clients you've seen too many times . . . the business associates that you've always wanted to get . . . to do anything . . . that you want them to. Think about friends . . . and lovers . . . think about times and places . . . in your future . . . that are places worthy . . . of taking these learnings and understandings . . . and having them spontaneously emerge. . . .

Because while your conscious mind has worked diligently during the past three days . . . to understand something that isn't about *it*, but about the rest of each of you . . . your unconscious mind has been collecting information . . . in the way that it knows how to . . . and can't avoid. . . . And you can allow that information . . . to settle in your unconscious . . . and you unconsciously know . . . how to sort through that information . . . to make changes in yourself . . . changes that although you may or may not notice them . . . can be lasting and pervasive.

Now, some of you have not yet made good enough friends . . . with your unconscious process . . . and we want you to realize . . . that your unconscious is not a person . . . it's a part of *you*. . . . It's not a part of you as a piece is a part. . . . It's a part of you because it works differently . . . than your conscious mind. Your unconscious, for one thing, is much more lethargic. . . . It only does things for a *purpose*. . . . And the purpose of sorting through the learnings of the Grand Ballroom . . . is so that your conscious mind . . . can be surprised delightfully . . . when it finds itself doing new things . . . and not knowing exactly *how* . . . and especially not *why*, it is. . . . And as long as there is a Grand Ballroom, the learnings of the Grand Ballroom will go with you. . . .

Goodbye.

Appendix I

Eye Accessing Cues

While most people lump all of their internal information processing together and call it "thinking," Bandler and Grinder have noted that it can be very useful to divide thinking into the different sensory modalities in which it occurs. When we process information internally, we can do it visually, auditorily, kinesthetically, olfactorily, or gustatorily. As you read the word "circus," you may know what it means by seeing images of circus rings, elephants, or trapeze artists; by hearing carnival music; by feeling excited; or by smelling and tasting popcorn or cotton candy. It is possible to access the meaning of a word in any one, or any combination, of the five sensory channels.

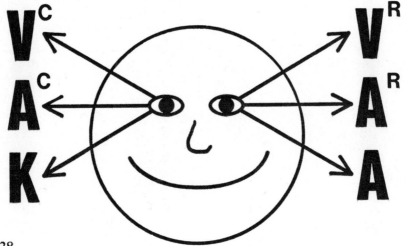

Bandler and Grinder have observed that people move their eyes in systematic directions, depending upon the kind of thinking they are doing. These movements are called eye accessing cues. The chart (left) indicates the kind of processing most people do when moving their eyes in a particular direction. A small percentage of individuals are "reversed," that is, they move their eyes in a mirror image of this chart. Eye accessing cues are discussed in chapter I of *Frogs into Princes*, and an in-depth discussion of how this information can be used appears in *Neuro-Linguistic Programming, Volume I*.

This chart is easiest to use if you simply superimpose it over someone's face, so that as you see her looking in a particular direction you can also visualize the label for that eye accessing cue.

V^r *Visual remembered:* seeing images of things seen before, in the way they were seen before. Sample questions that usually elicit this kind of processing include: "What color are your mother's eyes?" "What does your coat look like?"

V^c *Visual constructed:* seeing images of things never seen before, or seeing things differently than they were seen before. Questions that usually elicit this kind of processing include: "What would an orange hippopotamus with purple spots look like?" "What would you look like from the other side of the room?"

A^r *Auditory remembered:* remembering sounds heard before. Questions that usually elicit this kind of processing include: "What's the last thing I said?" "What does your alarm clock sound like?"

A^c *Auditory constructed:* hearing sounds not heard before. Questions that tend to elicit this kind of processing include: "What would the sound of clapping turning into the sound of birds singing sound like?" "What would your name sound like backwards?"

A_d *Auditory digital:* Talking to oneself. Questions that tend to elicit this kind of processing include: "Say something to yourself that you often say to yourself." "Recite the Pledge of Allegiance."

K   *Kinesthetic:* Feeling emotions, tactile sensations (sense of touch), or proprioceptive feelings (feelings of muscle movement). Questions to elicit this kind of processing include: "What does it feel like to be happy?" "What is the feeling of touching a pine cone?" "What does it feel like to run?"

Appendix II

Hypnotic Language Patterns: The Milton-Model

Milton Erickson used language very systematically in his hypnotic work, often in unusual ways. These patterns were first described by Richard Bandler and John Grinder in their book, *Patterns of the Hypnotic Techniques of Milton H. Erickson, M.D., Vol. I.*

Using this "Milton-Model" is a prerequisite to effective hypnotic communication, and all of the induction examples in this book have used these language patterns. Many readers will unconsciously begin to learn the hypnotic language patterns by reading the many examples of inductions in this book. This appendix makes these patterns more explicit, so that you can practice using one pattern at a time, in order to systematically incorporate them all into your behavior.

I Inverse Meta-Model Patterns

Often the Milton-Model has been called the reverse of the Meta-Model. The Meta-Model is described fully in *The Structure of Magic, Vol. I,* by Bandler and Grinder, and there is an excellent 12-page summary of it in an appendix to *They Lived Happily Ever After,* by Leslie Cameron-Bandler. The Meta-Model is a set of language patterns that can be used to specify experience more fully. In contrast, the Milton-Model provides the user with ways of being "artfully vague." Being artfully vague allows a communicator to make statements that sound specific and yet are general enough to be an adequate pace for the listener's experience, no matter what that is. The Meta-Model pro-
240

vides ways of recovering specific information that is deleted in any sentence; the Milton-Model provides ways of constructing sentences in which almost all specific information is deleted. This requires the listener to fill in the deletions from her own unique internal experience. The Meta-Model can be conveniently divided into three chunks: A. Gathering Information, B. Semantic Ill-formedness, and C. Limits of the Speaker's Model.

A. Gathering Information

As part of the Milton-Model, this chunk is called *Deleting Information,* and is the most useful of the three chunks for hypnotic purposes The four sub-categories follow.

1) Nominalizations: Nominalizations are words that take the place of a noun in a sentence, but they are not tangible—they cannot be touched, felt, or heard. The test for a nominalization is "Can you put it in a wheelbarrow?" If a word is a noun and it cannot be put in a wheelbarrow, it is a nominalization. Words like *curiosity, hypnosis, learnings, love,* etc. are nominalizations. They are used as nouns, but they are actually process words.

Whenever a nominalization is used, much information is deleted. If I say "Emily has a lot of *knowledge,*" I've deleted what exactly she knows and how she knows it. Nominalizations are very effective in hypnotic inductions because they allow the speaker to be vague and require the listener to search through her experience for the most appropriate meaning. Milton Erickson's inductions are filled with them.

In the following example, the nominalizations are in italics:

"I know that you have a certain *difficulty* in your *life* that you would like to bring to a satisfactory *resolution* . . . and I'm not sure exactly what personal *resources* you would find most useful in resolving this *difficulty,* but I do know that your *unconscious mind* is better able than you to search through your *experience* for exactly that *resource.* . . ."

In this paragraph nothing specific is mentioned, but if this kind of statement is made to a client who has come in to resolve a problem, she will provide specific personal meanings for the nominalizations used. By using nominalizations, the hypnotist can provide useful instructions without running the risk of saying something that runs counter to the listener's internal experience.

2) Unspecified Verbs. No verb is completely specified, but verbs can be more or less specified. If a hypnotist uses relatively unspecified verbs, the listener is again forced to supply the meaning in order to understand the sentence. Words like *do, fix, solve, move, change, wonder, think, sense, know, experience, understand, remember, become aware of,* etc., are relatively unspecified.

The sentence "I *think* this is true" is less specified than "I *feel* this is true." In the latter sentence, we are informed as to how the person thinks. If I say "I want you to *learn,*" I am using a very unspecified verb, since I'm not explaining how I want you to learn, or what specifically I want you to learn about what.

3) Unspecified Referential Index. This means that the noun being talked about is not specified.

"*People* can relax."

"*This* can be easily learned."

"You can notice a *certain sensation.*"

Statements like these give the listener the opportunity to easily apply the sentence to themselves in order to understand it.

4) Deletion. This category refers to sentences in which a major noun phrase is completely missing.

For example "I know you are curious."

The object of that sentence is missing completely. The listener does not know what he is supposedly curious about. Again, the listener can fill in the blanks with whatever is relevant in her experience.

B. Semantic Ill-formedness

1) Causal Modeling, or Linkage. Using words that imply a cause-effect relationship between something that is occuring and something the communicator wants to occur invites the listener to respond as if one thing did indeed "cause" the other. There are three kinds of linkage, with varying degrees of strength.

a) The weakest kind of linkage makes use of conjunctions to connect otherwise unrelated phenomena.

"You are listening to the sound of my voice, *and* you can begin to relax."

"You are breathing in and out *and* you are curious about what you might learn."

b) The second kind of linkage makes use of words like *as, when, during,* and *while* to connect statements by establishing a connection in time.

"*As* you sit there smiling, you can begin to go into a trance."

"*While* you sway back and forth, you can relax more completely."

c) The third and strongest kind of linkage uses words actually stating causality. Words such as *makes, causes, forces,* and *requires* can be used here.

"The nodding of your head will *make* you relax more completely."

Notice that when using each kind of linkage, the communicator begins with something that is already occurring and connects to it something she wants to occur. The communicator will be most effective if she begins with the weakest form of linkage and gradually moves to a stronger form.

These forms of linkage work by implying or stating that what is occurring will cause something else to occur, and by making a gradual transition for the listener between what is occurring and some other experience. Chapters I and II of this book contain more detailed descriptions of the use of causal modeling.

2) Mind-Reading. Acting as if you know the internal experience of another person can be an effective tool to build the credibility of the hypnotist as long as the mind-reading makes use of generalized language patterns. If the mind-reading is too specific, the communicator runs the risk of saying something counter to the listener's experience, and thereby losing rapport.

"You may be wondering what I'll say next."

"You're curious about hypnosis."

3) Lost Performative. Evaluative statements in which the person making the evaluation is missing (lost) from the sentence are called Lost Performatives. Statements using lost performatives can be an effective way of delivering presuppositions, as in the examples which follow.

"It's good that you can relax so easily."

"It's not important that you sink all the way down in your chair."

C. Limits of the Speaker's Model

This chunk of the Meta-Model is the least significant chunk as a part of the Milton-Model. Its two categories can be used to limit the listener's model in ways that produce trance as well as other outcomes.

1) Universal Quantifiers. Words such as *all, every, always, never, nobody*, etc., are universal quantifiers. These words usually indicate overgeneralization.

"And now you can go *all* the way into a trance."

"*Every* thought that you have can assist you in going deeper into a trance."

2) Modal Operators. Modal operators are words such as *should, must, have to, can't, won't*, etc., that indicate lack of choice.

"Have you noticed that you *can't* open your eyes?"

II. Additional Milton-Model Patterns

In addition to the inverse Meta-Model patterns, the Milton-Model includes a number of other important language patterns. The most important of these is the use of presuppositions.

A. Presuppositions

The way to determine what is presupposed and not open to question in a sentence is to negate the sentence and find out what is still true. The simplest kind of presupposition is existence. In the sentence "Jack ate the food" it is presupposed that "Jack" and "food" exist. If you negate the sentence and say "No, Jack didn't eat the food" the fact that Jack and the food exist is still not questioned.

Presuppositions are the most powerful of the language patterns, when used by a communicator who *presupposes what she doesn't want to have questioned*. A general principle is to give the person lots of choices, and yet have all of the choices presuppose the response you want.

Examples of specific kinds of presuppositions that are particularly useful in hypnotic work follow. There is a complete list of presuppositional forms in the appendix to *Patterns I*.

1) Subordinate Clauses of Time. Such clauses begin with words such as *before, after, during, as, since, prior, when, while*, etc.

"Do you want to sit down *while* you go into trance?" This directs the listener's attention to the question of sitting down or not, and presupposes that she will go into trance.

"I'd like to discuss something with you *before* you complete this project." This presupposes that you will complete this project.

2) Ordinal Numerals. Words such as *another, first, second, third,* etc. indicate order.

"You may wonder which side of your body will begin to relax *first*." This presupposes that both sides of your body will relax; the only question is which will be first.

3) Use of "Or." The word "or" can be used to presuppose that at least one of several alternatives will take place.

"I don't know if your right *or* your left hand will lift with unconscious movement." This presupposes that one of your hands will rise; the only question is if I know which one it will be.

"Would you rather brush your teeth before *or* after you take a bath?" This presupposes that you will take a bath and brush your teeth; the only question is in what order.

4) Awareness Predicates. Words like *know, aware, realize, notice,* etc. can be used to presuppose the rest of the sentence. The only question is if the listener is *aware* of whatever point you are making.

"Do you *realize* that your unconscious mind has already begun to learn. . . ."

"Did you *know* that you have already been in a trance many times in your life?"

"Have you *noticed* the attractive effect this painting has on your living room?"

5) Adverbs and Adjectives: Such words can be used to presuppose a major clause in a sentence.

"Are you *curious* about your developing trance state?" This presupposes that you are developing a trance state; the only question is if you are curious about it or not.

"Are you *deeply* in a trance?" This presupposes that you are in a trance; the only question is if you are in deeply or not.

"How *easily* can you begin to relax?" This presupposes that you can relax; the only question is how easy it will be.

6) Change of Time Verbs and Adverbs: *Begin, end, stop, start, continue, proceed, already, yet, still, anymore,* etc.

"You can *continue* to relax." This presupposes that you are already relaxing.

"Are you *still* interested in hypnosis?" This presupposes that you were interested in hypnosis in the past.

7) Commentary Adjectives and Adverbs: *Fortunately, luckily, innocently, happily, necessarily,* etc.

"*Fortunately,* there's no need for me to know the details of what you want in order for me to help you get it." This presupposes everything after the first word.

Stacking many kinds of presuppositions in the same sentence makes them particularly powerful. The more that is presupposed, the more difficult it is for the listener to unravel the sentence and question any one presupposition. Some of the presupposition sentences listed above contain several kinds of presuppositions, and those sentences will be more powerful. The following sentence is an example of the use of many presuppositions stacked together.

"*And I don't know how soon you'll realize the learnings your unconscious has already made, because it's not important that you know before you've comfortably continued the process of relaxation and allowed the other you to learn something else of use and delight to you.*"

B. Indirect Elicitation Patterns

The next group of Milton-Model patterns are particularly useful in getting specific responses indirectly, without overtly asking for them.

1) Embedded Commands. Rather than giving instructions directly, the hypnotist can embed directives within a larger sentence structure.

"You can begin to *relax.*"

"I don't know how soon you'll *feel better.*"

When you embed directives within a larger sentence, you can deliver them more smoothly and gracefully, and the listener will not consciously realize that directives have been given. The above messages are likely to have a much more graceful impact than if you were to give the directives alone: "Relax." "Feel better."

2) Analogue Marking. Embedded commands are particularly powerful when used with analogue marking. Analogue marking means that you set the directive apart from the rest of the sentence with some nonverbal analogue behavior. You could do this by raising the volume of your voice when delivering the directive, by pausing before and after the directive, by changing your voice tone, by gesturing with one of your hands, or by raising your eyebrows. You can use any behavior that is perceptible to the other person to mark out a directive for special attention. The other person does not need to notice your marking consciously; in fact she will often respond more fully when your marking is perceived but not consciously recognized.

3) Embedded Questions. Questions, like commands, can be embedded within a larger sentence structure.

"I'm curious to know what you would like to gain from hypnosis."

"I'm wondering what you would prefer to drink."

Typically people will respond to the embedded question in the first example, "What would you like to gain from hypnosis?" without realizing that the question was not asked directly. The listener doesn't refuse to answer the question, because it is embedded within a statement about the speaker's curiosity. This provides a very gentle and graceful way to gather information.

4) Negative Commands. When a command is given in its negative form, the positive instruction is generally what is *responded* to. For example, if someone says "*Don't* think of pink polka dots" you have to think of pink polka dots to understand the sentence. Negation does not exist in primary experience of sights, sounds, and feelings; Negation exists only in secondary experiences: symbolic representations such as language and mathematics.

Negative commands can be used effectively by stating what you *do* want to occur and preceding this statement with the word "don't."

"I *don't* want you to feel too comfortable."

"*Don't* have too much fun practicing negative commands."

Generally the listener will respond by experiencing what it's like to feel comfortable or to have fun practicing negative commands as a way of understanding the sentence.

5) Conversational Postulates. Conversational postulates are yes/no questions that typically elicit a response rather than a literal answer. For example, if you approach someone on the street and ask "Do you have the time?" the person generally won't say "yes" or "no." She will tell you what time it is.

If you ask someone "Do you know what's on TV tonight?" it's likely that she will tell you the evening's programming rather than say "yes" or "no."

To make conversational postulates, you first think of the response you want. As an example, let's say you want someone to close the door.

The second step is to identify at least one thing that must be true if that person shuts the door. In other words you are identifying what your outcome presupposes. In this case it presupposes (a) the person is able to shut the door, and (b) the door is now open.

The third step is to take one of these presuppositions and turn it into a yes/no question. "Can you shut the door?" "Is the door open?" You now have a question that will typically get you a response without directly asking for it.

6) Ambiguity. Ambiguity occurs when one sentence, phrase, or word has more than one possible meaning. Ambiguity is an important tool that can result in a mild confusion and disorientation which is useful in inducing altered states. In a normal conversation, unambiguous statements are highly valued; in hypnosis, the opposite is often true. Any ambiguity makes it possible for the listener to internally process a message in more than one way. This requires that the person actively participate in creating the meaning of the message, which increases the probability that the meaning will be appropriate for her. In addition, it is likely that one or more of the meanings will remain at the unconscious level. The first four patterns described in this appendix (Nominalizations, Unspecified Verbs, Unspecified Referential Index, and Deletion) all function to increase the ambiguity of the message.

a) Phonological ambiguity. Words that sound alike but have different meanings create phonological ambiguity. Such words include. *right/write/rite; I/eye; insecurity/in security; red/read; there/their/they're; weight/wait; knows/nose; here/hear.*

The following words similarly have two meanings, although

they both sound alike and are spelled alike: *left, duck, down, light.*

Other phonological ambiguities can be found in words which can either be used as an active verb "Lift your arm," or a nominalized verb "Give me a lift." Other examples are: *push, pull, point, touch, rest, nod, move, talk, hand, feel.*

Words that have phonological ambiguity can be marked out analogically and combined with other words to form a separate message. For example, "*I* don't know how *close* you are to understanding *now* the meaning of trance." The message marked out can be heard as "*eye close now.*"

b) Syntactic ambiguity. A classic example of syntactic ambiguity is the following: "Hypnotizing hypnotists can be tricky." This sentence can mean either that hypnotists practicing hypnosis can be tricky, or that putting hypnotists in a trance can be tricky.

The following sentence has the same form: "They were milking cows." The pronoun "they" could refer to people milking cows, or to the cows themselves.

This kind of ambiguity is based on taking a transitive verb, adding "ing," and placing it before a noun. The verb + ing can then serve either as an adjective or as a verb.

c) Scope ambiguity. Scope ambiguity occurs when it is unclear how much of the sentence an adjective, verb, or adverb applies to.

"We'll go with the charming men and women." This could mean we'll go with the charming men and the women (who may or may not be charming), or we'll go with the men who are charming and the women who are charming.

"I don't know how soon you will fully *realize* that you are sitting here comfortably, listening to the sound of my voice, and you are going into a deep trance only as quickly as your unconscious mind wants. . . ." Here it is unclear whether the verb "realize" applies to the entire sentence or only to what precedes the word "and." If "realize" applies to the whole sentence, everything following "realize" is presupposed.

d) Punctuation ambiguity. This kind of ambiguity is created by putting two sentences together that end and begin with the same word.

"Your coat looks like it is made of goose *down* deeply into trance." Here the word "down" is the end of the first sentence, "Your coat looks like it is made of goose down" and also the beginning of the following phrase "down deeply into trance."

"That's *right* now you've already begun to relax."

"I'm speaking clearly to make sure that you can *hear* you are, in the process of hypnosis."

"How *are you* able to go into a deep trance?"

C. Patterns in Metaphor

The final set of patterns is particularly useful when using metaphorical communication, as well as when using other kinds of hypnosis. There are many other patterns that are useful in effective story-telling. However, the following two are generally thought of as part of the Milton-Model.

1) Selectional Restriction Violations. This refers to the attribution of qualities to something or someone which by definition could not possess those qualities. For example, if I talk about a rock that was very sad or a man who is pregnant, I am violating selectional restriction, since rocks do not experience feelings and men do not get pregnant. The listener needs to find some way of making sense out of statements like this. If I talk about the experiences the sad rock had, and the changes it made, the listener is likely to make sense out of my statements by applying them to himself. "The rock can't be sad, so it must be me." This process is not a conscious one, but an automatic way of understanding what is said.

2) Quotes. This pattern involves making any statement you want to make to another person as if you are reporting in quotes what someone else said at another time and place.

Quotes can be used to deliver any message without taking responsibility for the message. Since you are apparently talking about what someone else said at another time, your listener will often respond to the message, but not consciously identify what he is responding to, or who is responsible for the message.

You can talk to someone about a client of Milton Erickson's who wanted to really learn about hypnosis. He listened to Erickson talk about hypnosis and thought that he understood. Then Erickson turned to him and said emphatically *"You don't really know something until you've practiced every piece of it thoroughly!"*

Note

It is a common experience with many people when they are introduced to Neuro-Linguistic Programming and first begin to learn the techniques, to be cautious and concerned with the possible uses and misuses of the technology. We fully recognize the great power of the information presented in this book and whole-heartedly recommend that you exercise caution as you learn and apply these techniques of a practitioner of NLP, as a protection for you and those around you. It is for this reason that we also urge you to attend only those seminars, workshops and training programs that have been officially designed and certified by Richard Bandler and John Grinder. These will be most often presented under the auspices of Grinder, DeLozier & Associates or Richard Bandler and Associates.

Writing both the following addresses is the only way to insure both Richard Bandler and John Grinders' full endorsement of the quality of services and/or training represented as NLP.

Richard Bandler
2912 Daubenbiss Ave #20
Soquel, CA 95073

Grinder, DeLozier & Associates
1077 Smith Grade
Bonny Doon, CA 95060

251